COMMUNITY DEVELOPMENT

A Critical and Radical Approach

Third edition

Margaret Ledwith

First published in Great Britain in 2020

Policy Press
University of Bristol
1–9 Old Park Hill
Bristol
BS2 8BB
UK
t: +44 (0)117 954 5940
pp-info@bristol.ac.uk
www.policypress.co.uk

North America office:
Policy Press
c/o The University of Chicago Press
1427 East 60th Street
Chicago, IL 60637, USA
t: +1 773 702 7700
f: +1 773-702-9756
sales@press.uchicago.edu
www.press.uchicago.edu

British Library Cataloguing in Publication Data
A catalogue record for this book is available from the British Library

Library of Congress Cataloging-in-Publication Data
A catalog record for this book has been requested

ISBN 978-1-4473-4817-7 paperback
ISBN 978-1-4473-4818-4 ePub
ISBN 978-1-4473-4820-7 epdf

Cover design by Policy Press
Front cover image: istock
Printed and bound in Great Britain by CMP, Poole
Policy Press uses environmentally responsible print partners

For all those children and young adults rising
with confidence and bravery to stand alongside
Greta Thunberg under the banner 'School Strike for
Climate', including my amazing granddaughter,
Grace. They are our hope for the future.

Contents

List of figures and boxes

Figures

Boxes

Acknowledgements

My heartfelt thanks go to Sarah Bird for her unfailingly generous interest and enthusiasm, a source of energy and vitality that inspires the very best. Jo Morton has been my travelling companion through the latter stages of this book; much more than a production editor, she is an outstanding source of expertise and inspiration, with boundless energy and dedication to producing a work that communicates ideas in words, graphics, illustrations that are compelling enough to challenge the depths of meaning. Thank you both for your friendship. As ever, this is teamwork, and the Policy Press team are a joy to work with – Emily Watt, Isobel Bainton, Dave Worth, Caroline Astley-Brown and Amelia Watts-Jones – you have all contributed to the excellent quality of this book, I am so very grateful.

My gratitude also goes to the storytellers who are so willing to share their ideas and practice, not only to bring key concepts alive, but to inspire others who are working for freedom and equality – from Iran: Manizheh Najm Araghi, Ali Sedaghati Khayaat and Delaram Ali; from Scotland: Selma Angestad, Orlaith McAree, Barbara Munro and Luke Campbell; from Australia: Sandra Sewell; and from England: Ali Melling, Paul Wilkinson, Diane Watt and Gary Craig.

Finally, Steve Casstles, whose extraordinary qualities of caring and kindness nurture me to keep going through the tough bits, and little Seb, who makes me laugh – both fill me with joy!

Glossary

Abjection: social abjection theory explains the way that the state targets some social groups as disgusting and unworthy, reinforced by the media and normalised in everyday conversations. The powerful are represented as worthy, deserving subjects; the disempowered as unworthy, undeserving objects. The one reinforces the other, justifying social divisions of poverty and privilege.

Action/reflection: the foundation of community development praxis, where our knowledge base is developed through reflection on action, and our subsequent action is informed by this analysis.

Alienation: power asserted over people results in a loss of personal control over life circumstances, a disconnection from society, and condemnation to the margins that dehumanises, resulting in the erosion of belonging.

Austerity: under neoliberal governments, 'austerity' is the political imposition of policies that have no apparent benefit other than to punish vulnerable social groups for their own poverty by cutting funding for housing, education, health, work and welfare, privatising public ownership, at the same time as giving tax cuts to and allowing tax avoidance for the rich. Throughout this book I often use inverted commas to denote that unnecessary, punitive 'austerity' measures have been imposed on the poor since the financial crisis of 2007–08 at the same time as the rich have got richer.

Banking education: this is Freire's term for the traditional approach to education in which a powerful teacher pours dominant knowledge into the unquestioning minds of passive learners, reinforcing dominant power interests. It is an approach to education which is controlling, which is why Freire also refers to it as 'domesticating'. Changing this system is the aim of the *knowledge democracy* movement so that subordinated knowledges are recognised and claimed as legitimate.

Civil society: in Gramscian theory, civil society is the site in which the dominant ideas of the ruling class invade our minds persuading us that their way of seeing the world is *common sense*. The institutions of civil society which engage us in life – the family, media, schools, religious organisations, community groups, and so forth – play a role in getting us to consent to ideas that favour the already privileged in society. It is also the site for grassroots action for change.

Codifications: in Freirean pedagogy, these are representations of familiar local situations that capture life experience in photographs, drawings, drama, story, poetry, music and so on, in order to 'see' a situation decontextualised from reality more critically as the focus for dialogue.

Common inheritance: every last one of us is indebted to those who have gone before us, and the natural world, for the advantages we are born into. From roads to fresh water, to hospitals and to developments in art, literature and science, the bedrock of all this is the biosphere that makes all else possible – energy, minerals, rivers, oceans, soil, plants, animals and the climate. We are but one small part and have no given entitlement. We have responsibility for reparation of the wrongs of the past and present – slavery, xenophobia, misogyny, racism and environmental degradation – all exploitations which live on through inheritance to continue to privilege some at the expense of others.

Common sense: dominant narratives are told with authority and repeated through the media until they become accepted as a form of common sense that is not challenged as nonsense! In this way, political strategies, such as 'austerity', designed to make the rich richer and the poor poorer, are accepted as inevitable, with the result that foodbanks become the order of the day in rich countries and social inequalities widen to push the poor towards destitution.

Conscientisation: translated from the Portuguese *conscientização*, Freire used this concept for the process of becoming critically aware of the structural forces of power which shape people's lives as a precondition for critical action for change.

Counternarratives: compelling stories that inspire hope and possibility for a different social reality based on values of equality, cooperation and connection running counter to the dominant narratives that justify inequality, competition and *alienation*.

Critical alliance: strategic alliances across *difference*, which are built on the collective strength of diversity in mutual collective action for social justice.

Critical analysis: refers to the theories and conceptual tools with which to analyse practice so that the contradictions we live by and accept as *common sense* get exposed and subsequent action is targeted at the source, not the symptoms, of oppression and therefore has the potential to bring about transformative change for social justice.

Critical consciousness: involves the 'dynamic between critical thought and critical action' (Shor, 1993: 32). This is the stage of consciousness needed for the empowerment to act collectively to bring about change in relation to the wider contexts of power from local to global.

Critical pedagogy: refers to that type of learning based on a mutual search rooted in a 'profound love for the world and for people' (Freire, 1996: 70). It is a democratic process of education that encourages *critical consciousness* as the basis of transformative collective action.

Culture circle: Freire's term for what we would call a community group, which provides the context for mutual, critical *dialogue* of equals intent on questioning life's contradictions in order to act collectively for change.

Culture of silence: Freire used this concept to capture the *dehumanisation*, apathy and disaffection that silence people into accepting their *alienation*. His challenge was to release their innate energy by teaching people to question lived reality, exposing the contradictions we live by.

Cultural invasion: is a Freirean concept which captures the way that the values, beliefs, ideology, cultural norms and practices of a dominant culture are superimposed on the culture of those it oppresses. It links to Gramsci's concept of *hegemony*.

Dehumanisation: people are robbed of the right to be fully human when they are stigmatised as worthless, incapable objects. Freire saw dehumanisation as an act of violence; his prime concern was humanisation – how to restore people's right to be fully human subjects in the world.

Democratic fascism: refers to the current extreme Far Right populist movement founded on old political and social values of violence, patriarchy, xenophobia and racism, wrapped up in a politics of hatred of ethnic minorities, women, the disabled, gay, refugees ... and all advocates of equality and social/environmental justice - intellectual activists, the judiciary, feminists, anti-racists, anti-poverty activists (see Tyler, 2017, discussed on p 57).

Dialogue: in Freirean pedagogy, is a mutual, respectful communication between people engaging the heart and mind, the intellect and emotions, which Freire saw as the basis of praxis.

Dichotomous thought: refers to a binary, either/or way of seeing the world that defines one thing in relation to its opposite, with a subject/object power implicit in the relationship, for example, working class/middle class, male/female, white/black. This is a limited understanding of power relations, which hides more than it reveals. *Intersectionality* challenges current thinking to embrace the complexity of interconnected oppressions as a system of domination.

Difference: is shorthand for the wide range of social differences that create our identities, and which are related to the process of *discrimination*, for example, race, class, gender, faith, ethnicity, age, sexuality, disability and so forth.

Discrimination: refers to the process by which people are disadvantaged by their social identity and therefore given unequal access to rights, resources, opportunities and power (Thompson, 2016).

Empowerment: people have their dignity and self-respect restored through empowerment, which is the consequence of critical consciousness: the understanding that life chances are prescribed by structural discrimination, an insight which brings with it the freedom to take action to bring about change for social justice. Empowerment is not fully achieved unless it becomes a collective process.

Environmental justice: calls for action to redress exploitation of the environment by capitalism which is destroying biodiversity and causing climate change, endangered species, pollution and degradation of land and water resources. The impact is experienced disproportionately by already disadvantaged communities and poorer nations, and so is inextricably linked to social justice.

False consciousness: refers to the unquestioning view of the world in which subordinate groups accept their reality in passive and fatalistic ways, leaving the power and privilege of dominant groups unchallenged.

False generosity: Freire saw this in empty gestures that give illusions of equality without changing structural discrimination. He saw charity, benevolence and tokenism as forms of violence that perpetuate poverty for the masses.

Feminism: feminist theory in community development places patriarchy as an all-consuming oppressive force, a system operating in an *intersectional* way over boundaries of class, race and other oppressions to maintain domination of the privileged and powerful. Feminist theory seeks to inform action for change for a diverse and biodiverse world where peace, cooperation, participation and sustainability are the imperatives to change the essentially exploitative system created by capitalism.

Generative theme: an issue that repeatedly crops up in the stories people tell about their lives. Freire referred to it as generative because its relevance generates an energy for action for change out of the hopelessness that is often a result of *alienation*.

Globalisation: refers to the acceleration of *neoliberal capitalism's* global reach by the most powerful systems in the West, not only exploiting the most vulnerable people and environments in the world for economic gain, but also invading other cultures with a Western ideology which reproduces *discrimination* on a complex global level within and between countries.

Hegemony: conceptualises the ways in which one class maintains dominance over the rest of society by a subtle system of coercion and consent. Coercion is maintained through the law, the police and armed forces, and through a parallel but mutual process of ideological persuasion. Gramsci's important contribution gives insight into the way that our minds are colonised by dominant ideas through the institutions of *civil society* – the family, religious organisations, schools and so on – persuading us to consent to our lot in life.

Intersectionality: the way that power relations of race, class, gender and all other differences overlap and intertwine as a complex whole to benefit the interests of white, patriarchal supremacy.

Knowledge democracy: seeks to claim multiple epistemologies and ontologies subsumed under the weight of a dominant truth as a legitimate right and key to the process of diversity and inclusion. This places cognitive justice as inextricably connected to social justice and environmental justice.

Liberating education: Freire's vision was the transformation of humanity to a participatory democracy founded on diversity and biodiversity, achieved by dispelling false consciousness for critical consciousness simply by teaching people to question. This frees people to see *discrimination* for what it is and to act collectively act for change. This process of liberating education is action for freedom, and runs counter to domesticating or *banking education*.

Magical consciousness: is Freire's concept of a fatalistic, disempowered and passive way of seeing the world.

Naive consciousness: is Freire's concept of partial empowerment that relates to the symptoms of oppression, engaging with single issues rather than the underlying roots of injustice.

Neoliberalism: refers to a free market non-interventionist ideology based on profit, individualism, competition, privatisation and the deregulation of trade and finance.

Neoliberal capitalism: refers to the accelerating system of modern capitalism that operates from a profit-over-people-and-planet imperative and has taken on global proportions.

Oppression: is the outcome of *discrimination*. While categories of discrimination can be seen as class, race, gender, ethnicity, and so forth, the forms of oppression which result are classism, racism, sexism, xenophobia and so forth, which are now seen in *intersectional* terms as a complex overlapping net of oppressions which act in the interests of the dominance of white, patriarchal supremacy.

Participation: true participation is achieved in community development through the empowerment of people to engage in collective action for justice and democracy from a critical perspective. Social change comes from bottom–up grassroots action, not top down.

Praxis: a unity of theory and practice, which, in community development, involves theory generated in action, the link between knowledge and power through critical consciousness which leads to critical action.

Prejudice: can be seen as the expression of discrimination at a personal level in overt or covert ways, and involves judgemental attitudes which are based on stereotyping and resist reason or evidence (Thompson, 2016).

Problematising: the essence of Freirean pedagogy; people are encouraged to ask thought-provoking questions and 'to question answers rather than merely to answer questions' (Shor, 1993: 26). This calls for strong democratic values as the basis of a mutual, transformative learning context where educators expect to be co-learners.

Radical community development: is committed to the role of community development in achieving transformative change for social, cognitive and environmental justice, and develops analysis and practice which move beyond local symptoms to the structural causes of *oppression*.

Social justice: for radical community development, social justice aims to create equal worth, equal rights, opportunities for all and the elimination of inequalities reinforced by poverty (Commission for Social Justice, 1994).

TINA: or 'There is no alternative', the mantra of Margaret Thatcher and rally cry of neoliberalism designed to persuade us to accept that this broken capitalist system is the only choice we have.

White privilege: refers to an invisible, assumed entitlement of whiteness as superior. It calls on us to engage with intersections of race, class, gender and all other discriminations including environmental degradation in order to understand, challenge and change whiteness as a political ideology that acts in the interests of the privileged.

Opening thoughts: community development in neoliberal times

Neoliberalism, the political system that has created austerity, and extreme social inequalities, has broken. Chaos reigns, as power attempts to defend itself with even more of the same. Alternatives based on different values have lacked a compelling counternarrative to put in its place. The failure lies, I feel, in not creating the spaces for critical conversations on the politics of everyday life, and the values that most people care about: those of community, connection, kindness, compassion and caring.

Politics is everything about life. It is built on the values we hold dear, the aspirations we have for ourselves and our world, the imagination to see the future we would like to live in, the ideas to create that future, and the freedom for each and every one of us to live that future. It is about human and environmental flourishing. Yet, we find ourselves in a world in crisis, unsustainable for people and for the planet. It is not a world we hold in common, but a world exploited by the few for their own self-interest. The few have taken over and told the many what to believe. We have been gullible, and now the stark consequences face us: we have a responsibility to heal the mess we find ourselves in.

This is not a time to feel defeated: it is an exciting opportunity for change, and we need to be bold. This book is all about seeing things differently. Read on!

> **If poverty is a political choice, then community development is inevitably a political activity!**

This social order is broken

The introduction to the second edition of this book talked about the twin crises of social justice and environmental sustainability created by neoliberal politics. Now, nine years later, we have reached peak inequality, the end of an era (Dorling, 2018a). In 2008, the effects of the global financial crash reverberated through the UK's economy. From 2010, the Coalition and Conservative governments relentlessly tore the fabric of society apart with 'austerity measures that inflicted great cruelty for no apparent economic benefit, but because of what appeared to be a political need to blame the poor … and any other, weaker group, including immigrants, who they could also find a reason to blame for not being rich, for not having tried hard enough' were targeted with spending cuts on public housing, education, health, work and welfare (Dorling, 2018a: 18). This politics of hatred was sold into the popular consciousness as unavoidable 'austerity measures' which

1

forced the poorest to pay the price for reckless, greedy bankers, who ducked under the radar and took home even bigger bonuses! All the while, this provided a smokescreen for the rich to get richer as the poor got poorer.

Eventually, policies of 'greed over need' started to raise questions. In 2009, Wilkinson and Pickett's *The Spirit Level* provided wide-ranging evidence on the costs of inequality, and the connections between social and environmental sustainability. 'It is fortunate that just when the human species discovers that the environment cannot absorb further increases in emissions, we also learn that further economic growth in the developed world no longer improves health, happiness or measures of wellbeing' (Wilkinson and Pickett, 2009: 219).

Gradually, in the UK, we are emerging from a long darkness, coming to realise that profit equates with greed more than equality and that Margaret Thatcher's favourite refrain 'There Is No Alternative' (shortened to TINA) is the anthem of the rich and a death knell for the rest of us. Exposing the harm that extreme inequality inflicts is the beginning of a new dawning. Poverty is a human rights issue. We have been seduced into accepting the inordinate increases in the wealth of the rich at the same time as access to decent housing, education, health, work, law centres, legal aid, child protection, libraries, youth centres, community centres and parks, and our general quality of life and freedom of choice have deteriorated dramatically. And now, as I write this, the evidence is there for all to see, with northern towns – Barnsley, Liverpool, Doncaster, Wakefield, Newcastle … – paying a much higher price in austerity cuts than the south of the country (perpetuating the North/South polarisation started by Thatcher with her war on the miners in 1984–85). Roads in the north are disintegrating, the environment increasingly looks like a litter-strewn, plastic wasteland, with a proliferation of foodbanks, charity shops and doorways occupied by the dispossessed and dehumanised. How long can we continue to say that people deserve to be treated like this, in the fifth-richest economy in the world?

> **'If increasing austerity alongside high and rising economic inequality had been a medical trial, that trial would have had to be halted on ethical grounds.'**
> Dorling (2018a: 18)

Seeing things differently

We have reached a turning point in history, and a crisis presents opportunities to do things differently if we want to avoid more of the same. This book is about seeing things differently in order to do things differently. Community development is predicated on principles of social and environmental justice. But, however much we aspire to these principles, without adequately critiquing the dominant neoliberal narrative, situating local lives in their wider political context, we simply cannot make a difference. At the same time, a counternarrative is called for, a kinder story, based on respect for each other and for the ecosystem we occupy, capable of replacing this atrocious story of dominance, self-importance, individualism and greed.

'People make politics, it does not just happen.'
(Dorling, 2018a: 27)

The forces of discrimination are structural: they reach from political systems into personal lives in community. If we fail to situate local practice in its wider political context, we don't have the understanding we need to develop practice that can bring about change. We do no more than scratch around on the surface, plastering over the cracks. We need to lift the lid and go down deep enough to discover the root causes of oppression if we want to meet our aspirations for social justice. Otherwise, by making life just a little more tolerable we are in danger of erring on the side of discrimination rather than liberation. Don't get me wrong. I fully support immediate action to keep people alive, like foodbanks and homeless shelters. My challenge is that at the same time we need to ask why there should be the need for foodbanks and why so many people are sleeping in doorways in such a rich society. The answers we come up with will then determine the action we need to take to bring about sustainable change for a fairer and more just future.

Stories hold the answer to theory and practice

I have long talked about the power of story in constructing reality. Much more powerful than statistics, stories involve imagination and draw people into them. Stories are the beginning and end of everything; they tell the tales of human suffering and human wellbeing, and hold the political answers to change that we need to act on. I want to begin this book by telling you the story of a week in my life, here in the north-west of England, in November 2018.

 A week in my life that changed my understanding forever

Monday: Far Right rising

I am shocked! Still reeling from the latest move towards Far Right politics when, at the end of October, Brazil elected Jair Bolsonaro as president, with his misogynistic, homophobic, fascist leanings. Those sectors of Brazil fighting for liberation, in the very country that produced Paulo Freire, are despairing of the hard-line neoliberal political agenda that lies ahead for them. Bolsonaro won by identifying the fear vote, emphasising rising crime and political and economic chaos, and offering a radical alternative for the disillusioned. This follows the same pattern we have witnessed with the uprising of white supremacists and right-wing extremists in Brexit Britain and in Trump's USA, where long-term austerity measures foisted on the poor together with immigration crises have created a niche for tapping into hopelessness. But the same pattern is also playing out in Hungary, Greece, Italy, France and a range of other countries that perceive threats of one sort or another... Austria, Romania, the Netherlands, Denmark, Poland, Sweden, Switzerland, Bulgaria ... What in the world is going on? My belief is that this swing is driven by the pendulum of white supremacy in fear of losing power to equality, diversity and biodiversity.

Tuesday: Brexit

Drowning in Brexit, I held my head in despair at hearing Theresa May and her Tory pals infighting over the terms of the UK leaving the European Union, the result of a referendum influenced by lies and corruption. Nigel Farage unveiled UKIP's anti-EU poster showing thousands of refugees supposedly heading for Britain under the caption 'Breaking Point', the result of which was an escalation of racial hatred; Boris Johnson's Tory battle bus was emblazoned with a banner claiming that £350m a week would be diverted from the EU to the National Health Service, a widely acknowledged lie which influenced voting patterns; and we are still waiting for investigations into allegations of corruption based on corporate and foreign interests influencing voting patterns. These are stories targeting the electoral 'hopeless' and 'disillusioned' with the promise of making Britain great again by voting for more of the same neoliberal politics that has created the astonishing paradox of the fifth-richest economy in the world having the most extreme economic divisions in Europe! Already, the outcome has been a loss of those migrant workers who keep our health service, our agricultural industry, our tourist industry and many more functioning in this fearful country divided down the middle on continued membership of the European Union.

Wednesday: Michael Moore and Fahrenheit 11/9

I went to see Michael Moore's alarming documentary, *Fahrenheit 11/9*, an exposé of the fascist underbelly of Donald Trump's neoliberal American society. He presented a hard-hitting story of an openly misogynistic, xenophobic president who boasts of his ability to get away with racist and sexist behaviour and climate-change denial, appealing to new right populism with his outrageous schoolboy Twitter comments that incite a politics of hatred. A huge backlash has seen many – in particular women and notably black women – determined to speak out, stand for election and change the future. The fury of young people in Florida who had witnessed the gun crime massacre of 17 of their friends in school was ignited against right- wing politics, so they organised a national rally, 'Fighting for our Lives', attended by hundreds of thousands of young people demonstrating for Congress to tighten gun laws. Students from the newspaper of the school where the massacre took place were appointed special correspondents for *The Guardian* and have been guest-editing its US website. Moore's documentary is also filled with testaments to the story of the black town of Flint whose water is contaminated by lead in the interests of corrupt, profit-driven greed. I came out of the cinema reeling at this exposé of levels of corruption that are not held accountable. How can we be allowing this to happen after decades of fighting for human rights? I heard Michael Moore interviewed on BBC news saying that his hopes for the future lie in young people, women and black people. White, patriarchal supremacy is becoming more exposed as the scourge of equality.

Thursday: Mike Leigh and Peterloo

I went to see *Peterloo*, director Mike Leigh's portrayal of the Peterloo Massacre, interested by hearing him say he grew up a stone's throw from where it happened but not once did he ever learn about it at school. I had learnt about it in school, but somewhat dispassionately. The film brought the reality to life. On 16 August 1819, almost two hundred years ago, a peaceful, pro-democracy rally of over 60,000 women, children and men gathered in St Peter's Field in the centre of Manchester, some walking 10 miles or more to get there. These people were living in squalor and were under threat of starvation, but turned out in orderly bands, dressed in their Sunday best for a picnic and to hear what the speaker, Orator Hunt, had to say on the right to vote to improve lives for everyone. Only 2% of the population had the vote at the time, and poverty was endemic in Manchester, centre of the world's textile industry and the first industrialised city in Britain. This poverty had been worsened by the economic depression that followed the end of the Napoleonic Wars in 1815; with wages cut, famine and unemployment escalated. The organisers asked them not to bring any weapons to defend themselves against trouble, but to come in the spirit of peace, and this was what they did. In the midst of this peaceful gathering, trapped in an enclosed area, there was a carefully planned attack by the government yeomanry on horseback, charging into the defenceless crowd. Eighteen people were killed, and 700 people were severely injured, maliciously and deliberately. The speakers were tried for treason and journalists at the event were arrested. The military were congratulated. But it marked a turning point in democracy: it was the spawning ground for *The Manchester Guardian*, Chartists and the Suffragette movement. My thought here is that this is yet another example of power defending itself with all the might it can muster when it feels threatened.

Friday: UN rapporteur reports on 'austerity' in the UK after a visit to see for himself!

A stark truth hit the headlines on Friday. In a 42-page report due to be presented to the UN Human Rights Council in Geneva (see undocs.org), Philip Alston, a human rights lawyer and the UN rapporteur on extreme poverty and human rights, highlighted how austerity measures imposed on people in the UK have violated four UN human rights agreements in relation to:

• women
• children
• disabled people, and
• economic and human rights.

If you got a group of misogynists in a room and said how can we make this system work for men and not for women, they would not have come up with too many ideas that are not already in place. (Alston, quoted in Booth and Butler, 2018: 1)

Alston highlights that:

- the UK is world's fifth-largest economy with levels of child poverty that are 'not just a disgrace, but a social calamity and an economic disaster';
- 14 million people – one fifth of the population – live in poverty;
- 1.5 million people are destitute;
- 40% of UK children live in poverty, predicted to rise to 47% by 2022;
- the limit on benefit payments to only the first two children in a family punishes families with a third child;
- cuts of 50% to council budgets are slashing at Britain's 'culture of local concern' and 'damaging the fabric of society';
- the middle classes will 'find themselves in an increasingly hostile and unwelcoming society because community roots are being broken'.

Alston visited towns and cities across the UK over two weeks, and says that the problems are 'obvious to anyone who opens their eyes to see the immense growth in food banks and the queues waiting outside them, the people sleeping rough in the streets, the growth of homelessness, the sense of deep despair that lead even the government to appoint a minister for suicide prevention and civil society to report on the unheard of levels of loneliness and isolation' (Alston, quoted in Booth and Butler, 2018: 1). Yet, the UK government spokesperson on Channel 4 news on 16 November 2018 said that the government disagrees with Alston's report, incomes are at a record high, income inequality has fallen, and universal credit is supporting people into work faster. This is indeed the age of post-truth politics!

Saturday: Extinction Rebellion

After a week of non-violent action, Extinction Rebellion demonstrators blocked five major bridges in London to draw attention to the urgent measures needed to counter climate change, demanding that government acknowledges the crisis and acts on it. The organisers feel that despite marches, lobbying and petitions, nothing is being taken seriously. George Monbiot, in conversation with one of the women involved, suggested that change needs to be gradual, but her response was that, as a 20-year-old mother, she wants a future for her children, there is no time left. In his own words, he had no reply! This is a climate emergency. In October, the Intergovernmental Panel on Climate Change Special Report from leading world climate scientists warned that we have 12 years to limit global warming to 1.5°C to avoid drought, floods, extreme heat and poverty for millions of people. We need to stop using fossil fuels, yet the UK government has overridden the decision of local Lancashire people and local government against fracking, going against community in favour of profit, granting fracking rights to Cuadrilla, a private company, calling on police to control peaceful protestors, often with aggressive, violent tactics and, I ask myself, what is so very different from Peterloo?

Denial of climate change is another chapter in the neoliberal story. Neoliberalism has told a mythical story of no alternative to profit-driven, endless growth, unsustainable exploitation of the earth's resources, poverty, austerity, mass misery, species extinction … all to create a super-rich, privileging the few at the expense of the many.

Making sense of the stories

How can poverty and environmental injustice be a political choice in a democracy, you may ask? How can we get to such desperate levels of human and environmental distress when we have the means to do things differently? Well, it appears that those who tell the most compelling stories create a paradoxical truth. In this case, the dominant ideology, since the onslaught of neoliberalism, has told bigger and better stories about welfare scroungers – work-shy scoundrels: the detritus of society – in an attempt to dehumanise the most vulnerable as a foil for creating a super-rich. The poor are characterised as worthless in this story, so they begin to believe that they really are unworthy; the population at large hears these stories of worthlessness repeated in the media so often that they are accepted as a real truth; and this appalling untruth escalates in such proportions that the rich convince themselves that their self-interested lies are indeed true. The levels of hopelessness that exist as a consequence of 10 years of invented 'austerity', in which the welfare state and the public sector have been mercilessly targeted as a smokescreen for the rich to get richer, resulted in an incredibly strange paradox when some of those most disenfranchised voted in the Brexit referendum for the very form of politics that created their poverty and despair in the first place. Gramsci's concept of hegemony comes to mind, the power of persuasion of dominant narratives in selling a 'common sense' that makes no sense at all. These powerful stories told by the dominant ideology filter into the minds of the many, persuading them to act in the interests of the few!

CRITICAL REFLECTION: What in the world is going on?

Take a few minutes to develop your own reflective thoughts on some of Philip Alston's key comments on the state of the UK from a human rights' perspective:

• **Austerity:** Alston described austerity as a 'punitive, mean-spirited and callous' approach to cuts and reforms, highlighting the Chancellor's decision to hand a tax cut to the rich in the November 2018 budget rather than ease poverty for millions of people – 'austerity could easily have spared the poor, if the political will had existed to do so'.

- **Universal credit:** The government's attempt to simplify the benefits system was a good idea in principle but 'fast falling into universal discredit'. It was too punitive and should be overhauled.

- **Brexit:** The most vulnerable and disadvantaged members of society will take the biggest hit. People feel their homes, jobs and communities are at risk. 'Ironically it was these very fears and insecurity that contributed significantly to the Brexit vote.'

- **Who suffers:** 'Changes to taxes and benefits have taken the highest toll on those least able to bear it.' The cost of austerity has fallen disproportionately on the poor, women, ethnic minorities, children, single parents, asylum seekers and people with disabilities. 'He met people who didn't have a safe place for their children to sleep, who had sold sex for money or shelter, young people who felt gangs were the only way out of destitution and people with disabilities who were being told they needed to go back to work or lose support, against their doctors' orders' (Booth and Butler, 2018: 5).

- **Holes in the safety net:** Libraries, parks and youth centre closures are 'damaging the fabric' of society.

- **Poverty:** 'There is a striking and almost complete disconnect between what I heard from the government and what I consistently heard from many people directly across the country.'

Problematise this paradox: take quotes from the Alston Report (available at undocs.org) and use them as provocations to stimulate dialogue. Identify the contradictions between what Alston is saying from a human rights perspective and the government's response. A decade of so-called 'austerity' cuts to the welfare state and public services have disproportionately impacted on people who are poor, black, disabled, women and children, yet the government tells us that incomes are at a record high. Where is the real truth? During this long period of 'austerity' measures, wealth has been flowing away from the poor into the pockets of the rich. Why would this be happening, when we remain such a rich economy in the world?

Reclaiming the radical agenda

This book overflows with relevant and exciting ideas for all those committed to social justice. It includes important new ideas on what is going on in current times, ideas that will transform your understanding of the political context, and therefore transform the potential of your practice to bring about sustainable change. 'Never has there been a time of greater challenge and opportunity for community development' were my opening words to the second edition. Since then chaos has erupted.

But this current rupture is an opportunity to work for change, for a future that holds hope for everyone. Community is a microcosm of society. The forces of discrimination reach from the structures of society into communities, making some lives appear more important than others, giving some lives greater chances than others. The process of social change begins in communities. But, to bring about anything more than superficial change, the social action from below has to identify the root sources of dominant power from above that are creating such vast injustices. At this point, my focus is on what I identify as the weak points in practice: critiquing the political context that is creating injustice; and developing compelling counternarratives to replace the dehumanising dominant narrative that is destroying so many lives. And it all starts with stories!

A historical juncture

We are at a crossroads in world history, embroiled in a form of neoliberal political ideology so powerful that we do not know which way to turn for the best. We have been left standing, bewildered, failing to analyse what is happening and lacking the imagination to put together a new story of what could be – and we have become stuck. The emphatic story known as TINA ('There Is No Alternative') has silenced us into submission (Dorling, 2018). Our imaginations have frozen.

So, my first point is voice values! Be familiar with the values that inform community development, discuss them regularly with everyone involved in the process, and use them as a system of checks and balances that frame everything: human dignity, mutual respect, trust, reciprocity, mutuality, equality, cooperation.

Next, critique of the current system is vital for effective practice, but critique alone cannot dismantle the power of the neoliberal story; we urgently need counternarratives of hope and possibility inspired by the values we place at the heart of the future we would like to see, a future based on a common good that benefits everyone. George Monbiot talks about the need to go beyond 'an unintelligible cacophony' of fragmented parts to tell 'a coherent and stabilising narrative' (Monbiot, 2017: 6), one that is embedded in the values we would aspire to live by. 'You cannot take away someone's story without giving them a new one' (2017: 1). So, you see, failure to come up with a counternarrative has created a space for Far Right politics to flourish. 'Political failure is, in essence, a failure of imagination' (2017: 6). So, therein lies our challenge!

'Those who tell the stories run the world' (Monbiot, 2017: 1)

We live by stories. They help us to make sense of our world and they create our reality. Dominant narratives are no different from any other story that presents us with a way of seeing the world. They are more convincing than facts or figures. They can persuade us to make sense of nonsense by persuading us to accept unjust contradictions. They can persuade us to believe lies and untruths. They can persuade us to believe that there is no alternative to the failing *status quo*. And in all these ways they manipulate our behaviour, and power maintains control of the masses.

But counternarratives can plant the seeds of change. This is why Paulo Freire (1970) emphasises the importance of social change beginning in the stories of the people. This is the point at which grassroots theory emerges out of lived reality. Through a process of critical consciousness, in dialogue with local people, community development questions the dominant story and exposes its contradictions. Once we begin to question, we see things differently. Why would we continue to vote for a system that is acting against our interests? There are alternatives! We need to work together to create a different story based on the values we hold dear, a counternarrative of diversity and biodiversity, of human flourishing and a happy planet. And if we make this counternarrative convincing, compelling and confident, discussing it in everyday conversations in every public space, we create a new story as the basis for a new reality. Now, in order to understand the need for a new story, let's look at the one that needs replacing.

The neoliberal story

Neoliberalism took hold from the 1980s onwards. In the UK, Margaret Thatcher, Conservative prime minister at the time, told a different story from the post-war narrative of a common good that had given rise to the British welfare state. That story was based on collective responsibility for the wellbeing of all, and on principles of equality of opportunity and equitable distribution of wealth for a good life. The state took responsibility for health, housing, education, employment and overall welfare of the people, and policies reflected these values and principles.

Margaret Thatcher's story ran counter to this. It was based on individualism, telling everyone there is no such thing as society, only individuals and their families. It was a story told with such vehemence that its impact was immediate. What it failed to achieve by conviction, such as the dismantling of working-class solidarity, it achieved by state violence, most notably in the war against the miners in 1984–85, with a move to dismantle the right to freedom of association for the biggest remaining trade union (Milne, 1994). This was reinforced by policy changes that prevented people meeting in 'public assemblies' under the Public Order Act 1986. A 'public assembly' had previously been defined as 20 or more people meeting in a public place wholly or partly in open air, but the Anti-social Behaviour Act 2003 extended this to assemblies of two or more persons. Given that freedom of critique is the key to deepening democracy, we see freedoms being eroded by the back door.

The neoliberal story continued. Its focal point, the free market, emphasises profit over people. We were told that the rich needed to get rich in order for everyone to flourish. The message for those at the bottom of the pile was to tighten belts and wait for the 'trickle-down' effect. Nothing trickled! It simply gave permission for the rich to get even richer, justified by a politics of hatred, which began with the story of the 'welfare scrounger'.

So, we tease out a story of profit rather than people, of individualism rather than collectivism, a free market rather than a fair market, and a small state rather than a responsible state. The promise to deliver a prosperous future for everyone has failed. The rich have become even greedier, and this has had a dehumanising effect on society as a whole, with social mobility stagnating.

The dominant story, told loudly and convincingly enough, becomes a real truth in the minds of the many. Since Thatcherism, we have heard tales about the undeserving poor, the wasters and the feckless who 'rip off' the welfare state. But now, the stories have extended to include immigrants, travellers, Muslims, and have unleashed a fear and hatred so powerful that we see overt discrimination acted out in the public domain with impunity (Tyler, 2013; 2015). This sways public opinion to consent to policies that are acting against the interests of those who vote for them. It is precisely why critical education is at the heart of the matter.

Since the banking crisis of 2007–08, we have heard the concept of 'austerity' sung from the hilltops as an inevitable and undeniable truth. Because so few understand what is really going on, it has come to haunt us as an untruth that distracts from wildly escalating social divisions, the signs of a fragmented and unhealthy society. 'Austerity' measures are not inevitable, they merely mask the way the poor are being made to underwrite the risks taken by corporate interests, at the same time as the rich become unacceptably wealthy, now holding more in common with a global super-rich than with their own culture. Poverty becomes normalised, not seen as a violation of human rights. The reality, however, is that poverty is a political choice.

Even more worrying is the fact that neoliberal ideology has gained hold in numerous countries of the world to create the same excesses for the rich and disenfranchisement of the many. This is at the basis of a crisis in democracy. As the common good is eroded, it gives way to justification for greed. Resources held in common are privatised into the pockets of the rich, and poor children are reduced to living with hunger when there is no need. As neoliberalism flags up its message of inevitability, that there is no alternative, just more of the same, we need to question why we would want to retain a system that has failed people and the planet so miserably.

As Gramsci so powerfully expressed: 'The crisis consists precisely in the fact that the old is dying and the new cannot be born' (Gramsci, 1971: 276). The new cannot be born because we have failed to understand what is going on in the present, as social and economic divisions widen and crises escalate. Equally importantly we have lacked the imagination needed for an alternative story. It is time for a counternarrative fuelled by hope and possibility, one that rejects competition in favour of cooperation, connecting people across difference and diversity from a kind heart. I have some good ideas on a way forward, and none of them are difficult, so read on!

In changing the story we change the course of history

Community development is founded on values of dignity, respect, mutuality, equality, reciprocity and trust. It is driven by principles of social justice and environmental sustainability. This is why it is essential to understand the political context in which we practise. In fact, without this our practice is placatory at best, addressing the surface symptoms of an unjust system, but failing to go deep enough to identify and change the root sources of injustice. This means that we could be culpable: without the necessary analysis to inform why we are doing what we do, we could be guilty of acting in the interests of power, against the interests of the powerless. Our values provide a foundation for a counternarrative; they emphasise the kind of principles we want to live by that will form the structure for a new story. For instance, in your practice it might be that in dialogue with people you repeatedly hear, 'We want to live in a community that is safe, where people accept each other, feel confident and cared for'. This could be the basis for teasing out the first steps to identify what is preventing this and the next steps to creating a counternarrative which identifies the changes needed to create the reality.

A counternarrative has to be compelling, clear and concise, but needs to critique what is wrong in order to change it for the better. For instance, the neoliberal story has weakened our connections with community and contributed to a sense of alienation, isolation and loneliness. This then becomes the basis for making changes that connect people, and by connecting people they not only become happier and healthier, but they become confident that they can work together to change things for the better. The beginning of macro change will come from grassroots communities demanding that change and demonstrating the first steps.

This third edition will provide you with new ideas for practice that could change the course of history!

1

Power and the political context

> The absence of a coherent political project, it is claimed, inhibits the
> development of a more radical paradigm in community work. (Cooke
> and Shaw, 1996: 9)

Reclaiming the radical agenda involves situating practice in its political context,
it is about understanding the structures of power that reach into people's personal
lives to determine their life chances.

Politics is about life itself. Without locating personal lives in their political
context, there is no change. Without a political analysis, radical concepts, like
empowerment, are reduced to ameliorative rather than transformative levels. So,
we need a past–present–future continuum: looking at where we have come from
in order to understand where we are and to steer a course to the future we want
to create. Without this, we are swaying in the breeze, directionless. Worse still,
we are unwittingly the purveyors of the very politics we deplore! We cannot
begin to talk about the concept of empowerment without an analysis of power
and the way that it works to disempower. Let's take a fascinating look at where
we have come from in order to understand where we are today.

The subtle nuances of the concept of empowerment are fundamental to community
development analysis, determining whether practice is informed by pathologising
or liberating theories. I am going to use this focus of power and empowerment to
explore the changing political contexts that have informed the theory and practice
of community development. By these means, my intention is to illustrate the ways
in which dominant ideology influences policy and practice, which, without a
critical dimension, skews us towards amelioration rather than transformation.
For those of us who take social justice seriously, those competing interests in these
turbulent political times demand vigilance: the creation of 'democratic spaces' in
which to engage in critical dissent dialogue are vital to the realignment of our
principles and our practice.

Beveridge and the welfare state

People were ready for change after the harshness and fear of the war years; they
did not want to go back to the austerity of the pre-war economic depression.
Based on the recommendations of the Beveridge Report (1942), which identified
the five giant evils of society as poverty, poor health, unemployment, poor
housing and poor education, a 'cradle to grave' welfare state, based on a collective
responsibility for the health and wellbeing of all, was planned to provide social

security, a national health service, free education and council housing, with a promise of full employment with decent wages and conditions. This was a major landmark in social justice thought and action; a revolutionary ideology that changed the face of the country. It was an acknowledgment that we all have collective responsibility for contributing to a common good.

However, democracy is a contested concept and therefore needs to be constantly critiqued and questioned. Whilst Beveridge dealt with the five evils related to class, he overlooked 'the giants Racism and Sexism, and the fights against them, behind statues to the Nation and the White Family'(Williams, 1989: 162). This was a time when women who had done so much in the workplace in the war years were forced to return to the confines of home and family to make jobs available for 'returning heroes'. It was also a time when British recruitment offices were opened in Caribbean countries to encourage immigration to the UK to help rebuild Britain. The first boat to dock was the MV *Empire Windrush*, arriving at Tilbury Docks in 1948 with workers from Jamaica, Trinidad and Tobago, and other Caribbean islands. This was the start of the large-scale immigration programme from 1948 to 1971, when Caribbean people – now known as the Windrush generation – who fought for Britain in World War II and who felt proud to be part of the British Empire, came to fill the UK's labour shortage. Their anticipated welcome was short-lived when they were met with overt hostility in the streets (Draper, 2015), by 1968 this was expressed politically in Enoch Powell's 'Rivers of Blood' speech, and to our shame has continued in the targeting of the 'Windrush generation' by immigration authorities today. Racism, sexism and all the other '-isms' that we were to understand in greater depth structurally as part of our culture in the new social movements of the 1980s were yet to penetrate our consciousness and lay somewhat concealed in that layer of everyday-taken-for-grantedness, what Freire would call 'naïve consciousness', yet to become critical.

Another significant focus of Beveridge, alongside his 'five giants', was his emphasis on 'absolute' poverty. In 1965, Peter Townsend and Brian Abel-Smith uncovered the damage done by 'relative' poverty (cited in Mack and Lansley, 1985), revealing the limitations of the welfare state. Relative poverty is related to social inequalities, so the wider the gaps between privilege and destitution in society, the more people are likely to be in relative poverty. Television documentaries such as *Cathy Come Home* (BBC, 1966) heightened public awareness of the reality of class oppression, even though this was yet to be related to what we now call intersectionality, the way that race, class, gender and other differences overlay and overlap to create multiple, intersecting oppressions. The important point here is to recognise how resilient our thinking is, how difficult it is to think outside the box to challenge and change. However, these new insights into the damaging impact of relative poverty prompted a Quaker initiative which led to the Child Poverty Action Group (CPAG) being formed in 1965, co-founded by Peter Townsend. (CPAG continues to be a vital source of poverty analyses and campaigns relevant to community development, linking grassroots projects with wider collective action.) This outcome is a good example of praxis, but it was not enough to sustain change, as we have found out to our cost.

The British welfare state was a flagship for the world. The idea of universal welfare was fundamental to an ideology of a common good, based on values of cooperation and mutuality. What was to follow could not have been anticipated. An unprecedented swing away from these values of cooperation to competition was made possible by a crisis of welfare spending, coupled with a global economic recession that took hold from 1973, exposing a space for change. Out of that space emerged a very different story, the story of neoliberalism, and this marked the beginning of the vast social and economic inequalities that we find ourselves facing today.

The birth of neoliberalism

Forty years ago, extreme inequality was unimaginable!

The founders of neoliberal thought were Friedrich Hayek and Milton Friedman, both 'firm believers in the power of ideas' (Bregman, 2018: 244). They tackled the idea of a free society as an intellectual adventure in search of a liberal Utopia, believing that the ideas of economists and philosophers are stronger than those of business and politics. The next stopping point in my version of this story is a little village in Switzerland where, on 1 April 1947, 40 philosophers, historians and economists gathered, at a meeting initiated by Hayek and attended by Friedman, to form 'a corps of capitalist resistance fighters against socialist supremacy' (Bregman, 2018: 245). This became known as the Mont Pelerin Society, after the village. The society firmed up its message, blaming problems on government and promoting the free market as the solution. Get rid of the minimum wage. Privatise education. Privatise healthcare. In fact, let the market reign supreme. They waited for a crisis to open up an opportunity, and that came in 1973 when oil prices were raised by 70 per cent by the Organisation of Arab Petroleum Exporting Countries, together with an embargo on exports to the US and the Netherlands. 'Western economies spiraled into recession' (Bregman, 2018: 247). Understanding the power of ideas is important: Friedman forever emphasised that the success of his neoliberal project was due to those ideas formed in that little Swiss village all those years ago.

> 'The rise of neoliberalism played out like a relay race, with think tanks passing the baton to journalists, who handed it off to politicians. Running the anchor leg were two of the most powerful leaders in the Western world, Ronald Reagan and Margaret Thatcher.'
> Bregman (2018: 247)

Neoliberalism went global: within a period of less than 50 years, the neoliberal idea that had been seen as marginal, even ridiculous, had found its niche and came to rule the world. It raises thoughts in my mind about the power of these ideas to sell themselves as a form of social control, a 'class project … an ideology which aims to restore and consolidate class power' (Tyler, 2013: 7). To that end, it is capable of dismantling compassion and all responsibility for a common good, stultifying the imagination and persuading people that there is no alternative to a way of life that harms everyone and the natural world.

> 'But the inability to imagine a world in which things are different is evidence only of a poor imagination, not of the impossibility of change.'
> Bregman (2018: 199)

What is neoliberal ideology?

Founded on the market controlling society, rather than society controlling the market, neoliberalism operates on a guiding principle that competition is the only way to organise society. It promotes deregulated economies, an uncontrolled market free to trade and driven by profit, and a small government controlling society by 'austerity' and privatisation. This is the ideology that informs the policies that shape our society today. Compare this with the ideology of the welfare state, and you begin to see that it was a shocking change from the thinking behind the welfare state based on cooperation and a common good. Even the International Monetary Fund (IMF), originally one of the significant proponents of neoliberalism, now has the temerity to admit that 'there is statistical evidence for the spread of neoliberal policies since 1980, and their correlation with economic growth, boom–and–bust cycles and inequality' (Metcalf, 2018). As Metcalf says, 'it is the reigning ideology of our era – one that venerates the logic of the market and strips away the things that make us human'. As a consequence of putting the interests of profit above the wellbeing of people and the planet, this ideology has had a disastrous impact on both. Metcalf stresses the importance of recognising neoliberalism as a human invention, just as the welfare state was, but its pervasiveness has permeated all aspects of human behaviour, persuading us to see individual wants as more important than collective needs. As practitioners committed to social justice, it is vital that we understand how its power works in order to change it!

How does neoliberalism work?

The political interpretation of neoliberalism is much more than profit-generated free-trade. It has been sold to us lock, stock and barrel, changing the horizontal axis of *cooperation,* the basis of a common good, to a vertical axis based on *competition,* a complete coup entailing the 'reordering of social reality, and ... rethinking our status as individuals' (Metcalf, 2018). It is a wonderful example of Gramsci's concept of the power of ideological persuasion (explained in depth in Chapter 6). Competition, as previously applied within the study of economics, has pervaded every nook and cranny of society, not only in our homes and communities, but under the surface of our skin to affect all we believe. It has become the organising principle for our thinking and being.

The process of neoliberal globalisation accelerated throughout the 1990s, increasingly projecting its free trade profit imperative across the world. Profit without constraints inevitably implies exploitation, and this began to make an impact on people and on the planet in crisis proportions. Neoliberal globalisation is the 'market-organized and imposed expansion of production that emphasizes comparative advantage, free trade, export orientations, the social and spatial divisions of labour, and the absolute mobility of corporations' (Fisher and Ponniah, 2003: 28). In other words, we find ourselves in a world where capitalism has re-formed on a global level, exploiting people and degrading environments in the interests of the dominant and privileged. It is a form of corporate capitalism where the most powerful systems of the West not only dominate the world economically, but also invade other cultures with a Western worldview that works by aggravating political, cultural, racial, gendered, sexual, ecological and epistemological differences. In the name of a free market economy, not only is labour exploited in the interests of capital (class), but the same structures of oppression that subordinate groups of people according to race, gender, age, sexuality, faith, ethnicity and disability are reproduced on a global level.

> Neoliberal globalization is not simply economic domination of the world but also the imposition of a monolithic thought (*pensamento unico*) that consolidates vertical forms of difference and prohibits the public from imagining diversity in egalitarian, horizontal terms. Capitalism, imperialism, monoculturalism, patriarchy, white supremacism and the domination of biodiversity have coalesced under the current form of globalization. (Fisher and Ponniah, 2003: 10)

Wealth is increasingly transferred from poor to rich countries by exploiting the labour and resources of the developing world in order to feed the consumerist greed of the West. The consequence is increased social divisions both within and between countries, with some corporations becoming wealthier than some of the world's poorest countries, and rich countries increasingly privileging the already privileged while abandoning swelling numbers of people to lives in poverty. Globalisation presents anti-discriminatory practice with increasingly complex, interlinking and overlapping oppressions that are poorly understood and therefore infrequently challenged. In this way, poverty becomes increasingly convoluted, and oppression becomes distant and even more concealed. It is not possible to take a critical approach to community development without having an analysis of the way in which all communities are inextricably linked on this global dimension. For example, it is Giroux's critique of the 'politics of disposability' (Giroux, 2006) as a central project of neoliberal globalisation's profit imperative that has led to our understanding of the full impact of an ideology of the market, and the way that our worth as human beings became ranked according to our potential as consumers and producers. The result is an increasingly divided world, one that is both environmentally unsustainable and socially unjust.

Neoliberal emphasis on deregulation and privatisation of a state's economic activities creates a niche for multinational companies to gain control over national economies. This benefits corporate interests, siphoning money out of local communities to profit big businesses. Kane likens this activity to that of 'a kind of international loan shark' (Kane, 2008: 196). Let's trace the beginnings of this preposterous narrative as it unfolded in the UK where Thatcherism gave it a foothold at a particular moment in time.

Thatcherism

The story of Thatcherism starts in 1975, when, during a meeting held shortly after being elected Conservative Party leader in the UK, Margaret Thatcher is said to have decisively thumped Hayek's *The Constitution of Liberty* onto the table and announced, 'This is what we believe' (Monbiot, 2017: 34). It became her rulebook to the letter when she was elected prime minister in 1979. She plunged herself into the sudden and immediate application of Hayek's principles, which included not only tax cuts to benefit the rich, the dismantling of trade unions, deregulation, privatisation, outsourcing and competition in public services, and fees for education, but also moves to dismantle the welfare state and end free universal healthcare. Luckily, she was restrained by her own party from the full implementation of her plans (Monbiot, 2017).

Ronald Reagan became US President in 1980, and took up the neoliberal cudgels. Reagan and Thatcher became political pals, and between them they aimed to destroy workers' rights to give free unharnessed rein to profit and free trade. Neoliberal ideologies emerged from obscurity to control the world nurtured by Thatcher in the UK, Reagan in the US and Pinochet in Chile, with the

International Monetary Fund (IMF), the World Bank, the Maastricht Treaty and the World Trade Organization (WTO) playing key roles in this story. From the election of the Thatcher government in 1979, the full and unmitigated ascendance of New Right politics was in full swing by the mid-1980s. New Right rhetoric, blaming the victims of poverty for their own suffering, painted evocative stereotypes of the 'welfare scrounger' that divided the poor into 'deserving' and 'undeserving'. This was reinforced by such bizarre parliamentary behaviour as Norman Tebbit's 'On yer bike' message to abandon community ties in the search for employment, and the demonisation of single parents by Peter Lilley in his rendition to Parliament of Gilbert and Sullivan: "I've got a little list, I've got a little list of young ladies who get pregnant just to jump the housing list". These divide-and-rule politics set people in poverty against each other and created a divided Britain. It was a clever and powerful ideology that captured the public imagination, paving the way for major policy change as working-class solidarity gave way to a widespread culture of individualism.

This conceptual paradox, one of *need* set against *greed*, made an immediate impact on communities. Social welfare became perceived as a burden rather than a collective responsibility and a moral right. Notions of collective social responsibility, which had formed the bedrock for the post-war welfare state, gave way to a competitive culture of individual greed driven by consumerism. The 'Thatcher revolution', an abrupt swing to the Far Right, brought about comprehensive social, political and economic change by a 'dismantling of the protective elements of state welfare, to breaking the power of the organised labour movement and to a reaffirmation of market forces that would bring poverty and unemployment to unprecedented levels' (Novak, 1988: 176).

Under Thatcherism, social reforms devoured rights and reduced benefits for some of the most vulnerable groups in society. These risks of poverty were further exacerbated by class, race, ethnicity, gender, age and disability, 'yet to suggest that poverty is evidence of structural rather than personal failing is to swim against the modern-day tide of individualism' (Witcher, quoted in Oppenheim and Harker, 1996: vii).

As a society, we became complicit, allowing the most vulnerable to be exploited in the interests of the powerful. 'Between the 1980s and 1990s, the number of people who could objectively be described as living in poverty increased by almost 50 per cent' (Gordon and Pantazis, 1997: 21). There was a massive transfer of wealth from the poor to the rich, with the income of the wealthiest tenth of the UK's population being equal to that of the poorest half (Goodman et al, 1997). The indictment of this period is the way that poverty targeted children. From only one in ten children in 1979, by 1997 one in every three children in Britain was growing up in poverty (Flaherty et al, 2004).

'Freedom' as the central tenet of neoliberalism

> 'Freedom from trade unions and collective bargaining means the freedom to suppress wages. Freedom from regulation means the freedom to poison rivers, endanger workers, charge iniquitous rates of interest and design exotic financial instruments. Freedom from tax means freedom from the distribution of wealth that binds society together.'
>
> Monbiot (2017: 37)

The British trade union movement was a beacon of hope to workers around the world. In action, we witnessed Thatcher's war against the miners. The miners' strike of 1984–85 was a pivotal point in UK history as Margaret Thatcher targeted the National Union of Mineworkers (NUM), determined to dismantle the largest remaining force of organised labour in Britain. The story of the miners' struggle against the might of the state is one of the greatest examples of collective grassroots action in recent history. Mining communities, built around the pitheads to serve the industry, had seen generations of families and neighbours grow up side by side, sharing lifetimes together in the face of the danger and adversity of mining conditions. Closing the mines closed the communities and ended a culture. Alan Brown from Barnsley talks about the Battle of Orgreave:

 **The Battle of Orgreave**

'I came away that day with a black eye and a cut on my face but there were many worse off than me, especially the lad who was beaten in front of the TV cameras. He had brain damage after this and still to this day suffers from the beating he got. No one was brought to book over this even though everyone saw the cop who did this but before the police got to Orgreave they all took their numbers off their uniforms.

On our first day back to work we marched from Darton to Woolley pit with everyone clapping us. I was walking with my late father, Jack, and had tears in my eyes all the way. When we got to the pit we were told that there was a list of names and if you were not on the list your job wasn't there any more. But transfers to other pits were open to anyone who wanted it. So before the Christmas holiday I signed on at Riccall pit in the Selby coalfield and started after the holidays. I still live in Barnsley and our old pit is now a housing estate but I think our town isn't the same without all the pits around it. And I will never forget Thatcher for what she did.'

Source: 'Your Miners' Strike stories', BBC, 24 August 2009, available at news.bbc.co.uk (accessed 21/05/18).

I was a grassroots community worker at the time, and witnessed Margaret Thatcher's ideology in action. At the same time as police were being drafted from other parts of the country to use direct force to break the miners' union, poor people were told to tighten their belts, as it was necessary to make rich people richer in order to get a trickle-down effect to benefit the poor. Divide-and-rule politics turned people against each other. We heard a great deal about welfare scroungers and rip-off lone parents, but we heard nothing at all about the unacceptability of poverty. In these ways, working-class solidarity was brought to an abrupt end and we were all caught in the headlights of state brutality and the power of persuasion to silence people, Gramsci-style.

Only in the course of time have the dirty tricks of the state been exposed: full power was vented on the National Union of Mineworkers, not to reform the economics of coal, but to target the right to organise (Milne, 1994). Margaret Thatcher perceived her hairsbreadth victory as a triumph over the power of collective organisation, and it gave her government a head of steam to bring in other major reforms. For instance, the Social Security Act 1986 promised welfare changes unsurpassed since Beveridge, but the results were devastating, forcing vulnerable groups further onto the margins of society while the rich got richer. It was a sudden, revolutionary move to the Right, with disastrous results. Economic growth in the UK and the USA slowed down, and inequalities of income and wealth accelerated after a long period of greater equality.

Community development practitioners were alarmed by Thatcher's abrupt change from collectivism to individualism, telling convincing tales of "no such thing as society, only individuals and their families". For me, the biggest shock of all was to see the sudden and immediate impact of these stories on communities that had previously prided themselves on working-class solidarity. One minute the word on the block was that you never violate your own, though it was almost OK to randomly redistribute resources by robbing the rich outlying communities, the next minute crime turned in on the community itself. Conversations in the community centre began to include such statements as "If you've got any sense, you just see to yourself". The driver had become self-preservation and the sacrifice was community. It was the beginning of the severance of the social connection, a necessary part of the human condition. Nevertheless, there were still those who operated from a kind heart and worked together ...

Blair: centrist politics and the end of class

Tony Blair is associated with the centre politics of New Labour, the dawn of which was the landslide election of the Blair government in 1997. It was neither on the Left nor the Right, but in the centre; apparently, we were all on the same side. Blair also told us it was the end of class, 'the class war is over [but] he meant we should accept the victory of the rich.... Never mind unearned income and the unequal division of labour, job shortages or the lottery of birth in a highly unequal society: class is reduced to a matter of character and effort. Now the

Conservatives counterpose "hard-working people" and "strivers" to "skivers"' (Sayer, 2018: 296).

From the rhetoric, we believed that at last this marked a distinct shift from Thatcher's 'no such thing as society', and we heaved a sigh of relief. Not long after his election, Prime Minister Blair wrote:

> we all depend on collective goods for our independence; and all our lives are enriched – or impoverished – by the communities to which we belong.... A key challenge of progressive politics is to use the state as an enabling force, protecting effective communities and voluntary organisations and encouraging their growth to tackle new needs, in partnership, as appropriate. (Blair, 1998: 4)

This ideology was informed by the thinking of Anthony Giddens (1998). New Labour combined strands of communitarianism: community as a life with meaning based on the mutual interdependence of individuals, and the role of the state in partnership with community in creating a quality of life. For the first time, we found the language of partnership with community, of bold anti-poverty statements, of a preoccupation with regeneration projects, of widening access to education. In this context, community development gained more policy recognition than it had known before. But radical community development was alerted to the increasing repositioning of Left and Right towards the centre, removing the dialectical relations of traditional political parties to suggest that we are all on the same side in mutual partnership. Without this adversarial positioning, policies and practice became flawed by the absence of a structural analysis of inequality and injustice. The rhetoric of communitarianism, that of autonomous, flourishing communities founded on mutuality and reciprocity, took on an edge of state authoritarianism. Zero tolerance policing, punitive approaches to asylum seekers, and on-the-spot fines for anti-social behaviour were indicative of policy approaches that circumvented a bottom-up empowerment model to impose top-down interventionist approaches to community (Calder, 2003).

New Labour and child poverty

At Toynbee Hall, in March 1999, Tony Blair delivered a speech on the legacy of Sir William Beveridge, the unanticipated high spot of which was his own personal and political commitment to end child poverty within 20 years. The absence of 'poverty' from political discourse throughout Thatcherism had created a smokescreen for what was happening in reality, so Tony Blair's public declaration to end child poverty brought an upsurge of optimism from the social justice lobby, and a raft of policies appeared on child poverty, unemployment, neighbourhood deprivation and inequalities in health and educational achievement. CPAG found itself for the first time working with a government that acknowledged the unacceptability of soaring child poverty rates, and was encouraged by an abundance of anti-poverty policies directed at children and poor families. But, just below the surface, contradictions emerged between the interests of the state and the rights and responsibilities of parents. As Tess Ridge (2004) pointed out, a state interest in children as future workers leads to policies that are qualitatively different from those that are concerned with creating happy childhoods:

> Children who are poor are not a homogeneous group, although they are often represented as being so. Their experiences of being poor will be mediated by, among other things, their age, gender, ethnicity, health and whether or not they are disabled. In addition, children will interpret their experiences of poverty in the context of a diverse range of social, geographical and cultural settings. (Ridge, 2004: 5)

More than this, we now know that poverty damages children's cognitive development in the early years (Dickerson and Popli, 2015), so no amount of schooling is going to put that right!

Those of us fighting for social justice celebrated Blair for putting child poverty on his personal and political agenda. We were exuberant and optimistic that the horrors of inequality would be put right. But Blair's principles were flawed: he did not care enough about inequality. Owen Jones (2016: 100) critiques New Labour for taking working-class voters for granted, allowing them 'to tailor their policies to privileged voters'. Astonishingly, the rise in inequality triggered by Thatcher continued. New Labour's centre politics resulted in disillusionment; voters felt there was little to choose between any of the main parties. Blair proved that his rhetoric was empty: he was not too concerned about reducing inequality as long as the rich paid taxes. 'During Tony Blair's time in office, the top 1% carried on taking more and more each year as compared to the year before, just as fast as they had done during the Thatcher years' (Dorling, 2018: 18).

A betrayal of socialism

Tony Blair was a warmonger. He will be remembered for his alliance with Bush on the USA's 'war on terror', and the delusional justification of weapons of mass destruction. In 2001, he joined forces with the USA for the invasion of Afghanistan and in 2003 for the invasion of Iraq, flying in the face of popular protest. In his first six years, Blair ordered British troops into battle five times – more than any other prime minister in British history. He was the Labour Party's longest-serving prime minister, the only person to have led the Labour Party to three consecutive general election victories, but his anti-democratic stance on war was to be his downfall and his legacy. He was succeeded as Prime Minister on 27 June 2007 by Gordon Brown.

Blair's premiership is now seen as a betrayal of socialism, an abandonment of the political Left's commitment to workers, in favour of pandering to the privileged.

Despite all his rhetoric of a commitment to ending child poverty, his achievement was a deplorable rise in inequality (Metcalf, 2017).

CRITICAL REFLECTION: Tony Blair

Despite indications of a commitment to social justice, and his impressive stand on child poverty, Sayer critiques Tony Blair's analysis as naïve from the time he talked about his lack of concern for the gap between rich and poor in the 2001 general election campaign. Sayer draws on a later interview in March 2005 in which Blair justified this statement:

> 'What I meant by that was not that I don't care about the gap, so much as I don't care if there are people who earn a lot of money. They are not my concern. I do care about people who are without opportunity, disadvantaged and poor. We've got to lift those people but we don't necessarily do that by hammering the people who are successful.' (Lazzarato, 2012: 20, cited in Sayer, 2016: 164)

Reflect on Blair's choice of words, 'the people who are successful'. Sayer suggests that using the concept 'successful' distracts from questioning the source of riches, for example whether the money is inheritance or unearned income, whether it has come from unethical sources or whether it is inflated income differential. Importantly, Blair's suggestion that it is 'not his concern' diverts attention from the relationship between poverty and wealth, which is vital for understanding the way that power works by blaming the poor for their own poverty. Does this encourage us to unquestioningly accept the rich? If we do that, we also accept poverty as a failure rather than a structural discrimination. Instead of looking at increasing income inequalities as a problem for society, by dismissing the rich as being 'of no concern' lays the problem at the feet of the poor. This ideology led to policies that ignored economic justice and the nature of advantage to focus on disadvantage as the problem: the unemployed needed to be helped back to work through training programmes for jobs that did not exist; poor children needed to work hard at school in order to get jobs as adults, overlooking the cognitive and emotional damage that growing up poor inflicts on children in the early years. This is similar to looking at racism without looking into the nature of white privilege; it ducks the central issues of power. Think about these points and, in dialogue with local people or colleagues, pose the questions that Sayer raises.

Perhaps the key to understanding Blair lies in the words of Margaret Thatcher:

> When asked what she considered to be her greatest victory, Thatcher's reply was 'New Labour': under the leadership of neoliberal Tony Blair, even her social democratic rivals in the Labour Party had come around to her worldview. (Bregman, 2018: 249)

Cameron's 'Big Society'

Much to the dismay of those of us committed to social justice, Gordon Brown, the Labour leader, withdrew from the coalition debate after the inconclusive general election of 2010, leaving the way clear for an alliance between David Cameron, the Conservative leader, and Nick Clegg, leader of the Liberal Democrats. The 'Big Society' was the flagship policy of the Conservative Party, and became the driver of the coalition government, aiming to decentralise state power and hand power over to communities and local people.

The concept of the 'Big Society' was, it claimed, about participatory democracy and community empowerment. The paradox became apparent when the transference of power to communities was accompanied by 'austerity' cuts in public sector provision, targeting the poorest in general, and women, children and older people in particular. The Trades Union Congress, in the most comprehensive analysis of public spending ever undertaken, *Where the Money Goes* (available at www.tuc.org), forecast that the public sector cuts in health, social and education services would hit the poorest 13 times harder than the richest, with most impact felt by women, children and older people. Vanessa Baird (2010) identified a major contradiction by questioning the wisdom of prioritising community credit unions as anti-poverty strategies without setting this in juxtaposition with the need for redistributive wealth. The 'small state' was absolving its democratic responsibilities to the poorest in society by making 'austerity' cuts in public services at the same time as making the poorest responsible for their own poverty.

The country was confused. What, precisely, did this mean in relation to everyday lives? Then the impact of major funding cuts was made public. The 'Big Society' was exposed as a metaphor for targeting the poor. In February 2011, as pro-democracy grassroots protests demonstrated the power of collective action throughout the Middle East, Cameron gave a public speech defending his 'Big Society', claiming it had nothing to do with financial cuts, it was about the social recovery of the 'broken society', it was about making people responsible, about mending broken families, about giving communities power by reducing public services, devolving state power and increasing charitable giving.

The 'small state' in handing over power to the 'Big Society' effectively labelled communities as both the problem and the solution (Craig, 2011). Community development is a process of empowerment that leads to autonomous communities. This is precisely why Thatcher's concept of 'care in the community' and Cameron's 'Big Society' need to be critiqued for 'community engagement [being] used as an excuse for social dumping' (Monbiot, 2017: 81). Both of these initiatives were based on using community as an alternative to state responsibility. Community development's role is not to provide an alternative to state responsibility: this fudges the issue of inequality. Critique and dissent are vital to deepening democracy, identifying unjust concentrations of wealth and power in order to force the state to be a protector of democracy by ensuring fair distribution of resources, maintaining rights and keeping a balance of power between the powerful and powerless (Coote, 2010). This all went badly wrong!

The Brexit referendum

> The Brexiteers' promise during the 2016 EU referendum was that the United Kingdom would 'take back control'. The ensuing two and a half years have shown how unfit Britain is to do so. As well as demonstrating that the UK has no coherent strategy for leaving the EU, the Brexit debacle has exposed its economic, social, political and constitutional frailties and fractures. For a country historically governed by parliamentary sovereignty, the Leave vote was a subversive event … all the more disruptive since two of the UK's four nations (England and Wales) voted for Brexit, while two (Scotland and Northern Ireland) voted against. ('Leader: Ill fares the land' in *The New Statesman*, 25–31 January 2019)

Brexit is one of the most remarkable stories in British political history (Mosbacher and Wiseman, 2016). David Cameron courted the votes of Eurosceptic Conservative MPs during his party leadership election pitch in 2005. This planted the seed of his eventual political downfall. He resisted the idea of an in/out EU referendum, but his failure to win a majority in the 2010 general election, and his decision to enter into a coalition with the Liberal Democrats under Nick Clegg, resulted in a coalition agreement to bind it, and any subsequent government, to a referendum if a European treaty transferred any (rather vague) powers from the UK to the EU: 'We will amend the 1972 European Communities Act so that any proposed future treaty that transferred areas of power, or competences, would be subject to a referendum on that treaty – a "referendum lock"' (Cameron and Clegg, 2010:19). Opposed by Labour and struggling through the House of Lords, this somewhat vague measure became law in 2011, primarily as a means to allow the two coalition parties to agree to disagree on Europe. It was designed to placate opposing views at a time when the likelihood of a referendum in the UK was seen as minimal.

By the summer of 2012 Cameron had changed his position on an in/out EU referendum and went public on this in 2013. A backbench proposal for a referendum had resulted in an unanticipated parliamentary rebellion on Europe against a government-imposed three-line whip on its MPs to oppose the proposal. Cameron wrongly believed that a referendum could be won by the 'in' vote and so as not to antagonise the 'out' rebels, and under increasing pressure from outside parliament with the growing threat of the UK Independence Party (UKIP), he gave a pledge that a referendum would be implemented after the 2015 general election, assuming the Conservatives were still in office.

The Leave and Remain campaigns were conducted very differently. Dominic Cummings, Campaign Director of Vote Leave, saw an opportunity: the case for

Leave had to be emotive and specific, based on the slogan 'Take Back Control'. Public imagination was captured by Boris Johnson's 'battle bus' imagery of the (alleged) £350m weekly cost of EU membership diverted to funding a failing National Health Service (NHS), coupled with fear stoked by Nigel Farage's anti-immigrant 'Breaking Point' poster which appeared to suggest that Turkey joining the EU would escalate UK immigration by enabling refugees to cross EU borders. 'What the Brexiteers understood was the need for simplicity and emotional resonance: a narrative that would give visceral meaning to a decision that might otherwise appear technical and abstract' (D'Ancona, 2017: 17). We are understanding Far Right rhetoric, and its use of outrage, chaos and confusion, a lot better in retrospect. 'A debate about whether it's appropriate to brand a law preventing a no-deal Brexit as "the Surrender Act" works well for Johnson, just as the row over the bogus £350m did in 2016, not least because it ensures the idea gets repeated on the airwaves ad nauseam; surrender, surrender, surrender' (Freedland, 2019). In these ways, the dominant narrative gets embedded in popular consciousness.

Remain did not understand this need for a simple counternarrative with emotional resonance and concentrated instead on facts and figures and experts, drowning a public, already sceptic of experts, in indigestible statistics. Story matters more than facts when it comes to engaging with people and the issues that concern them. Even though the Remain arguments were supported by a majority of economists, thinktanks, business leaders, diplomats and professional bodies, the Leave campaign was quick to dismiss any evidence-based arguments, including those from the Bank of England, and the BBC played a questionable role in giving excess air time to this Far Right campaign (Behr, 2016).

Nevertheless, all the forecasts on referendum polling day, 23 June 2016, pointed to a Brexit defeat, so much so that many of us went to bed confident that leaving the EU would be unthinkable. At breakfast, the result shocked the nation: 51.9% voted Leave; 48.1% Remain (Mosbacher and Wiseman, 2016).

BORIS JOHNSON'S BREXIT BATTLE BUS

However did we get into this Brexit mess?

Despite loud proclamations of 'Leave means Leave, the British people have voted', what came to be known as Brexit went ahead on a very narrowly won margin a referendum based on a simplistic yes/no vote informed by a lot of emotive lies and few facts on the implications of this enormous constitutional change to the everyday lives of people in the UK. The reality is that it was an inconclusive vote, dividing the country, causing chaos, confusion and fear. Under the leadership of Theresa May, the Conservative Party continued to steer a rocky course towards leaving the peace and cooperation the EU had brought to Britain, surrounded by uncertainty as to the future and its outcome. As I write, the UK has still not left the EU. Neither Theresa May nor Boris Johnson was democratically elected as prime minister. Theresa May, having failed to get a Brexit agreement through parliament, was rejected in favour of Boris Johnson by the Conservative Party membership. The antics of Boris Johnson's no-majority government in railroading an exit from the EU without maintaining good relations with our nearest neighbours and trading partners has been alarming. So far a disastrous no-deal Brexit has been averted by a hair's breadth, but the situation still hangs in the balance, and the chaos continues. A general election has been set for 12 December 2019. It is a juncture in history, and we wait to see a future direction in a climate of fear and social unrest. So, however did we get into this Brexit mess?

There are the plausible allegations of dirty tricks. The UK public was misled by lies such as Boris Johnson's 'battle bus' promise and propaganda such as Nigel Farage's blatantly anti-immigrant 'Breaking Point' poster, appearing to depict a long queue of Syrian refugees waiting to enter the UK, fuelling Muslim discrimination. There are ongoing investigations into corruption (including the exposé by Channel 4 News of Farage being bankrolled throughout the campaign and since the referendum by Far Right millionaire Arron Banks [www.channel4. com, 16 May 2019]).

General research carried out by Vyacheslav Polonski, a network scientist at the University of Oxford, into social media's part in influencing the vote reveals that Instagram was used by twice as many Brexit supporters, who were five times more active than Remain activists. There was a similar pattern on Twitter, with Leave supporters outnumbering Remain by 7:1. The impact was reflected in the support that social media generated for Leave: 26% more likes and 20% more comments. The most active users were campaigning for Leave. In Polonski's opinion, the evidence suggested that, 'Using the Internet, the Leave camp was able to create the perception of wide-ranging public support for their cause that acted like a self-fulfilling prophecy, attracting many more voters to back Brexit' (Polonski, 2016). In terms of social media influence on the referendum vote, Facebook has launched an investigation into claims that Russia used the social network to influence the Brexit referendum, and the whole debacle surrounded by post-truth arrogance, lies and dirty tricks rumbles on.

A series of further surprises

In the face of this shock defeat on the EU question, David Cameron left us to it! Only a few hours after the referendum result, standing outside 10 Downing Street, visibly shaken, he said that his country needed 'fresh leadership':

> Although leaving Europe was not the path I recommended, I am the first to praise our incredible strengths. I said before that Britain can survive outside the European Union and indeed that we could find a way. Now the decision has been made to leave, we need to find the best way and I will do everything I can to help. (Cameron, cited in Mosbacher and Wiseman, 2016: 122)

It was a great surprise that Theresa May, a firm Remainer in the Brexit referendum, was chosen to succeed Cameron to lead Brexit. An even greater surprise came when she called a general election in April 2017, expecting to increase the Conservatives' majority from 12 to over 100. 'Then something extraordinary happened' (Monbiot, 2017: 52).

Labour's draft manifesto was leaked, revealing radical policy ambitions under new leader, Jeremy Corbyn, such as reversing the neoliberal drive for private ownership by taking railways, water, mail and energy back into the public sphere, as well as increasing public spending, free university education, workers' and unemployed rights, landlord controls to protect tenants, stronger environmental protections and much more. It was seen to be so socially radical as to sound the death knell for Labour, but then came the greatest surprise. This was a narrative that connected with the British public so compellingly, it brought about 'perhaps the most dramatic political turnaround in modern democratic history' (Monbiot, 2017: 52). Importantly, young people, one of the most disillusioned political groups, rose up, voted Labour and joined the Party.

Call for a counternarrative

> The government threw the biggest possible question at an electorate that had almost no experience of direct democracy. Instead of building towards the decision with a series of small but participatory events, such as citizens' juries, in which people might have had a chance to work through the issues together, voters were rushed towards judgement day on a ridiculously short timetable, with no preparation except a series of humungous lies. (Monbiot, 2017: 150)

Throwing such responsibility at the general public without any critical education into the issues at stake, in a naïve yes/no vote, has, unsurprisingly, not only let the country down, but destabilised it. The Far Right targeted the vote of the hopeless, those who were disillusioned by the way that politics had failed them and were prepared to take risks on the unknown.

Matthew D'Ancona explains this:

> For those who would win back the voters that were driven to support (Trump or) Brexit by a sense of disenfranchisement, the mission is both clear and daunting. They must find an alternative to the 'deep story' of disillusionment ... acknowledging the anxieties of those who feel left behind without appeasing the bigotries fed by this disquiet ... Such a counter-narrative must be constructed with great delicacy. It needs to take account of the alienation spawned by the pace of global change, without deceiving the public that this pace is likely to slow ... What is required now is a discourse rooted in generous confidence, not tribal fear, one that emphasises the benefits of well-managed immigration and recognises that admission to a country entails responsibilities as well as rights to be treated as a fully fledged citizen. (D'Ancona, 2017: 134–5)

The age of post truth

> Nations and peoples are largely the stories they feed themselves. If they tell themselves stories that are lies, they will suffer the future consequences of those lies. If they tell themselves stories that face their own truths, they will free their histories for future flowerings. (Okri, 2015)

'Austerity' is one of those lies. It has been used as a smokescreen for the banking crisis of 2007–08, created by excessive corporate greed and inappropriate risk-taking, exposed the fragility of capitalism, plunging us into a world recession. We saw national governments bailing out banks, and entire nations teetering on the brink of bankruptcy. Economists have suggested that this will prove to be the worst financial crisis since the Great Depression of the 1930s. This is the key to understanding the way in which those in power have abused their authority to use 'austerity' measures as a way of convincing the poorer members of society that they need to tighten their belts to pay for the financial risk-taking of the rich. During a 10-year period, we have seen social divisions widen within and between countries. Most importantly, we have seen wealthy countries continue to deny life chances to their more vulnerable people while the richest of all continue to benefit from the resistance of governments to apply fair taxation measures across their nations as a whole, while turning a blind eye to the many loopholes that encourage tax avoidance among the rich. The state has underwritten businesses, protecting them from failure, with the businesses taking the profit and the state taking the risk (see for instance the bailouts of Royal Bank of Scotland and Northern Rock). Power is transferred from the state to corporate business, with the state acting as risk insurer with taxpayers' money. As state power is reduced so is the power of our vote. A crisis of democracy has erupted from this power swing to the rich away from the rest:

> The result is a disempowerment of the poor and middle. As parties across the political spectrum adopt similar neoliberal policies, disempowerment turns to disenfranchisement. If their dominant ideology stops governments from challenging social outcomes and delivering social justice, they can no longer respond to the needs of the electorate. Politics becomes irrelevant to people's lives, debate is reduced to the yabber of a remote elite. (Monbiot, 2017: 39)

The cost of disillusionment

Barack Obama inspired the world with hope for a future founded on equality and diversity. His fundamental mistake was to invest in the same economic power that had been the result of the 'irresponsible and often fraudulent practices' that led to the financial crisis: by bailing out banks, he left the victims to fend for themselves, a 'powerful symbol of abandonment, of both people and values' by choosing to protect criminality rather than vulnerability (Monbiot, 2017: 49). Another mistake Obama made was in relation to the Transatlantic Trade and Investment Partnership (TTIP) that the EU was actively negotiating with the US, and which played a role in driving British people to favour Brexit. The tendency of both Democrat and Republican Parties to curry favour with the privileged continued to alienate masses of Americans, and contributed to Hillary Clinton's failure to succeed Obama as US President in 2016. The poor were left without a sense of representation in politics. Coupled with the lack of a compelling counternarrative of hope and possibility, or any powerful social organisation, this resulted in despair, hopelessness and alienation. 'Donald Trump became elected president of the United States because his opponent provided no convincing or relevant alternative' (Monbiot, 2017: 70).

Alienation includes people's loss of control over their circumstances, loss of control over their work, loss of connection with community and society, as well as a loss of trust in politicians, all impacting on public health and wellbeing, and producing a general lack of trust that affects us all. And 'at the heart of this global trend is a crash in the value of truth' (D'Ancona, 2017: 8). Donald Trump, leader of the free world, is known to operate on 69% untruth (D'Ancona, 2017). In the UK, the Brexit referendum provided Trump with a model of disillusionment against the establishment that would secure his own success. The secret of Trump's success was in recognising that the story matters more than facts, and he constructed a narrative that connected emotionally with a disillusioned public to create a politics of hatred towards subordinated groups – a ban on Muslim immigration, a wall along the Mexican border, Make America Great Again and Take Back Control

– and at the heart of the story was Trump, who has brazened out his misogyny, racial hatred and low morals to cast himself as the hero of the hour.

I hope that, at this point, it becomes apparent as to why Andrew Sayer (2016) says that we can't afford the rich, and why George Monbiot says that 'Those who tell the stories run the world' (Monbiot, 2017: 1). It bring us full circle as to why community development has lacked the tools of analysis to understand the impact of the political context on personal lives and, in turn, why we lack the imagination to work with people to create a counternarrative, one which imagines a future based on equality.

Here is a story of what happens when a dominant ideology puts profit before people.

Grenfell Tower: a story of profit over people

On Wednesday, 14 June 2017, just after 1.00 am, a fire broke out on the fourth floor of Grenfell Tower, a 24-storey council housing apartment block owned by Kensington and Chelsea London Borough Council. Advanced neoliberalism encouraged even greater disregard for the vulnerable, and it was this disregard that turned what was essentially a house fire into a human disaster. In that moment, 'housing became the defining political issue of our times' (Dorling, 2018a: 87). Kensington and Chelsea covers areas of housing where the very rich and the very poor live side by side. The councillors who make decisions on housing the poorest are among the privileged who have benefited from neoliberal policies and, having no understanding of their poor neighbours, made decisions about their housing based on stigma (Tyler, 2013; 2015) and profit (Dorling, 2018a).

 **Whose lives matter?**

Fire from the fourth floor had reached an outside wall of the tower and within 15 minutes the entire building was a blazing inferno. At least 320 people were inside. There was no audible communal fire alarm in Grenfell Tower. It also had no sprinklers: the law in England requiring sprinklers in buildings taller than 100 feet applied only to new buildings. A newsletter, distributed around the tower in 2014, described emergency policy as 'stay put' in the event of a fire. The thinking (fire brigade-endorsed) is that by remaining where they are for as long as a fire is out of sight, residents won't flee from an area of relative safety into one of threat. Of course, this thinking means nothing if fire is able to spread up the side of a building, away from its concrete core.

There were people of all ethnicities in the tower, people who did every sort of job: teachers, pupils, hairdresser, caterer, security guard, artist, graduates and refugees. People died in their homes, on the stairs and on the ground, jumping when all else failed.

Construction in Britain is among those industries subject to much fiddly and costly regulation – but many of these regulations are safety laws, in place to protect society at large, and in particular society's voiceless and vulnerable. It would emerge later that well over 100 tower blocks and buildings around Britain had been clad in materials that, like those used at Grenfell, failed basic fire-safety tests. There is now an effort to peel the flammable skin from these buildings, but it has not been quick work. Wherever such de-cladding gets under way, there usually remains a population of residents still living inside – closing their eyes, just imagining the worst.

It took until November 2017 before investigators could provide a final toll of the dead at Grenfell: 71. The last visible human remains had been removed from the tower in early July, the work after that continuing with fingertips, with sieves, with archaeologists, with a hired American official who'd done comparably dire work in the aftermath of 9/11. The Grenfell fire, at its peak, burned at 1,800 degrees Fahrenheit. What was left to recovery workers was tons and tons of ash.

On 19 July, five weeks after the fire, survivors from Grenfell attended a public meeting at Kensington and Chelsea Council's headquarters. Some were invited up to microphones in the council's main chamber to speak, but the majority were put in a gallery above. A small group of survivors, exasperated by this, tried to get down to the chamber. "We fear being burned to death in our homes," councillors were told that afternoon, by a North Kensington resident. "You fear being shouted at!"

Around the country, shaken councils and landlords directed new scrutiny at the fire-safety measures in their own buildings. Cladding, square miles of the stuff, kept being peeled from other high-rises. In North Kensington, plans were under way to cover the ruined Grenfell with a tarp, until such a time this unmeant mausoleum could be demolished entirely.

Source: Adapted from Lamont (2017).

Two inquiries (one political, one criminal) have been launched to determine causes and contributing factors; these will continue into 2020. A BBC investigation conducted shortly after the fire suggested that the aluminum-composite cladding used at Grenfell was an inferior – and cheaper – variety, and was not officially classified as fire-retardant. A 75-page preliminary report compiled by a group called Architects for Social Housing, or ASH, focused on the fact that Grenfell had been *doubly* clad during its refurbishment: firstly, with squares of dense foam insulation, to keep the building warm; and secondly, with squares of aluminum-composite rain-screen panelling, to keep it dry. The ASH report (2017), which drew on the informed speculation of dozens of experts, proposed a likelihood of cavities between the double layer of cladding. If oxygen lurked in these cavities, it would have been there that the fire at Grenfell spread most aggressively. The outer aluminum rain screen, slower to burn than the insulation, might even have kept water from adequately dousing the worst of the fire. One year on from the fire, it emerged that the manufacturers of the cladding and insulation made an active bid to work on Grenfell's refurbishment. They knowingly misled on the use of their materials, saying that they were suitable for high-rise buildings despite the fact that they had never been tested on tower blocks and that the two products had never been tested together. In the aftermath of the fire, it was discovered that the cladding melts and ignites the insulation. So, effectively, the building had been wrapped in flammable material. It was a disaster waiting to happen, and the residents had expressed fears of this kind since the refurbishment. It is suspected that a faulty fridge-freezer in a flat on the fourth floor was the original source of the fire, which spread to the 22nd floor in 15 minutes and burned for 60 hours, giving off toxic fumes containing cyanide. Most damningly, it is suggested that a cheaper, more flammable version of the material was chosen by the management committee to keep the price down. Grenfell needs to act as a catalyst for the way we see society, as does Stephen Lawrence's murder, the Windrush debacle and all those other shameful events that should not be forgotten. To tell the truth is an act of courage with a revolutionary intention!

Ridiculing of the conquered by the conqueror

> The demonization of the working class is the ridiculing of the conquered by the conqueror. (Jones, 2016: 247)

Stigmatising the poor as layabouts has dehumanised the most vulnerable groups in society. The dismantling of trade union power – the real objective of Thatcher in her war with the miners – has robbed the working class of a means of organising protection of their rights. This was all part of a systematic plan that unfolded together with Thatcher's much-repeated story of the 'welfare scrounger'.

Along with this came the 'right to buy'. When I was a grassroots community worker, I saw the impact of these policies take effect. Good quality council housing was sold at rock bottom prices, lost forever as a public housing resource. It was a route to powerlessness for the poor. Speculators roamed council housing areas knocking on doors to offer to pay for the purchase of flats and houses, and to pay more to get tenants to move out. Taking apart the stock of council housing triggered soaring house prices, 'creating a housing bubble that is now imploding, and injecting record levels of debt into the economy' (Jones, 2016: 257). The housing crisis has created an escalation in homelessness, with increases in youth homelessness, particularly, to levels that violate human rights. By 2014, it was possible to see that housing had become a major factor in inequality. Today, London is the most divided city in the UK, marked by large numbers of unoccupied homes bought as profit investments for the rich of the world, while the dispossessed live under arches and in doorways.

Chaos, crisis and confusion

We find ourselves in times of chaos and crisis, and without the tools of analysis to understand why things are changing we end up in confusion. Confusion is not an ideal basis on which to act!

'After decades of globalization our political system has become obsolete – and spasms of resurgent nationalism are a sign of its irreversible decline' (Dasgupta, 2018). Dasgupta refers not only to the UK, but also to the USA, France, Spain, Italy, Germany, and beyond Europe to Russia, Turkey, India, Hungary, Myanmar, China, Rwanda, Venezuela, Thailand, the Philippines and more. 'There is no coincidence. All countries today are embedded in the same system, which subjects them to the same pressures: and it is these that are squeezing and warping national political life everywhere' (Dasgupta, 2018). He points to an advanced state of political and moral decay from which it is impossible to escape. The nation state is in decline, he argues, without any alternative to replace it. Wall-building and xenophobia, misogyny, racism, fear of difference, promises to go back to what was once seen as great are grasped in desperation. Social divisions are greater than ever, moral leadership has evaporated and the nation state system is reduced to a 'lawless gangland'. The nation state has not delivered the promised security and dignity that was hoped for; in fact, in some ways it has been a 'colossal failure'. Current symptoms mark the end of an era. 'Decades of globalisation, economics and information have grown beyond the authority of national governments' (Dasgupta, 2018) to a point that global wealth and resources are largely uncontrolled by politics.

But hope must spring from this dire situation because without political intervention there will be no democratic census, no controls over the abjection of greed and exploitation. It is urgent to imagine a political system capable of operating in a global arena, one that will serve human and planetary wellbeing. Impossible, you may think, but Dasgupta points out that at one point in history, and not so very long ago, the nation state was inconceivable. 'The real delusion is the belief that things can carry on as they are' (Dasgupta, 2018). The morbid symptoms that have come to define neoliberal capitalism are inevitable consequences of its ideology. This is why it is so hard to reform capitalism, to find its compassionate face when its purpose is to exploit for profit.

Dasgupta (2018) names three elements of the crisis we face: the breakdown of rich countries in the face of global forces; the volatility of the poorest countries and regions; and the lack of credibility of an international order that can aspire to a 'society of nations' governed by the rule of law. He suggests a set of directions based on: global financial regulation that deals with tax evasion; global flexible democracies, stable structures within which nation states are stacked, of which the EU is the major experiment to date; and new notions of citizenship which do not convey advantage by birth through inherited privilege. His hope is that the lessons from capitalism and its economic and technological advances offer the bedrock for building a new, integrated, global politics: we are just lacking the political imagination to produce the vision!

A new story for new times!

A crisis of these proportions signifies a conjuncture, a point at which social, political, economic and ideological contradictions are condensed into a historical moment. It offers an opportunity for change, but without the necessary critiques of power and a compelling counternarrative, any interventions are likely to fail. We need new stories for a new system! The *status quo* is resilient and comes up with many good reasons why we should stay with how things are. Constantly we hear dominant power insisting that 'there is no alternative', but this is simply a ploy to silence any dissenting voices or counternarratives of change, and it takes us on a trajectory of disaster. Take a moment to think about this. Neoliberal ideology has failed. It has crumbled and disintegrated. The banking crisis of 2007–08 has been used to justify 'austerity' measures that have forced the poorest to pay for the risks taken by the richest. Unsurprisingly, the poor have become even poorer, but, by stealth, the rich have become richer. This counter-process has created a more divided society than is either acceptable or sustainable. Almost one third of children in the UK, one of the richest countries in the world, have childhoods blighted by poverty. This means that, out of a schoolclass of 30, nine are growing up in poverty (www.cpag.org.uk). This is unacceptable and unnecessary. Why would a rich country fail to feed it poorest children, denying them the life chances to aspire to their full potential? It has long been recognised that the least divided societies are the healthiest and happiest (www.equalitytrust. org.uk/about–inequality/impacts).

So, now is the time to rise from the ashes of this failed system to challenge and change it to one that is better on every level, for everyone and everything. We have an opportunity to create a new system based on a common good with values of diversity and biodiversity in healthy balance, and this book will take you through how this is possible by simply changing our perceptions and aspirations. According to the Gramscian thinker, Stuart Hall, the first stage in effective interventions is to 'see' the forces of power critically (Williams, 2012). If we question what is happening, we begin to see things differently. When we see things differently, we act differently in the world. This chapter has critiqued the political context in order to see the forces of power critically.

Community development is inevitably a political activity because its principles of social justice and environmental justice embody its commitment to social change. The point I am making here is about connection and disconnection. Knowledge is the basis of action: without knowledge there is no struggle, no change. Ideas are the tools of struggle because they offer the key to understanding power and disempowerment, and this is vital for without understanding how power works to silence people into submission, how can we possibly know how to work for change? Conversely, power stays in place, impenetrable because there is no understanding of the way it works to maintain its dominance through the structures of capitalism, imperialism and patriarchy. So, going back to my point about disconnection, you will see that by preventing people from reading, meeting together, questioning and organising, we stop connections being made between the overlapping, intersecting forces of power that result in multiple oppressions of class, race and gender acted out through capitalism, colonialism and patriarchy being identified as the roots of struggle for human rights. These are the reasons for my first port of call being *power* and why I am now moving on to introduce new ideas that both critique neoliberal power and offer ideas that change the way we see the world.

2

Changing the story

Ideas change the course of history

Ideas change everything. They can turn the world upside down in an instant. So, I want to give you a taste of some ideas that are capable of stimulating your imagination and changing your practice. They are not fanciful: they are crucial additions to the eclectic body of community development knowledge and they build on Paulo Freire's foundation to develop powerful ideas for our times. Only by situating practice within a critique of its current political times and developing a counternarrative of hope and possibility will community development play its radical role in shaping a future worthy of aspiration.

Paulo Freire and the radical agenda

Paulo Freire is 'one of the most influential educational philosophers of the twentieth century' (Darder, 2018: 1). His life was shaped by the Brazilian politics of the early 20th century, one with a legacy of Portuguese colonialism that thrived on the poverty of the many. Freire was shocked by the moral silence around human suffering. He was determined 'to intentionally shift the focus away from a dehumanizing epistemology of knowledge construction toward a liberating and humanizing one [that] linked the material conditions of oppression to the brutal impact of cultural invasion imposed on the oppressed' (Darder, 2018: x).

Freire's first and, arguably, most influential book, *Pedagogy of the Oppressed*, was first published in the USA, in English, in 1970 (only later being published in Portuguese), and its impact was huge. But in Brazil, 'Paulo's name could not be spoken in public spaces, at the time. It was forbidden.… At the universities, Paulo's work could not be discussed as it was prohibited. It was forbidden in schools as well, and it was forbidden in the mainstream media' (Nita Freire, in Darder, 2018: 154–5). It was forbidden because it encouraged people to think and to question power relations! In the preface to *Pedagogy of the Oppressed*, Paulo Freire was emphatic that the work was not abstract in thought and study, but 'rooted in concrete situations' giving evidence from the outset of the importance of the political context. It provided practitioners and activists with a theory of liberation based on analyses of power, *conscientisation* and social action. Freire triggered community development's radical agenda, and still forms the bedrock of its knowledge base and practice.

His critical praxis remains as important at this major conjuncture in time, a point at which social, political, economic and ideological contradictions are condensed into a historical moment created by the crumbling of neoliberalism and its politics of disposability.

> Grave changes are warranted in our political civilization … freeing us to reclaim our stolen humanity. Freire's struggle was to be humble enough to wonder yet courageous enough to defy, to be sufficiently self-assured to rebel yet possess enough self-doubt to keep from backsliding, to have the audacity to be creative yet remain unburdened by socio-cultural dogma, to be vigilant against the new faces of tyranny yet ever conscious of the flaws and insufficiencies of our own struggles. (McLaren, 2015: 34)

Paulo Freire's ideas changed community development from being a placatory occupation to aspire to a transformative potential. He was a Brazilian critical educator, working with the poorest and most marginalised people of his country in the favelas. He challenged the knowledge that is poured into the heads of people as a real truth, beyond question. Instead, he discerned that relevant knowledge comes from questioning lived experience. Freirean dialogue is generated in knowing through questioning: What is happening? To whom? By whom? Why is it happening? In whose interests? How? Where? When? In a process of reflection and mutual dialogue, information is sought and new knowledge is co-created; a deeper understanding of the world emerges providing the basis for action to change the world for the better, for everyone. Unthinking practice is dangerous. It can be reinforcing the very structures of society that discriminate and create inequality by working unquestioningly within a dominant ideology that favours privilege:

> … according to Paulo, our *critical awareness of the world* tells us that we *know,* and can *know more.* In the continuous dynamic of departing from the practice of what is known, and seeking the theory that explains it, and practising again, brings with it the learning, the common sense, the institutions and the emotions. This is what Paulo called '*the right thinking,* the need to think the practice, to practice better, and *to learn more,* and to learn better'. (Freire, N., 2015: xvii)

This is the essence of Freirean pedagogy: a problem-posing education that is critical, empowering and transformative, in an approach to praxis that has both reflection and action at its heart.

Freire's problem-posing approach

Freire's problem-posing approach to education for social justice was revolutionary in its time and remains so more than ever today. Freire was clear that the only escape from dehumanising 'emotional dependence' is to be involved in our own struggle for freedom. This is the key to self-belief. But it cannot be abstract intellectualism, actionless thought, nor can it be thoughtless action: it involves action that comes from 'serious reflection'. This is critical praxis. Dialogue is the key to praxis. 'The content of that dialogue can and should vary in accordance with historical conditions and the level at which the oppressed perceive reality … Attempting to liberate the oppressed without their reflective participation in the act of liberation is to treat them as objects which must be saved from a burning building!' (Freire, 2018: 65).

Freire never intended *Pedagogy of the Oppressed* to be an academic text, but more the sharing of his reflections on his experience of working together with marginalised groups of people in their communities. What he produced was revolutionary, and has stood the test of time for the following reasons.

- It provided a theory and practice, a critical praxis from his own lived experience of working with community groups developing critical adult literacy for 15 years before the coup in Brazil.
- He offered this as the basis from which we could develop the critical praxis for our own historical time and place.
- The very first page laid out his stand on *dehumanisation* and the process of *humanisation*, claiming back the right to be fully human in the world.
- Values inform every dimension of this process of freedom: the right to human dignity, mutual respect, trust, reciprocity, everyone's intellectual capacity to become fully human and engaged in the world as a subject, not object.
- It included a detailed practice for popular education based on a critique of the controlling purpose of traditional education: posing problems using generative themes captured in codifications, a mutual dialogue emerges in the culture circle (community group), ideas are explored in trusting, reciprocal relations with educator-as-student and student-as-educator, and lived reality is questioned with the purpose of freeing critical consciousness as the basis for collective action – theory in action and action as theory = critical praxis.
- This approach spoke to a multitude of practices and movements emerging at the time: community development, teaching, social work, liberation theology, health and many others engaged in anti-racist, feminist and anti-poverty action for equality, democracy and social justice.
- Education is politics: it can never be neutral. All approaches to education produce consciousness of one sort or another, based on the ideology of the approach. Without questioning the *status quo*, it is endorsed!
- A counternarrative challenges the dominant hegemony (see Chapter 6) by providing the possibility of an alternative world based on values of human dignity and human worth.

> For Paulo, throughout his life and work, the essential questions of this famous book remained: What kind of world do we live in? Why is

it like that? What kind of world do we want? How do we get there from here? (Shor, 2018: 188)

Paulo Freire was influenced by an eclectic range of thinkers, but perhaps the most significant was Antonio Gramsci, who was imprisoned and died in fascist Italy for teaching people to think critically. It was Gramsci's ideas that helped Freire to understand life in the favelas. There is a great deal more in this book about Freire and Gramsci, but this brief acknowledgement is designed to emphasise the theoretical bedrock of radical community development knowledge as the basis for introducing some of the new ideas which have influenced my thinking and which add relevant knowledge to the body of community development theory.

Towards a compelling counternarrative: inspiration from 14 current intellectual activists

The neoliberal project has so badly failed people and planet, with disastrous results. We have lacked the insight to come up with an adequate critique and have lacked the imagination to come up with a compelling counternarrative of connection, possibility and hope. We need to emerge from this context of alienation and destruction with renewed determination to create a future that is informed by diversity and biodiversity, a world in balance founded on mutual respect.

So, with the centrality of critique and the crucial role of counternarrative in mind, this chapter builds on a strong Freirean foundation by incorporating ideas selected from some current key intellectual activists. Read on!

'Austerity is a tactic to deliver the goals of the neoliberal project.'
Kerry-Anne Mendoza (2016: 10)

Austerity is not a short-term disruption to balance the books. It is the controlled demolition of the welfare state – transferring the UK from a social democracy to a corporate state. Austerity has been presented as necessary, constructive and temporary by governments across the world, the UK included. By the end of this book, it will be clear to the reader that it is unnecessary, destructive and intended as a permanent break with the traditions of social democracy.' (Mendoza, 2016: 7)

In *Austerity: The Demolition of the Welfare State and the Rise of the Zombie Economy* (2016), Mendoza argues that austerity is a deliberate strategy employed to deliver the goals of the neoliberal project, a move from the colonial state to an international corporate power, which employs the structural power of the state to deliver a corporate empire. Picture, for instance, the way that the risks taken by bankers which resulted in the financial collapse of 2007–08 were underwritten by austerity measures being imposed not on the bankers who were reckless, but on the poorest in the country. Within this model, power is transferred from the state to private institutions and corporations, and vulnerable people are persuaded to serve the interests of power. The International Monetary Fund (IMF) invented 'austerity' by creating the debt trap, using predatory lending to hold on to the powers of colonialism and 'the shackles of slavery' (2016: 13). The IMF imposed neoliberal economic policies in the developing world through structural adjustment programmes, using emergency loans to enable poor countries to pay off unaffordable existing loans, thereby tying debtor nations in to conditions that have been 'extraordinarily profitable for the creditor nations and institutions' (2016: 16), while continually resisting any calls for debt forgiveness. Avoiding ethical responsibility and brushing aside democratic accountability, it hoovered up state-owned industries and exploitation rights to natural resources, allowing private interests to make enormous profits by selling them off cheaply at the same time as depressing living standards, wages, civil liberties and employment rights to provide malleable, impoverished labour forces (2016: 15).

Critique how the system works. For example, for decades leading up to the banking crisis of 2007–08, a partnership between governments and the financial services industry had neglected responsible regulation to protect people, leaving banks, brokers and insurance companies free to exploit debt. 'High-street banks and mortgage providers, credit-card companies and other debt merchants chased the custom of individuals with little or no regard for their ability to pay back the loans' (Mendoza, 2016: 18). The debts were sold to investment banks and then sold on to pension companies as creditworthy, at the same time as the banks insured themselves against the risks they were creating, known as credit default swaps (CDS). 'This is the equivalent of an estate agent selling you a house, knowing he[/she] had set a fire under the floorboards, then taking out an insurance policy on the house being burned down – and then every estate agent in the country doing exactly the same thing' (2016: 18). In 2007–08, the whole lot imploded! What is astonishing, and of vital consequence, is that 'this extraordinary mountain of toxic private debt' did not result in the corporations collapsing but was transferred into public debt by the government bailing out the banks. This particular move is important to note: for the first time we had government insuring the risk-taking of corporate, profit-making interests, diverting public money that belongs to all of us into the pockets of the rich. This alarming failure of the neoliberal project was smoke-screened by 'austerity': 'Austerity is Structural Adjustment with a new name' (2016: 19).

The systematic erosion of any commitment to a common good and the welfare state system that supports it was, and continues to be, achieved by applying the notion of 'weakness' and 'worthlessness' to anyone who fails to perform a role in profit-generation. It deflects attention away from the failings of neoliberalism by blaming the people destroyed by the system rather than the system itself. 'Lies repeated often enough become the truth and a climate of suspicion forms around those who find themselves reliant on the welfare system' (Mendoza, 2016: 119). Once an ideology takes root, it becomes normalised, embedded in policy and institutionalised. Mendoza draws on economics professor Steve Keen to capture the ideological cleansing of universities in the field of economics by teaching students nothing but neoliberal theories, and selecting only those academics who endorse neoliberal theories to be awarded research grants or publication opportunities in leading journals. 'Anyone suggesting that this might not be the most effective, efficient or ethical way of running things is treated not as a critical thinker, but as a heretic' (Mendoza, 2016: 120). When critique and dissent are silenced, democracy is weakened and freedom is curtailed: 'There has been a failure, to date, fully to communicate the real-life, daily impacts of corporate fascism' (Mendoza, 2016: 120).

Corporate fascism is the endgame of neoliberalism, and with it comes the end of civilisation as we know it. 'The only way out is to abandon capitalism, in all its forms' (Mendoza, 2016: 178). There are those who argue that capitalism is synonymous with trade, property ownership, or profit. It is not. It is simply a paradigm, an ideological framework for how we go about these things. Capitalism has only been around for 400 years, and its neoliberal brand for 50 years. It is not how we have always done things, this is simply untrue!

Civilisation in its truest sense is measured by the people's ability to benefit from the collective developments of that civilisation. Andrew Sayer is referring to this when he talks about our *common inheritance*, ie the way we all have a right to benefit from what has gone before us, and no one should take more than their fair share, as highlighted in the next section. In this sense, civilisation can be measured according to human rights, a work–life balance, a fair justice system, an income that reflects the cost of living, access to good quality, relevant education, a welfare state, decent and affordable homes, controls over the exploitation of children and adults, and more. Hard-won gains in these areas have not been due to capitalism. Far from it, they have been wrought from capitalism by people in movement, fighting for the right to decent lives. Gains have only taken place in recent history:

> The right to unionize, bargain for pay and conditions collectively, and withdraw labour through strike: this co-operative approach to holding corporate power to account brought workers rising wages, reduced hours, the concept of work–life balance, the weekend, health and safety in the workplace, and an end to the slave-like conditions working people endured through the 18th, 19th and early 20th century. (Mendoza, 2016: 121)

In the latter part of the 20th century and to the present day, this is precisely why governments led by Edward Heath, Margaret Thatcher, John Major, Tony Blair, David Cameron, Theresa May and now Boris Johnson have all warred against the unions, downplaying the fact that these are ordinary working people striving for their rights.

Neoliberalism reframed the ideology of capitalism to shatter the pillars at the heart of civilisation. The result is unsustainable divisions in society as economic and political power is handed over to the inordinately wealthy few who use that power in the name of corporate fascism. Mendoza draws on US President Franklin Roosevelt to offer a definition of the term:

> The liberty of a democracy is not safe if the people tolerate the growth of private power to a point where it becomes stronger that the democratic state itself. That in its essence is fascism: ownership of government by an individual, by a group, or any controlling private power. (2016: 179)

Mendoza (2016: 179) cites the words of Owen, a character representing the voice of reason in Robert Tressell's (1914) *The Ragged Trousered Philanthropists*: 'What I call poverty is when people are not able to secure for themselves all the benefits of civilization; the necessaries, comforts, pleasures and refinements of life, leisure, books, theatres, pictures, music, holidays, travel, good and beautiful homes, good clothes, good and pleasant food'. We have allowed neoliberalism to drain all the hard-earned quality of life – a common good that current and previous generations alike have struggled for – away from the majority to feed the insatiable greed of an elite minority. Now we need to imagine a different story, one informed by values of reciprocity and mutuality, a paradigm shift that offers everyone and everything dignity, the chance to flourish in a world where we belong and which we respect. Mendoza describes us as the cavalry, and it is our emerging campaigns and institutions that can dismantle the existing institutions that have been created to serve neoliberalism. Far from rule by a market based on the exploitative greed of the few, we need a vision of a new economics. Critique starts the ball rolling, so here are ten economic myths contributed by Dinyar Godrej and David Ransom in the new material Mendoza includes in the 2016 edition of her book.

Box 2.1: 10 economic myths
1. Austerity will lead to 'jobs and growth'.
2. Deficit reduction is the only way out of a slump.
3. Taxing the rich scares off investors and stalls economic performance.
4. Economic migrants are a drain on rich world economies.
5. The private sector is more efficient than the public sector.
6. Fossil fuels are more economically viable than renewables.
7. Financial regulation will destroy a profitable banking sector.
8. Organised labour is regressive.
9. Everyone has to pay their debts.
10. Growth is the only way.
Source: Adapted from Godrej and Ransom, in Mendoza (2016).

REFLECTION: Myth-busting

Reflect on the power of these myths. They are messages that generate fears of any alternative, of market collapse and of job losses. These messages go deep into public consciousness, channelling behaviour to produce more of the same. Devise a myth-busting dialogue session in which these are used as provocations to get people questioning. You may want to use the 10 myth-busting provocations in combination with Kate Raworth's Doughnut introduced on p 65.

Read the story of Richer Sounds. This is the story of one man who is trying to make a difference. Yes, he is rich and has benefited from the capitalist system, and yes, he believes that capitalism can be reformed. But, what do you make of his ideas?

 **Richer Sounds**

Julian Richer made a decision to hand over control of his business to his 500-plus staff to give him time to focus on fighting 'uncontrolled' capitalism:

> Capitalism is inherently evil because it's based on greed so you have to rely on people to do the right thing. I'm doing the right thing because I sleep better at night, and my business is better off because of it, but a lot of people don't and that is why the state needs to be firmer.

He had decided to hand back a third of the £9.2 million he received for his stake in the business, paying staff £1,000 for every year's service they had given to the business. At his store manager conference, held in a Salvation Army hall in London, he announced an average payment to employees of £8,000. Zoe Wood, writing in the *Guardian*, says that 'the announcement was initially met with hushed silence but within a short space of time Richer would receive a standing ovation from cheering staff'.

Richer founded Richer Sounds in 1978 at the age of 19, and over four decades has been working on providing job security and decent pay because 'he believes a happy workforce is key to business success'. At a time when austerity has come to justify zero-hours contracts, with no promise of any work let alone a fair income, he has created a business where loyalty and respect are high on the agenda. 'At the conference employees reel off examples of the support he had given them through personal crises such as battles with cancer.'

Richer is preoccupied with finding ways to make the world a better place by tackling inequality and sharing prosperity. He agrees that capitalism is in crisis, and is looking for an idea to shake up the status quo. Currently, he has established Taxwatch, a non-profit organisation which investigates the finances of multinational companies. He is also attempting to construct a test case against zero-hours contracts. And he has developed a Good Business charter that challenges business interests to be more ethical.

Richer Sounds has 52 stores that are small and in busy areas just a step away from the high street prime sites that command extortionate rents. Richer made an early decision to buy the freeholds so that he was in control of his shops, so this meant that even with the advent of online shopping the survival of his business and the livelihoods of his employees were secure. He describes the key influences on his thinking as a socialist housemaster at his boarding school in childhood and, in later life, his faith, which he calls 'practical Christianity'. "I just want to try and make the world a better place."

Source: Adapted from Wood (2019).

~~~~~~~~~~~~~~~~~~~~~~~~~~~~~~~~~~~~~~~

From here, let's take a look at Andrew Sayer whose ideas are inspirational, not only his provocation 'We can't afford the rich', but his counternarrative based on common inheritance, which changed the way I see the world.

> **'Nature needs respect and a sense of wonder, not plunder.'**
> Andrew Sayer (2016: 347)

We can't afford the rich and the systems that are supporting them, Sayer argues in *Why We Can't Afford the Rich* (2016). 'They are living beyond our means and those of the planet, and their interests are at odds with those of the 99% and the environment' (2016: 366).

> We need an economy that can function on the concept of *enough*, instead of insatiable acquisitiveness. Much more equal societies are desirable in themselves for allowing all to develop their capacities and to develop a sense of the public good, and of mutual respect, solidarity and care. (2016: 341)

Economies are meant to serve the wellbeing of the many rather than the greed of the few.

> [A] truly developed society is one that makes it possible for all to contribute what they can. The neoliberal dream of a society of self–reliant individuals, able to avoid any dependence on others beyond what that can pay for, is absurd and deceitful. (2016: 345)

Neoliberalism is a power-based economy that thrives on dehumanising the majority on the strength of a message that says it is only through hard work and self-reliance that we achieve success. But none of us is self-reliant: it is a delusion. We are social beings, interconnected and interdependent; we need each other and we are reliant on each other.

> And the rich continue to get richer, even in the worst crisis for 80 years – they can still laugh all the way to their banks and tax havens as the little people bail out the banks that have failed. (2016: 1)

For me, Sayer's analysis of our *common inheritance*, or *the commons*, is immensely thought-provoking. His key point is that there is nothing we do from scratch, solely from our own endeavours, we are always enormously indebted to those who have gone before. We build on what society inherits from all its yesterdays and by drawing on nature's resources. Our common inheritance includes the accumulated experience, intelligence, inventions, investments and hard work of previous generations that have created the advantages and ease of lifestyle that we have now in the West.

> Most of what we so easily attribute to our own intelligence and efforts is the hard-won product of previous generations' thought and labour, to which any one of us can rarely add more than a little. (2016: 140)

So, if we explore this perspective, we get the inspiration of a new way of seeing the world that shatters the illusion of self-importance, the 'because-I-deserve-it' mentality that so easily falls into greed and status!

> Innovation does not come out of the blue but from new combinations of what already exists. (2016: 141)

So, the commons extends from what we take for granted in our everyday lives (for example our roads and sewage systems) to outstanding works of art and science.

Next – and, Sayer says, most fundamentally – it is important to recognise that the commons includes the environment. The biosphere – energy, minerals, rivers, oceans, soil, flora and fauna and the climate – is not only central to the commons, but is the basis for the rest. 'The environment constrains and enables everything that we do' (2016: 142). And the environmental argument for equality is that 'no one has the right to more of the earth's resources … than the total of those resources divided by the world's population' (2016: 341).

Unequal exchange is the next point. Inequalities that privilege the powerful over the less powerful are due to inequalities in the development of the commons, often linked to slavery and exploitation. All of us in rich countries benefit from cheap goods – coffee, cotton, jeans, computers, and so on - from poor countries, based on the power that comes from common inheritance. This is unequal trade and is based on cheap labour in poor countries being exploited to supply consumerism in the West. In these ways, we can see how neoliberalism exploits its own poorer populations within countries, but equally we see that global exploitation keeps countries unequal.

Here, we begin to understand the connectedness of the commons, our debts to those who have gone before to create our common inheritance. I think we also need to address reparation for the wrongs of the past, a point raised by Eddo-Lodge (2018), not only to make amends for the generations that suffered exploitation and slavery, but to be mindful of the way that many people are still benefiting from the proceeds of that suffering, and that many are still suffering the wrongs of modern-day slavery and exploitation.

So, we see from these points that when someone claims 'I deserve it' they are laying more importance on themselves than they really merit.

Where do we begin to create a counternarrative of connection? Clearly addressing common inheritance raises issues of fairness, and moves us towards a mutual, respectful and sustainable future. We need not only to tax the rich to redistribute the wealth that has been stolen from the rest, but we must identify and stop the sources of unearned income that create privilege. To do this, we need to look at three key areas:

1. **Rent:** 'Nationalise land and minerals, so that rent comes under democratic control … it need not prevent people owning buildings and benefitting from improving them and the land; it's just a matter of recovering for society the gains made from the privatisation of nature and space itself' (2016: 351).
2. **Interest and credit money:** Interest, especially at high rates, is the problem, not credit. Credit facilitates development and makes sure that money is put to use. But it should *not* be used as a device by which the rich can take advantage of the rest through excessive interest. The most important function of credit should be to fund sustainable investments and projects.
3. **Profit:** When the rich profit from ownership of businesses, the employees who produce the goods and services have no say in how the profits are used. 'Democracy stops at the workplace door … it is essential that this situation is reversed, both as a matter of justice and to ensure that workers' interests are aligned with those of their organisation' (2016: 351).

> Under neoliberalism, the political interests of the rich are masked as merely economic considerations, but there's nothing apolitical about cutting top rates of tax, cutting tax-evasion investigators, allowing private utilities companies to siphon off public money to shareholders and supporting asset inflation. (2016: 351)

Where do we begin to organise an economy that is fair, focused on human wellbeing and sustainability? To start with, it means questioning our way of life and wealth:

Real development means creating circumstances that allow everyone simultaneously to be able to have and do the things necessary for a good life: having enough food, shelter and health services; having security and freedom from threat and violence, including sexual violence; being able to develop their capacities through education and access to a range of activities; being able to participate in political decisions that affect them and having free speech and conscience; being able to care for others and be cared for; being able to have respect and interact with others without coercion, exploitation, stigma or neglect; and so on.' (2016: 344)

This is our challenge.

A crackdown on tax avoidance, tax havens and an emphasis on redistributive taxation would be a fair place to start: 'we cannot afford to leave the financial sector in the hands of those with an interest in not fixing it' (2016: 281).

'Like goldfish swimming in a bowl of dirty water'
Dorling (2018b: 31)

Danny Dorling warns that we have reached peak inequality in Britain.

The gap between the very rich and the rest is wider in Britain than in any other large country in Europe, and society is the most unequal it has been since shortly after the First World War.' (Dorling, 2018b: 31)

He suggests that we have accepted inequality as 'normal', failing to see that we are 'like goldfish swimming in a bowl of dirty water': we are 'swimming in the dirtiest of fish tanks' failing to see its unacceptability and inhumanity.

It was the Occupy Movement's 'We are the 99%' in September 2011, followed up by *The Economist* on 21st January 2012, asking 'Who exactly are the 1%?' that focused attention on how much the richest had helped themselves to wealth generated by austerity, creating the level of inequalities that lead to unhealthy, unhappy societies – the answer was that increasingly they are those involved in the finance sector! (Dorling, 2018a: 23)

Dorling cites the 1987 film, *Eat the Rich,* which opens in a fictitious restaurant with a TV projecting a fictitious Home Secretary: 'Some people in this country are very, very rich, but most of you are very, very poor. You know why? It's because you're all lazy bastards' (2018a: 351). This scene was a warning of things to come, a shock exposé of the stigma politics researched by Imogen Tyler (2013,

2015); we laughed but did not heed. It's a scam. The demonisation of the poor as lazy skivers is a good story, it paints the poor as poor because they are workshy and lazy, and the rich as rich because, by comparison, they claim to work hard to justify their excess wealth. It promises the same wealth to all those who work hard, but apart from occasional tokenism, this is a lie. Income inequality has widened to a point that:

> 'Today the rich hold almost all of the world's wealth ... Should it continue to rise by 7% a year, then in just over 7 years from now (in the year 2021) the best-off 1% on the planet will own everything. Everybody else will have nothing, at which point eating the rich stops being a joke.' (Dorling, 2018a: 354)

Income is the most important measure of inequality; it gives us freedom to make choices and brings us respect and self-respect. Everyone benefits from greater equality, the poor and the rich alike, yet we have chosen to go down a route that has taken us from being the second most equal country in Europe to the most unequal. The decade 1968 to 1978 was pivotal in terms of potential for equality. After a previous peak of 71.5% of wealth held by the bottom 90% in 1968, UK equality peaked at 72.2% in 1978 (Dorling, 2018b: 32). Had we taken different decisions, we could have created a sovereign wealth fund for our future generations based on oil like Norway, could have been leaders in science and technology like Finland, or could have been as environmentally conscious as the Danes. But we made different choices under the Thatcher government and changed our future to one of massive inequality instead. There were good comprehensive schools, good housing, full employment, and a growing lack of deference to the class system. Then everything was shunted to the right: 'It happened because of a very British problem. Britain differed fundamentally from other countries in Europe in the 1960s and 1970s because its wealth had been built on a huge empire. And now the loss of our empire meant we were forced to get used to having less' (Dorling, 2018b: 32).

> And the rich do not have to fear the poor so much ... The irony is that greater equality helps the rich as well as the rest.' (Dorling, 2018b: 33)

We have a choice; we need no longer be the most economically unequal country in Europe. So, what's to be done?

REFLECTION: Stretch your imagination

Let's take Dorling's idea of looking forward 100 years from now to imagine the world that you would like to see:

• **Imagine** how we could be better housed if we see housing as a basic need, not an investment, and we concentrate on good quality eco-housing to look after our environment at the same time.

• **Imagine** what schools could be like if we had no private schools but one well-funded education system for all, based on the right for all children to have the best education possible, not one based on the appalling idea that some children are born clever and others lack the intelligence to do great things!

• **Imagine** how politics could be more democratic. To make it more inclusive 'we should expect people not to just be given the chance to vote once every five years at a general election, not just offered two electable candidates to choose between, and not be presented with insulting yes/no referenda' (Dorling, 2018a: 331).

• **Imagine** how might we control the rich, create greater diversity and opportunity, live in harmony with each other and Europe, elect our politicians, police ourselves, deal with terrorists, welcome immigrants and create full employment and 'without our current obsession with the market'.

Source: Adapted from Dorling (2018a: 327).

Dorling claims that inequality has harmed our imagination. It has left us stuck, believing 'there is no alternative', only more of the same. If we can free our imaginations then we will see much more easily what we need to do. Once we imagine the future we aspire to, then it will be easy to know how to create it. In this respect, counternarratives are urgent.

> **'Do we want to live in a society based on co-operation and reciprocity, or competition and rivalry?'**
> Richard Wilkinson and Kate Pickett (2009: 261)

More equal societies are happier and healthier, argued Wilkinson and Pickett in *The Spirit Level: Why Equality is Better for Everyone* (2009). This made a major impact on the thinking of those committed to a fair and just world. Large income gaps between rich and poor are much more likely to create societies that have extensive health problems (lower life expectancy, higher infant mortality, mental illness, illicit drug use and obesity) and social problems (violence, imprisonment, low levels of trust and weak community ties, low levels of child wellbeing, poor educational attainment, high teenage pregnancy and low social mobility) than those with greater equality. Research evidence suggests that inequality creates excessive reductions in wellbeing as a result of social stress created by status inferiority. Yet rich countries of the West are living testament that profit produces inequality when the values of society are skewed. Since Margaret Thatcher told us all to tighten our belts – that the rich needed to become richer in order for a trickle-down effect to make the poor richer – our happiness levels have not increased but inequality is now at its peak, and we still fail to ask why nothing has trickled down!

Wilkinson and Pickett's emphasis on future wellbeing not being about profit but about community and the way we treat each other was a direct challenge to the neoliberal project with its overt intention to privilege the rich at the expense of the poor. Their sequel, *The Inner Level: How More Equal Societies reduce Stress, Restore Sanity and Improve Everyone's Wellbeing* (2018) builds on *The Spirit Level* to deepen connections with the ways in which inequality invades our minds, increasing anxiety levels, and changing the way we think and feel and relate to each other. They offer insight into the significant links between health and social outcomes and income inequality, which is extremely revealing when viewed as a connected whole rather than disconnected parts:

This overview of the multiple costs to the nation of income inequality also helps us to understand that fragmented, piecemeal reforms will do nothing to bring about real change (see Figure 2.1). We begin to see that the success of neoliberal politics is ideological: outrageous, dehumanising stories have targeted people and the planet in a sustained, systemic way to justify the wealth of the few. The only way to claim back our world is to start from values, putting these at the heart of a counternarrative of possibility.

Wilkinson and Pickett emphasise that, based on rigorous evidence, profit cannot bring us the health, happiness and wellbeing we seek as human beings. They summarise four key areas to improve which would take us nearer to wellbeing and sustainability:

1. Greater social equality would reduce the need for status and the damage that class divisions create by cutting the levels of social anxiety, and improving confidence, self-esteem and positive social interaction. In turn, this would reduce drink and drug abuse and status consumerism, leading to more relaxed lifestyles with stronger communities that offer friendship and conviviality. There is such a lot to be gained if everyone was happier and had their basic needs met!

2. If each increase in productivity was used to reduce work demands and increase leisure we could leave status and consumption behind and relax. The New Economics Foundation suggests we should aim for a 21-hour week, based on international differentials in working hours making no difference to the GNP

Figure 2.1: Health and social outcomes of inequality

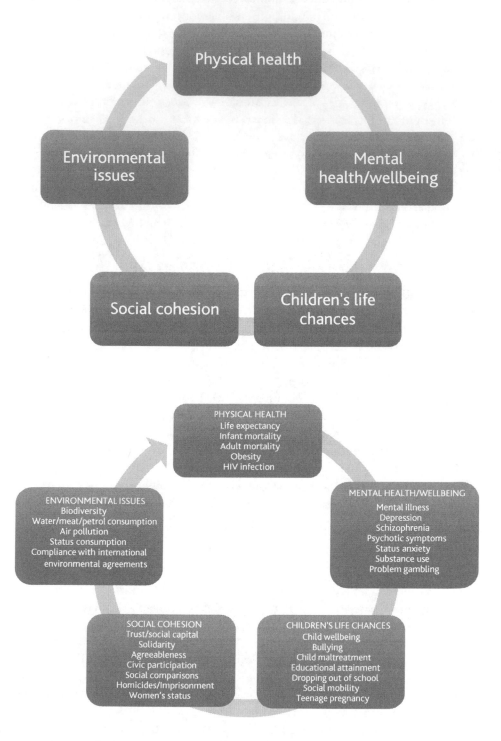

Source: Adapted from Wilkinson and Pickett (2018: 272).

(gross national product; see www.neweconomics.org). We need productivity to translate into reduced working hours rather than income and profit. We could have an extra day off per week within seven years, and the working week could be halved within 24 years as a result of increased automation and computerisation. This would trade quality of life for all for the inequality between unemployment and overwork.

3. Workplace democracy – that is, increased ownership of the workplace by employees – would reduce inequality and exploitation. Control of companies and employees by management hierarchies excludes workers from having any say. Democratic organisations, co-ops and employee-owned businesses change the balance of power so that management becomes accountable to employees. Hierarchies of management are replaced by social responsibility, and smaller pay differentials reduce status divisions. This increases employee confidence and self-worth, as well as enhancing potential.

4. The health and social benefits of a more equal society are transformative. There would be major reductions in physical and mental ill health, increases in childhood wellbeing, less violence, less drug addiction, less incarceration in prison, and more equal opportunities. This would benefit the common good, our relationships with each other would improve, status consumption and waste would decline and without the emphasis on individualism, community life would be strengthened.

These changes, urge Wilkinson and Pickett, are absolutely necessary in order to mend the damage inequality has done to our social fabric as well as to the environment. They would restore the principles of mutuality that have been subsumed under neoliberal self-interest.

> Greater equality is at the heart of creating a better society because it is fundamental to the quality of social relations in society at large. Social status systems among humans ... are orderings based on power; they ensure privileged access to resources for those at the top, regardless of the needs of others. The fact that humans, like members of any other species, all have the same basic needs means that there is always the question of whether or not to share access to scarce resources; whether to co-operate as allies or compete as rivals. Do we want to live in a society based on co-operation and reciprocity, or competition and rivalry? (Wilkinson and Pickett, 2018: 261)

So, let's steer our theoretical investigation towards where we have gone so badly wrong. To take our analysis deeper, let's consider Imogen Tyler's explanation of the use of stigma as a neoliberal class project to justify massive social inequalities.

> **'As governments have come to govern for the market they have also come to govern *against* the people.'**
> Imogen Tyler (2013: 6)

Imogen Tyler's ongoing research into the relationship between stigmatisation, inequalities and neoliberal capitalism is outstanding in its ability to connect dominant neoliberal narratives with dehumanising outcomes for targeted social groups. There is an urgent need to theorise the ways in which stigma functions in neoliberal free-market politics to create inequality and injustice by normalising poverty and austerity-driven welfare reforms as a smokescreen for the excesses of the rich, creating violent differentials in the value of human lives 'fuelled by the crafting of stigma, violence and hatred from above' (stigmamachine.com).

> The 'ascendance of far-right politicians and parties, the erosion of access to systems of legal justice and redress, deepening surveillance and policing powers, the limiting of press freedoms, expanding prison populations, and a marked increase in racist, disablist, misogynistic hate speech and violence in public forums' need to be understood if we are to halt the flow of injustice and find a new way forward based on greater compassion. (Tyler, blog site, available at stigmamachine.com).

In *Revolting Subjects: Social Abjection and Resistance in Neoliberal Britain* (2013), Imogen Tyler provides key insights for community development's understanding of power in society. She draws on Erving Goffman (1963), who first transformed understanding of the way that stigma is used as a form of social control to target and marginalise specific groups of people. Imogen Tyler sees Goffman's work as pivotal in its practical application to political movements, such as disability rights, HIV/AIDS and mental health, transforming public perceptions, but suggests that we need a much better understanding of stigma as a form of social control, as a class project, if we are going to get to grips with the way that free-market capitalism has created escalating inequalities of income, health, education and citizenship (Tyler, 2015).

Social abjection is a theory of 'power, subjugation and resistance'. In other words, Tyler offers analyses of the way power works to subordinate some social groups, but also offers ideas for action. She develops the concept of *abjection* as a lived social process that targets some social groups as the butt of violent disgust; unworthy *objects* on the margins of society. Stories of disgust, as we have seen with Thatcher's 'welfare scrounger', are reinforced by the media and enter everyday conversations as a given truth. Social abjection theory, in these ways, reveals the need for state power to constantly reproduce these relations of the powerful, worthy *subject* and the disempowered, unworthy *object*, a dialectical relationship in which one reinforces the other. Without one, the other would not exist. Hegemony is that fragile, relying on the strength of the stories it tells to maintain its power and legitimacy. By examining the neoliberal de/recomposition of class, deepening inequalities and poverty, work and precarity, sexual violence, disabilities, borders, citizenship and the differential value of human lives in the context of austerity, welfare reform and the 'migrant' crisis in Europe, Imogen Tyler presents the neoliberal project not as a 'free market' ideology, but as a 'politics of control'.

The way forward lies in collective action, global social movements that bring people together on common ground. First, we need a critique of what is happening: connections that illuminate links between so-called 'austerity measures' that favour the rich and the dismantling of welfare provision that removes protection from the poorest, and also racist and patriarchal violence and all other forms of violence against minority groups in a resurgence of white patriarchal supremacy and all it stands for.

At the same time, dissent has been undermined, and political protests that forged change in the 1970s and 1980s have been weakened and even criminalised in the guise of deepening democracy (Tyler, 2013). Tyler's thesis is that neoliberalism is a class project that uses stigmatisation as a form of legitimising increasing inequalities and injustices. She revisits class within the complexity of intersectionality by:

> focusing on not one but several different categories and groups of people 'laid to waste' by neoliberal economic, political and social polices (including asylum seekers and other unwanted irregular migrants, politically and economically disenfranchised young people, Gypsies and Travellers, people with disabilities), my intention is to produce an intersectional account of marginality and resistance that will deepen critical understandings of the *common* processes and practices of neoliberal governmentality both within Britain and beyond. (Tyler, 2013: 8)

Her recent analysis of the current political context goes much further than that of a temporary blip in world politics, to identify *democratic fascism*, a concept coined by Alain Baiou, with reference to the notion of an 'extinction-level event', a phrase used by Andrew Sullivan, political commentator, in relation to the election of Donald Trump as 45th US President. Tyler talks about the way that:

> Fascism pivots on racism but also incites hate against non-racialized minorities, the disabled, queers, women and fascism's political opponents, from refugee advocates to feminists, labour movements and intellectuals, to the judiciary. Democratic fascism is not only deepening an existing social and economic crisis, but has become the source of crisis, splintering social solidarity in ways unprecedented since the 1930s. (Imogen Tyler, blog post, 14 March 2017)

This gets to the heart of the role of stigma in maintaining dominance over more vulnerable social groups. Once again, the force of this analysis demonstrates the urgent need for a counternarrative of belonging, starting with identifying the values that most people hold dear.

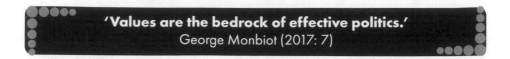

'Values are the bedrock of effective politics.'
George Monbiot (2017: 7)

George Monbiot (2017) puts values at the heart of everything. He continues: '[Values] represent the importance we place on fundamental ways of being, offering a guide to what we consider to be good and worthwhile' (2017: 7). Starting with a compelling analysis of our current crisis, he offers some practical ideas to move us towards *a politics of belonging*. I have chosen to concentrate on his ideas about the importance of placing values at the heart of a counternarrative for change, based on the notion that the only thing that can displace a dominant story is a different story. Human beings have a natural capacity to feel compassion and a need to feel connected in reciprocal relationships, but this is denied by the neoliberal emphasis on individualism and competition:

> ... we find it hard to imagine our way out of the reaction and helplessness to which we have succumbed ... To escape from this trap, we first need to perceive it. We need to name the power that has exacerbated our isolation and our collective loss of agency. This power is neoliberalism, the story it tells and the political programmes that arise from it. Our failure to tell a new story with which to replace it has allowed this power to persist and grow. By confronting the politics of alienation with a politics of belonging, we rekindle our imagination and discover our power to act. (Monbiot, 2017: 182–3)

Change the story and we change the course of history! Monbiot is not coming from a Freirean or a community development perspective, as far as I am aware, but his analysis of the need for a story that inspires hope and possibility for a new future, 'faithful to the facts, faithful to our values, and faithful to the narrative patterns to which we respond' (2017: 6) is in tune with our practice. The thrust of what he has to say is that our crisis is one of a failure of imagination, a failure to come up with an alternative story, a counternarrative, and the result is that hope evaporates and we sink into despair and disillusion. Hopelessness has left us wide open to the rise of fascism and Far Right politics based on xenophobia and misogyny in the UK, across Europe, in the US and, in October 2018, in Brazil, the homeland of Paulo Freire, where Jair Bolsonaro has been elected into power.

So let's explore what George Monbiot has to suggest about creating a counternarrative, 'a story that is positive and propositional rather than reactive and oppositional … with such a story, everything changes' (2017: 6).

This, of course, is precisely what community development does, but is not always very good at articulating. So, let me restate that our work is principled on social and environmental justice, and framed by values of human dignity, mutual respect, trust, reciprocity, equality, diversity, biodiversity … all those values that give rise to kindness, compassion, caring and connection towards people and planet. It is these values that inform everything about community development's politics, practice and theoretical base.

And the evidence is there: in the Common Cause Foundation's UK Values Survey (Common Cause Foundation, 2016) when people were asked what they care about, community, friendship, compassion, kindness and equality came top. The research evidence points to the fact that most people care deeply about each other and the world, but this is largely underestimated – we just do not realise how much people want a world framed by these values so it holds us back from using them to start a counternarrative. The survey found that those who understand the values that others hold dear are those who say they have a deeper connection to their communities, who are more likely to be motivated to get involved in community and more likely to support action on social or environmental issues, as well as having greater levels of wellbeing which they pass on to others by their actions (valuesandframes.org).

In the results of the *UK National Values Survey: Increasing Happiness by Understanding What People Value* (Barrett and Clothier, 2016), focusing on increasing happiness by understanding what people value, we find another revelation: there is a strong relationship between people's personal values and the culture they desire for the UK, yet strangely these values are absent from their perceptions of our current culture. The paradox is that we have created a culture that is at odds with what people want.

So, it seems that we have ready evidence that most people want a kinder world. The first step is to frame our counternarrative in these values, but more than this, we need to name these values clearly and confidently, understanding that they are the foundation of social change.

'A politics that has failed to articulate its values and principles leaves nothing to which people can attach themselves but policies', suggests Monbiot (2017: 12). This disconnect goes some way to explain how we have ended up with a world we don't want. We need to name our values and weave them compellingly through a story that instantly appeals to as many people as possible. It should critique the mess we are in, but offer clear and simple ways to get out of it that benefit the common good. This story needs to connect with the innate human capacity for caring, compassion and cooperation. Monbiot's ideas fit perfectly with the values and principles of our Freirean approach to community development. What we are discovering here is that this is precisely how most people describe the world they want to live in!

Figure 2.2: UK national values

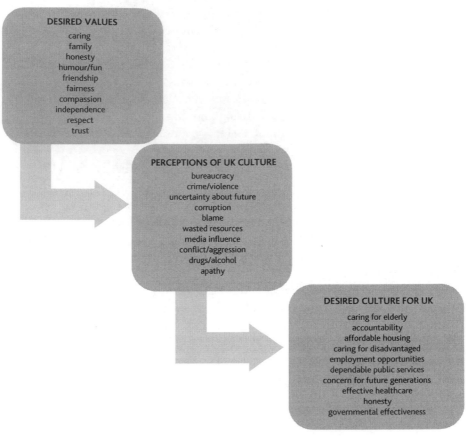

DESIRED VALUES
caring
family
honesty
humour/fun
friendship
fairness
compassion
independence
respect
trust

PERCEPTIONS OF UK CULTURE
bureaucracy
crime/violence
uncertainty about future
corruption
blame
wasted resources
media influence
conflict/aggression
drugs/alcohol
apathy

DESIRED CULTURE FOR UK
caring for elderly
accountability
affordable housing
caring for disadvantaged
employment opportunities
dependable public services
concern for future generations
effective healthcare
honesty
governmental effectiveness

Source: Adapted from Barrett and Clothier (2016).

Monbiot emphasises values as the basis of a politics of belonging developed by strong and confident local communities. By example, he offers the story of Barking and Dagenham, the most deprived borough in London, with extremely high unemployment, homelessness, teenage pregnancy, domestic violence and premature death. It has a high population turnover and was known to be a stronghold of the British National Party (BNP) until 2010. Despite all this, it has made its mark as a global leader in participation due to having a local council prepared to take risks, the inspiration of the Participatory City Foundation and the commitment of local residents to action for change (Monbiot, 2019). Throughout many years of imposed 'austerity', people's rights to welfare have been eroded and public sector provision has been dismantled. Much of this provision has removed the mainstay of community action, with youth and community centres disappearing, together with the presence of youth and community workers. At the same time, stigmatisation has been used to dehumanise targeted social groups, destroying lives and eroding community resilience. This, says Monbiot (2019), is 'leaving many people with the worst of both worlds: neither the top-down protection of government nor the bottom–up resilience of the community it replaced.'

Monbiot identifies two different approaches to building social networks: bonding networks, which strengthen community cohesion; and bridging networks, which actively bring different groups together across race, ethnicity, religion, age and so on. In this sense, bridging networks are essential for developing intersectional unity, a collective force for change across difference. Research suggests, says Monbiot, that this enhances a politics of belonging which reduces social problems and empowers people to have voice. Grassroots politics like this forms the basis of participatory democracy. Here is his inspiring story of community action.

 ## 'A bright light in a darkening world'

'There's a programme to turn boring patches of grass into community gardens, play corners and outdoor learning centres ... After routing the BNP, Labour councillors in Barking and Dagenham wanted to move from top-down service delivery to participation. This is when the Participatory City Foundation, led by Tessy Britton, came on the scene with a plan based on nine years of research into bridging networks. She persuaded the council to take a risk by part-funding a £7m, five-year experiment, called Every One, Every Day.

There are welcoming committees for new arrivals to the street, community potluck meals, cooking sessions and street lunches. There's a programme to turn boring patches of grass into community gardens, play corners and outdoor learning centres. There's a bee school and a chicken school (teaching urban animal husbandry), sewing and knitting sessions, places for freelance workers to meet and collaborate, computing and coding workshops, storytelling for children, singing sessions and a games café. A local football coach has started training people in the streets. There's a film studio and a DIY film festival too, tuition for spoken-word poets and a scheme for shutting streets to traffic so children can play after school. Local people have leapt on the opportunities the new system has created.

Yes, there is an alternative. These people have shown how to 'take back control'.

Source: Monbiot (2019).

Monbiot helped me to understand just how badly we have let people down by failing to create a compelling narrative, one that offers hope that a new world is possible. We fell into a trap of settling for critiquing neoliberalism without offering anything to put in its place. Little wonder that the neoliberal stories – of there being no alternative to us all being slaves to profit; of xenophobia, claiming immigrants and membership of the EU are the causes of poverty; of 'going back to when Britain was great' – a politics of hatred that feeds into isolationism, building walls and withdrawing from a collective future were repeatedly told to justify Brexit, and told as forcibly by Trump in the USA. We failed to imagine any alternative, and so gave rise to the hopelessness that was spotted by the Far Right as an opportunity!

> **'NO is not enough ... fiercely protect some space to dream and plan for a better world.'**
> Naomi Klein (2018: 259)

Naomi Klein is an environmentalist who for almost 20 years has been investigating neoliberal capitalism as a global phenomenon that urgently needs to be understood in a connected way. In *The Shock Doctrine* (2007) she identified that Thatcherism and Reaganism had grown into a global movement, that the profit-as-virtue ideology of neoliberalism had led us into a global economic revolution, the basis of her 'disaster capitalism' thesis. *No is Not Enough* (2018) hits harder and deeper. She opens by locating herself in Australia in a meeting between environmentalists, labour and social justice organisations focusing on this key insight. Compartmentalising global warming, racism, inequality, violations against human rights *fragments* the connections that are needed to analyse neoliberalism in sufficient depth in order to create a counter-movement of sufficient strength to dismantle the 'surge of authoritarian, xenophobic, right-wing politics – from Marine Le Pen in France, to Narendra Modi in India, to Rodrigo Duterte in the Philippines, to the UK Independence Party, to Recep Tayyip Erdogan in Turkey and all of their counterparts (some explicitly neo-fascist) threatening to take power around the world' (Klein, 2018: 17).

Klein believes that Trump is symbolic of a toxic global trend that threatens to privilege the few at the expense of the many, exploiting the most vulnerable with disregard for the planet. But despite what he stands for, she sees Trump as not the story of 'one dangerous and outrageous figure' but as representing a 'ferocious backlash against the rising power of overlapping social and political movements demanding a more just and safer world' (2018: 20), the fear of profiteers desperate to protect their ill-gotten gains. White patriarchal supremacy grappling to hold onto its power!

Time is short, so we need to regroup: 'to connect the dots among these movements ... in order to build a common agenda, and with it a winning progressive coalition – one grounded in an ethic of deep social inclusion and planetary care' (Klein, 2018: 20). For those of us who have fought for decades for human rights, this is our time to get to grips with an analysis that is capable of resistance together with a counternarrative of change sufficiently powerful to counter the disillusionment of those who have been taken in by the lies and false promises that enabled Trump's election and the Brexit vote, persuasive stories based on xenophobia, misogyny, racism and hatred of the poor.

One of Klein's most important concepts is that of 'shock':

> A state of shock is produced when a story is ruptured, when we have no idea what's going on. But … Trump is not a rupture at all, but rather the culmination - the logical end point – of a great many dangerous stories our culture has been telling for a very long time. That greed is good. That the market rules. That money is what matters in life. That white men are better than the rest. That the natural world is there for us to pillage. That the vulnerable deserve their fate and the one per cent deserve their golden towers. That anything public or commonly held is sinister and not worth protecting. That we are surrounded by danger and should only look after our own. That there is no alternative to any of this. (2018: 257–8)

But there have always been other stories, other subordinated knowledges that recognise that money is not all that is valuable, that all our futures are intertwined with each other and with the planet. The interface of these different value systems is where we locate power struggles against domination. But just saying *no* is not enough: we need to 'fiercely protect some space to dream and plan for a better world' (2018: 259). Extreme inequality, openly neo-fascist tendencies, and escalating climate change and environmental crises are driven by neoliberalism, and there needs to be a tangible plan, a boldness about change that engages with concepts like *redistribution* (of resources and wealth) and *reparation* (making amends for wrongs, such as slavery and colonialism), and an openness to challenge consumerism and its impact on the planet. It is not policies, but culture itself that needs to be confronted at its roots. People are ready for change: 'the spell of neoliberalism has been broken, crushed under the weight of lived experience and a mountain of evidence. What for decades was unsayable is now being said out loud by candidates who win millions of votes: *free college tuition, double the minimum wage, 100 per cent renewable energy as quickly as technology allows, demilitarize the police, prisons are no place for young people, refugees are welcome here, war makes us all less safe*' (2018: 263; Klein's italics).

> A very good start would be accepting the premise that widening economic inequality and climate disaster are inseparable from systems that have always ranked human life based on race and gender, while the capacity to pit populations against each other based on skin colour, religious faith, and sexuality has been the single most potent tool for protecting and sustaining this lethal order. (Klein, 2018: 263–4)

At this point, let's turn to Reni Eddo-Lodge to engage more deeply with issues of whiteness and its resistance to change.

> **'I'm no longer engaging with white people on the topic of race.'**
> Reni Eddo-Lodge (2018: ix)

Eddo-Lodge has produced a vital contribution to understanding the essence of white privilege and the absence of black history from our consciousness by emphasising the intersectionality of race, class and gender, all the more powerful because it is written from her own personal experience.

Eddo-Lodge, in a rarely expressed, direct and biting challenge to white people, levels the accusation that not only do we fail to recognise our assumed entitlement to white privilege, but we actively resist being open to hearing the black experience of white power. I talk in some depth about this, drawing on the work of Peggy McIntosh on page 219. Those of us born white have had the privilege to assume a power in society that comes with white skin. We do not need to listen, we do not want to listen, it is uncomfortable and exposes the range of undeserved assets we are rewarded with simply because of our colour. We would much rather normalise our privilege and overlook the black experience. Ignorance is convenient; it embeds racism more deeply into the structures of society and allows us to continue to amass unearned rewards that are not rightfully ours for the taking. We do not want to hear the reality of black experience; it is a story that faces us with the reality of our whiteness, so we become deaf, defensive and preoccupied with formulating a counterargument rather than being open to listen from the heart. It is an emotional disconnect that builds a wall between black and white people as true equals. This leaves black people with the responsibility of challenging structural racism without the full strength that comes from alliances across difference. By this, I mean that we need to listen and act, not only in our own interests, but in the interests of all humanity if we are truly committed to creating a better world. If something is wrong, we all need to stand together on eliminating its inhumanity, and we cannot do this without listening carefully to the thousands of daily microaggressions that give life to racism as a structurally embedded disgrace. Eddo-Lodge's challenge to white people is to become aware of the privilege of always having permission to speak, but never the responsibility to listen. For those white people committed to ending oppression and discrimination, be humble, listen, be open to challenge and brave enough to reflect and act on it.

Whiteness is a political ideology central to racism. It is vital to understand that we need to grapple with both sides of racism: the way that it works to disempower black people at the same time as empowering white people. Otherwise, its invisible dominance remains resilient to challenge and change and systemic racism gets acted out in personal lives with impunity, as with Stephen Lawrence, the talented 18-year-old who bled to death on a London street in 1993, his promising black life over in a matter of minutes – it took 19 years of determined struggle against the embedded racism of the system for Doreen Lawrence to get justice for her son's vicious racist murder that evening (Eddo-Lodge, 2018: 57–62).

Feminism is Eddo-Lodge's prime focus. It is a praxis: both a theory and a movement for change. At its heart, feminist theory engages with exposing the ways in which power interests actively create injustices in order to maintain power. Feminism, as a movement committed to creating a better future for everyone and everything, is duty bound to get to the heart of the economic, social, cultural and environmental injustices that affect the whole of humanity and the planet, diversity and biodiversity. Based on this, Eddo-Lodge legitimately questions the authenticity of white feminists conscious of sexism but ignorant of racism. This raises the importance of placing intersectionality on the table: the way that overlapping, intertwining injustices work together as a whole in the interests of the dominance of white, patriarchal supremacy. Eddo-Lodge's thesis is that white privilege reinforces racism to act in the interests of those who are white against the interests of those who are black in relations of empowerment/ disempowerment, but this is not a simple binary relationship; it calls for us to be open to complex questions that engage with the intersections of race, class and gender, as well as those of disability, religion, culture, age, sexuality and environmental degradation.

Whiteness is an overriding, intersecting political ideology that needs to be understood in relation to all injustices as an assumed, invisible privilege that affects all exploitation. It also connects with knowledge democracy, and the domination of white thought at the expense of subordinated knowledges. Aspects of these arguments are developed in Chapter 8 and Chapter 9. Tackling white privilege would take us a long way in pursuit of a world informed by values of diversity and biodiversity. When people are kinder to each other they are kinder to the natural world they occupy. So, in order to be in harmony with our natural predisposition for connection, kindness and compassion, let's see what Kate Raworth has to say about a new economy which is not driven by profit!

> 'What enables human beings to thrive? A world in which every person can lead their life with dignity, opportunity and community – and where we can all do so within the means of our life-giving planet.'
> Kate Raworth (2018: 43)

I was intrigued to read George Monbiot's enthusiasm for Kate Raworth and her development of an economic model meeting 'the needs of all within the means of the planet' (Monbiot, 2017: 123). This was enough to point me in the direction of *Doughnut Economics: Seven Ways to Think like a 21st-Century Economist*, and Raworth's development of the 'doughnut model', a model that comprehensively captures the parameters of diversity and biodiversity, a world within the boundaries of self-righting balance. Here, at last, is an economist who prioritises connection rather than competition. Let's forget profit as a driver of people and planet with no alternative to this chaos and catastrophe, she says, and start all over again, freeing our imaginations to discover what is possible. There are many alternatives to what we have created, so let's start a process of discovery by posing questions: 'What enables human beings to thrive? [How do we create] a world in which every person can lead their life with dignity, opportunity and community – and where we can all do so within the means of our life-giving planet?' (Raworth, 2018: 43).

Raworth pays attention to the basics of life: sufficient food; clean water and decent sanitation; access to energy and clean cooking facilities; access to education and to healthcare; decent housing; a minimum income and decent work; and access to networks of information and to networks of social support – all achieved with gender equality, social equity, political voice, and peace and justice (2018: 45).

The doughnut model is the visual encapsulation of her radical concept of diversity and biodiversity interconnecting life on earth for a future that provides for everyone at the same time as protecting the living world that accommodates us. It illustrates safe parameters for human and environmental flourishing, with delineated boundaries for identifying shortfalls in human wellbeing below the

Figure 2.3: The Doughnut: a 21st-century compass

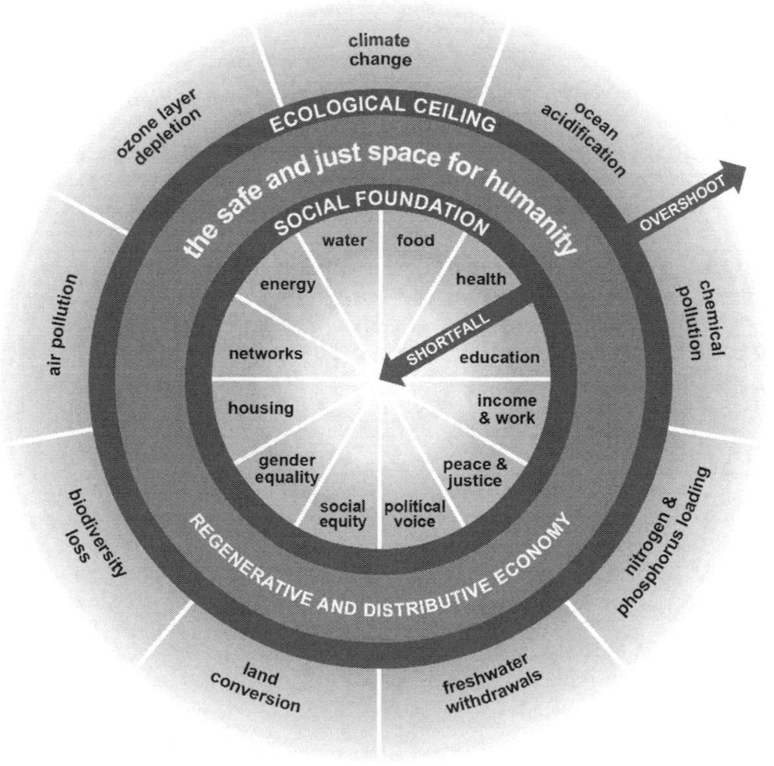

Source: Raworth (2018: 44) reproduced with permission.

social foundation (in the middle of the doughnut) and a danger zone (outside the doughnut) which goes beyond the ecological ceiling (Raworth, 2018: 44). It works as an integrated whole for monitoring humanity's needs within the needs of the planet. The inner ring is the social foundation, outlining the 12 basics of life of which no one should go short: sufficient food; clean water and decent sanitation; access to energy and clean cooking facilities; access to education and to healthcare; decent housing; a minimum income and decent work; and access to networks of information and to networks of social support – all to be achieved within gender equality, social equity, political voice, peace and justice, representing the minimum welfare standards stated in the UN Sustainable Development Goals. The void in the middle of the doughnut represents deprivation, a place into which no one should fall. The outer ring measures the environmental limits of the planet: climate change, ocean acidification, chemical pollution, nitrogen and phosphorous loading, freshwater withdrawals, land conversion, biodiversity loss, air pollution and ozone layer pollution.

The aim of a new economy should be to replace profit with both human and planetary flourishing:

> Currently, economic life transgresses both limits. Billions of people live below the social foundation, deprived of sufficient food, healthcare, energy, housing, peace, gender equality or political voice. Man-made

Figure 2.4: 'Hands off the commons'

Source: Photo by Margaret Ledwith, 22 January 2019.

climate change, the destruction of the biosphere, and water pollution by fertilisers extend far beyond the planetary boundaries. (Monbiot, 2017: 124)

'Redistributing land ownership has historically been one of the most direct ways to reduce land inequalities' (Raworth, 2018: 178). The 'Hands off the commons' action, photographed by me just a stroll from my home, visibly challenges everyone walking past to think about its meaning. The fury that generated the action came from the knowledge that this part of the commons had been sold to an overseas property speculator who is now wishing to cash in by selling the commons with planning permission for private houses. It is a local action with a global reach to counter neoliberalism's well-paved routes for the global super-rich to flourish by amassing land and property.

We are facing interlinked crises of climate change, violent conflict, forced migration, widening inequalities, raising xenophobia, and endemic financial instability (Raworth, 2018: 286). This calls for an interconnected, rather than disconnected, praxis.

> Doughnut economics sets out an optimistic vision of humanity's common future: a global economy that creates a thriving balance thanks to its distributive and regenerative design ... And we know full well, as an international community, that we have the technology, know-how and financial means to end extreme poverty in all its forms should we collectively choose to make that happen.' (2018: 286)

We can do this simply by changing our focus from profit to human and environmental flourishing. This is a view that sees diversity and biodiversity as inextricably connected, so the future has to be one of cooperation, not competition:

> ... to create economies that promote human prosperity in a flourishing web of life, so that we can thrive in balance within the Doughnut's safe and just space. It starts with recognising that every economy – local to global – is embedded within society and within the living world. It also means that the household, the commons, the market and the state can all be effective means of provisioning for our many needs and wants, and they tend to work best when they work together. By deepening our understanding of human nature we can create institutions and incentives that reinforce our social reciprocity and other-regarding values, rather than undermine them. (2018: 287)

The social foundation of Raworth's Doughnut encompasses the UN Sustainable Development Goals agreed by 193 member countries at the UN Summit, 2015, which came into force in 2016 as a 15-year universal agenda. By 2030, all countries, rich, poor and in-between, are called on to end poverty, put right inequalities and tackle climate change, leaving no one behind (www.un.org). It is well worth taking a look at the UN website for ideas, and you can link this to Naomi Klein's ideas, too.

BOX 2.2: Ideas for community projects inspired by UN Sustainable Development Goals

The 12 social dimensions defined by Raworth are derived from the social priorities in the UN Sustainable Development Goals, with some simple ideas for projects that could start the ball rolling in your community.

1. **Education:** access to good education; make learning fun; start a children's book library; support local children and adults to read and write; get teachers to train volunteers to work with reading skills; teach people to question the world...

2. **Income and work:** buy from green, equal opportunities, fair trade, environmentally sustainable companies; support people on low incomes to develop confidence and skills; liaise between employers and employees; offer people experience in volunteering to develop work skills; set up training workshops in your community; identify employers offering apprenticeships; set up a community credit union...

3. **Peace and justice:** change values; keep children safe and protected from witnessing violence; keep people hopeful and connected with their communities; stand up against gun crime and knife crime; make governments accountable; educate politicians...

4. **Political voice:** start a political discussion group using Freirean approaches; support people to vote; make politicians accountable and keep them informed of the issues; educate people in their rights and responsibilities to vote; climate change is linked to economics, public health, inequality and gender, and climate change-induced disasters affect women more than men underlining gender inequality...

5. **Social equity:** 836 million people live in extreme poverty – donate what you don't use; start a discussion group to discover why some people are rich and some poor; talk about values, child poverty, employment, education; join Child Poverty Action Group and End Child Poverty...

6. **Gender equality:** name and shame sexism; start a black and a white and a black/white women's group to look at race and gender issues; discover the facts on gender inequality; look at white privilege and the differences black women experience; encourage women in politics; find women's voices. Gender equality, social justice and environmental sustainability are interdependent: 'We know women will shape the future. In order to build the most liveable, equal and economically empowered cities, we need women

to lead. Unfortunately, women remain underrepresented in positions of power. That must change.' (Friends of the Earth and C40 Cities, 2018: xvii/2; join the conversation at hashtagwomen4climate)...

7. **Housing:** campaign for decent housing for everyone; work to support the young and homeless by developing a friendship scheme; liaise between housing providers and people in need of housing; involve newspapers in exposing unacceptable private landlords...

8. **Networks:** set up a local internet café for access to networks of information and to offer social support; support people to campaign, to be part of groups and movements for change; connect people in community and between communities and with communities in other countries; let people know you care, listen to their issues, hopes and aspirations – together we stand up stronger to tackle wrongs...

9. **Energy:** access to energy and clean cooking facilities; campaign for renewable, non-fossil fuels; start-up funding for solar panels; campaign against fracking; use energy efficient light bulbs; recycle cookers and cooking utensils for poor families; make sure everyone has access to cooking facilities and healthy food...

10. **Water:** 40% of the world is short of clean water and sanitation – start a save water campaign; tell the story of the town of Flint in Michael Moore's *Fahrenheit 11/9* which was exposed to lead poisoning from contaminated water by corruption and greed; use Liz Bonnin's *Drowning in Plastic* (BBC1) to educate and stimulate community debate on plastic pollution and start a campaign against plastic; use Stacey Dooley's exposure of the polluting impact of the fashion industry in *Fashion's Dirty Secrets* (BBC1) to educate and encourage change...

11. **Food:** Over a third of the world's food is wasted – start a campaign against food waste; offer healthy cooking classes; develop cooperation with local shops to take food that has passed the 'best before' date; start up a community-run shop for food basics; start a community café; grow food locally in gardens and allotments...

12. **Health:** Support access to healthcare; educate people in healthy living, encourage healthy diets, train people in relaxation techniques; start a mindfulness group; start a health campaign; set up a running, walking or cycling for fitness group; get health practitioners to base themselves in your centre and work with them to encourage vaccination

---

My enthusiasm for Raworth's (2018) Doughnut model is that it captures the integrated nature of social justice and environmental justice, diversity and biodiversity, to illustrate the interconnection between the two. Far from the dominant neoliberal message that there is no alternative, here is a simple alternative economic model based on meeting the needs of everyone within the means of the planet. It talks to me of the mutual interdependence needed for healthy people and a healthy planet to replace our profit-driven broken model which is lurching from crisis to crisis, and in its wake creating extreme inequalities in wealth and environmental destruction. With my interest in life on earth as an ecosystem in cooperation and balance, this is the most thorough representation of the basis for a counternarrative of social and environmental justice that I have encountered.

Among her many rich ideas for alternatives, Raworth endorses the idea of a Universal Basic Income (UBI):

> Contrary to concerns that a guaranteed basic income would make people lazy or even reckless, cross-country studies of cash transfer schemes show no such effect: if anything, people tend to work harder and seize more opportunities when they know they have a secure fallback. When it comes to delivering a basic income to the world's poorest people, the question is no longer 'how on earth?' but 'why on earth not?' (2018: 200)

Let's take the concept of UBI a stage further through the work of Annie Lowrey.

'Refocus the voices of people who are poor as central to the conversation on a basic income to ensure a movement that is inclusively built and led with people who are poor holding power.'
Annie Lowrey (2018: 198)

Imagine that a check showed up in your mailbox or your bank account every month. The money would be enough to live on, but just barely. It might cover a room in a shared apartment, food, and bus fare. It would save you from destitution if you had just gotten out of prison, needed to leave an abusive partner, or could not find work. But it would not be enough to live particularly well on. Let's say that you could do anything you wanted with the money. It would come with no strings attached. You could use it to pay your bills. You could use it to go to college, or save it up for a down payment on a house. You could spend it on cigarettes and booze, or finance a life spent playing Candy Crush in your mom's basement and noodling around on the Internet. Or you could use it to quit your job and make art, devote yourself to charitable works, or care for a sick child. Let's also say that you did not have to do anything to get the money. It would just show up every month, month after month, for as long as you lived. You would not have to be a specific age, have a child, own a home, or maintain a clean criminal record to get it. You just *would,* as would every other person in your community. (Lowrey, 2018: 4)

A universal basic income is simple, radical and elegant, according to Lowrey in *Give People Money: The Simple Idea to Solve Inequality and Revolutionise our Lives* (2018). 'Universal' means that everyone resident in a country qualifies for it without being means tested. It is basic inasmuch as it covers just enough to live on without hardship. It is an income. But it is not a new idea. Its roots lie in Tudor England, originating in the work of Thomas Paine, but it is an idea that keeps surfacing, often in economic crises, as it has done during this most recent global recession, with supporters ranging from Hillary Clinton to the Black Lives Matter movement, to Bill Gates, with interest shown by a wide range of countries, including Germany, the Netherlands, Finland, Canada, Kenya and India (Lowrey, 2018: 5).

A government would send every citizen an income each month, forever and regardless of individual circumstances. The popularity of and possibility for this fundamental change in social policy has vastly increased since the horrors of the banking crisis, when the greed of the rich and risks taken that are underwritten by the rest of us were brought to wider public attention by the Occupy Movement. For Lowrey, who has covered the development of UBI the world over, the more she found out, the more it raised questions about the legitimacy of our current systems. It is these questions that have taken her 'to villages in remote Kenya, to a wedding held amid monsoon rains in one of the poorest states in India, to homeless shelters, to senators' offices … I interviewed economists, politicians, subsistence farmers, and philosophers … travelled to a UBI conference in Korea to meet many of the idea's leading proponents and deepest thinkers … contemplating the terrifying, heartening, and profound effects of our policy choices' (Lowrey, 2018: 11).

A project in Kenya, run by the NGO GiveDirectly, lifted a village out of poverty in an instant, based solely on the insight that giving people cash is more effective than giving goods or services. It is about empowerment rather than dependency. Of course, questions arise from fears that it makes people lazy and workshy. But economists studying randomised control trials on UBI from Honduras, Indonesia, Morocco, Mexico, Nicaragua and the Philippines found quite the opposite – the only exception being that the elderly and those with dependants, quite rightly, worked less.

'The UBI idea has become a UBI movement' (Lowrey, 2018: 199). The theoretical foundations are developing and activists are pushing politicians to turn UBI into policy. The movement has provided funding for the Black American activist Mia Birdsong to conduct a 'listening tour' to 'refocus the voices of people who are poor as central to the conversation on a basic income to ensure a movement that is inclusively built and led with people who are poor holding power' (Lowrey, 2018: 198). Search youtube.com to hear Mia Birdsong talk from experience on UBI in relation to basic income and racial justice, and also to hear British economist and co-president of Basic Income Earth Network (BIEN) Guy Standing excellently explain about the lies told by neoliberalists, the corruption of capitalism, the political monster we have created – and the role of UBI in social and economic justice, and how we can make it happen.

> **'Knowledge democracy is about intentionally linking values of justice, fairness and action to the process of using knowledge.'**
> Budd Hall and Rajesh Tandon, retrieved 8 August 2016, from www.politicsofevidence.ca/349

Budd Hall and Rajesh Tandon pose profound questions on deepening democracy, calling for us to address the issue of whose knowledge counts and the relationship between knowledge and privilege. Biodiversity creates a healthy planet in balance; similarly diverse ways of being and diverse ways of knowing create humanity in balance, a fully engaged ecosystem. Knowledge democracy addresses the links between knowledge and power: whose knowledge is creating the world that we live in? This ties in with Freire's position on knowledge, but only recently has the area of cognitive justice been more forcibly linked with social and environmental justice. Budd Hall and Rajesh Tandon, describing their respective roles as a Northern university scholar and a Southern civil society leader, have played a central part for the past 40 years in developing the concept of knowledge democracy. The key text for this section is their article 'Decolonisation of knowledge, epistemicide, participatory research and higher education' (2017). I also draw on 'No more enclosures: knowledge democracy and social transformation' (Hall and Tandon, 2014), as well as the 2016 *World Social Science Report, Challenging inequalities: Pathways to a just world* (ISSC, IDS and UNESCO, 2016).

Ordinary people generate knowledge, and if we work together to co-create knowledge for a common good, this simple realisation could change the world for the better. This is yet another uncomfortable truth for those of us in the West! Hall and Tandon (2017) endorse De Sousa Santos's (2007: 10) claim that 'Global social injustice is therefore intimately linked to global cognitive injustice. The struggle for global social justice will, therefore, be a struggle for cognitive justice as well'. Put simply, this means that we cannot begin to address social justice without understanding the way that knowledge has been colonised, controlled and used as a commodity to benefit an elite at the same time as killing other knowledge systems.

Knowledge democracy as a concept embraces the following ideas:

- Diverse world knowledge systems have been excluded, marginalised and destroyed in favour of a dominant Western, white, patriarchal system.
- These diverse knowledge systems and different ways of knowing include the knowledge of the marginalised and excluded everywhere, encompassing the

knowledge of indigenous people as well as knowledge generated from lived experience and cultivated by social movements, such as black and feminist ways of knowing.

- Different ways of knowing may be captured in many forms other than text, for example stories, images, numbers, music, poetry, drama.
- Open access for the sharing of knowledge is vital for deepening democracy in the struggle for a fair and just world, for example knowledge should not be a commodity that is delivered to those with the privilege to go to university.
- Diverse knowledges are the foundation for taking action to deepen democracy for a fair and healthy world.
- These kinds of action for change honour human diversity by rejecting neoliberal globalisation as a dominant ideology.

The process of knowledge democracy is predicated on cooperation, compassion and conversation between ordinary people who take both power and knowledge into their own hands:

> Cognitive justice recognises the right of different forms of knowledge to co-exist, but adds that this plurality needs to go beyond tolerance or liberalism to an active recognition of the need for diversity. It demands recognition of knowledges, not only as methods but as ways of life. This presupposes that knowledge is embedded in ecology of knowledges where each knowledge has its place, its claim to a cosmology, its sense as a form of life. In this sense knowledge is not something to be abstracted from a culture as a life form; it is connected to livelihood, a life cycle, a lifestyle; it determines life chances. (Visvanathan, 2009)

Knowledge inequality intersects with other inequalities; the point being that it is impossible to bring about social change which is sufficient to divert the trajectory that threatens the survival of people and the planet without addressing the intersections of social justice, environmental justice and cognitive injustice. We have to roll back our questioning to focus on whose knowledge is seen as being at the centre of knowledge production and how it is being used to marginalise or eliminate other knowledges if we are to be more aware of 'inequalities in the construction of knowledge – which kinds of knowledge are produced, by whom and where' (ISSC, IDS and UNESCO, 2016: 274).

Hall and Tandon emphasise:

> fundamental to our thinking about knowledge democracy is understanding that knowledge is a powerful tool for taking action to deepen democracy and to struggle for a fairer and healthier world. From this we understand that everyone's knowledge is legitimate, accessible and necessary for deepening democracy as a precursor to action for social change. (Hall and Tandon, 2014)

They call on universities to debate what constitutes knowledge in the academy (whose knowledge counts?), to re-establish the centrality of attention to transformation in a world that every day grows more unequal, more un-loving and less sustainable and to create structures and processes for the co-creation of knowledge with social movements and civil society partners.

> Respecting the knowledge of the people for me is a political attitude consistent with the political choice of the educator if he or she thinks about a different kind of society. In other words, I cannot fight for a freer society if at the same time I don't respect the knowledge of the people. (Paulo Freire, in Horton and Freire, 1990)

> **'Be realistic, demand the impossible was the rally cry of the 1968 Paris demonstrators – think about ending slavery, emancipation of women, the welfare state – all seen as crazy and eventually accepted as common sense.'**
> Rutger Bregman (2018: 255–6)

Rutger Bregman took no prisoners when he challenged the participants at the Davos World Economic Forum to talk about taxes (30 January 2019, available at www.theguardian.com):

> 1500 jets have flown in here to hear Sir David Attenborough speak about how we're wrecking the planet. I hear the language of participation, justice, equality and transparency – but then almost no one raises the real issue of tax avoidance, right, and how the rich are just not paying their fair share. It feels as I'm at a firefighters' conference and no one is allowed to speak about water. This is not rocket science! We can talk for a very long time about all these stupid philanthropy schemes, and we can invite Bono once more, but come on, we've got to be talking about taxes. That's it, taxes, taxes, taxes. All the rest is bullshit in my opinion!

This is intellectual activism at its best, but also provides a mind-stretching basis for a counternarrative of change. Bregman accuses politicians of failing to come up with new ideas; he advocates UBI, open borders and a 15-hour working week for starters!

Bregman's *Utopia for Realists and How We Can Get There* is a provocative but simple challenge to aim high by thinking differently. 'In the past everything was worse. For roughly 99% of the world's history, 99% of humanity has been poor, hungry, dirty, afraid, stupid, sick and ugly' (2018: 1)! In 1820, 84% of the world's population lived in extreme poverty, by 1981 this had fallen to 44%, and now it has dropped to below 10%' (2018: 1). The paradox is that as extreme poverty has eased, relative poverty has increased, creating unacceptable, unsustainable inequalities that harm people and plunge the environment into crisis.

> A crisis can provide an opening for new ideas, but it can also shore up old convictions ... A crisis, then, should be a moment of truth, the juncture at which a fundamental choice is made. (2018: 242)

Our current condition is described by Bregman as more like a coma, an inability to imagine any possible alternative to such a degree that when the entire banking sector collapsed in 2007–08, we opted for more of the same system that had so badly failed us. We bought into the invented notion of 'austerity', a smokescreen for wringing the life out of poor and middle-income earners to divert wealth upwards into the pockets of the already wealthy. The result has been the creation of a global super-rich with insatiable greed for excessive consumption, disconnected from any mutual responsibility for humankind or the environment.

This disconnection began in the UK with Thatcher's repeated emphasis on individualism, disconnection from each other and the earth, and denial of any such thing as society and the mutual responsibility of a common good, but instead the privatisation of everything in public ownership, including spaces where people meet to talk, such as public squares, silencing any form of dissent or organised unionisation ... With the benefit of hindsight, it makes perfect sense as an imperative for the success of the neoliberal project. It stilted our collective imagination, leaving us gullible to believe that 'there is no alternative' to a system that has broken!

Bregman (2018) offers some brilliantly simple ideas for changing our stuck views, backed up by evidence, learning lessons from the past, he frees our imaginations to see a way to a better future: if we 'talk differently, think differently, and ... describe the problem differently' we quickly come to realise that not only is TINA (there is no alternative) a lie, but there are many better choices to be made (2018: 47).

In a convincing argument for making the impossible infinitely possible, Bregman reasons that 'it's precisely because we're richer than ever that it is now within our means to take the next step in the history of progress: to give each and every person the security of a basic income. It's what capitalism ought to have been striving for all along. See it as a dividend on progress, made possible by the blood, sweat, and tears of past generations' (2018: 46). The welfare state, once seen as a collective good, has descended into a system that shames and humiliates. Again among my chosen thinkers, I find enthusiasm for a universal, unconditional basic income which would give back dignity and be a form of redistributive fairness. If we begin to explore our choices from a different perspective, begin to recognise that only a fraction of our prosperity is due to our own exertions, the West is rich thanks to the institutions, knowledge and social capital amassed by our forebears – and, I would add, due to colonisation, exploitation and slavery – we could open our minds to reparation for the wrongs of the past and the wrongs of the present. 'This wealth belongs to us all. And a basic income allows all of us to share it' (2018: 46).

Ideas for change are immensely straightforward; they just require us to free the shackles of our imagination and talk differently, think differently. Take, for instance, Wilkinson and Pickett's evidence for the correlation of poverty and mental ill-health. It people's mental health problems are the consequence of poverty, says Bregman, then targeting poverty as the cause improves mental health as the symptom.

What can we do about it? Well, the first task is to free our imaginations. It's hard to imagine a future without paid work being at the centre of our lives, 'but the inability to imagine a world in which things are different is evidence only of a poor imagination, not of the impossibility of change' (2018: 199). But, things are changing. Jobs are become increasingly automated, changing the structure of paid work. 'Robots don't get sick, don't take time off, and never complain', and we need to be aware of this unless we want to end up with masses of people in poorly paid, dead-end jobs, the 'precariat as defined by British economist Guy Standing, a new social class on low pay, temporary jobs without a political voice' (2018: 192).

Redistribution is the answer. Bregman cites French economist Thomas Piketty, who declares the only answer is 'a worldwide, progressive tax on wealth'. "We have to save capitalism from itself"' (Piketty, in Bregman, 2018: 200).

Bregman talks about 'Politics' with a capital P, one that is about revolution, one that breaks free from rule by the powerful. The biggest problem during the Brexit debacle is that socialism has failed to tell a counter-story, a narrative of hope and possibility, in a compelling language that can inspire the millions of ordinary people that need to hear it. In relation to communicating ideas, Bregman issues a provocative challenge: 'The greatest sin of the academic left is that it has become fundamentally aristocratic, writing in bizarre jargon that makes simple matters dizzyingly complex. If you can't explain your ideal to a fairly intelligent twelve-year old, after all, it's probably your own fault' (Bregman, 2018: 258).

It makes sense if we realise that we can save more money by investing in homelessness, child poverty and healthcare, saving on benefits, policing, court costs … Think how empowering it would be if we gave everyone a basic income, allowing them the dignity and autonomy to take responsibility for their own lives. Utopia is within reach, we just need the conviction that ideas and hope, combined with ethics and a hard sell, can pump prime action. Do not listen to those who dismiss progressive ideas: we must aim for the outrageous and impossible if we really want to bring about change:

> Remember those who called for the abolition of slavery, for suffrage for women, and for same-sex marriage were also once branded lunatics. Until history proved them right. (2018: 264)

REFLECTION: Freeing the imagination to ask different questions

What if teachers were paid more than investment bankers?

What if the working week were three days long?

What if we all earned the same?

What if the government gave everyone enough money to live on?

What if well-being was the main purpose of economics?

What if the economy stopped growing?

What if work were fun?

What if we were all rich?

What if we were all paid what we are worth?

What if we all had to pay for damage to the planet?

Source: Boyle (2013).

There it is! My collection of intellectual activists selected for their profound insights which deepen the body of knowledge that informs radical community development. My next port of call is to look in some detail at what constitutes radical community development.

3

Radical community development and the role of stories

'Everything it takes to defeat injustice lies in the mind. So what matters most is how we think.' (Dorling, 2010: 320)

How we live is not predetermined: a 'collection of movements will achieve the change we wish to see in the world' (Dorling, 2010: 320). First comes critical thought followed by grassroots action. Democracy is an engaged practice calling for participation, making debate, dialogue and deliberation central to community development's radical agenda. As Giroux (2009) warns us, a society that neither questions itself nor can imagine any alternative to itself often falls into traps of becoming complicit with the forms of power it condemns. Radical practice 'provides a starting point for linking knowledge to power and a commitment to developing forms of community life that take seriously the struggle for democracy and social justice' (McLaren, 1995: 34). This is precisely why community development is a political activity.

Radical community development as critical praxis

Radical community development is in the business of questioning everything; rather than dealing with symptoms that appear on the surface, we go deeper into discovering the root causes of discrimination and oppression by questioning the contradictions of everyday life that we are persuaded to accept as 'normal'.

Community development is an integrated praxis: its theory informs its action and its action develops its theory. It is constantly questioning itself and its political context. Without this critical dimension, practice can so easily reinforce the *status quo* by making life just a little bit better around the edges, failing to get to the heart of the matter. On the surface, we hear well-rehearsed neoliberal stories, told with authority, that blame a diversity of poor and marginalised social groups – working class, women, ethnic groups, migrants, travellers – for their own suffering, labelling them in their entirety as feckless, no good scroungers. They become feared and despised. But, if we dig deep enough and open our minds wide enough, we see how structural power uses these stories in its own interests to maintain relations of domination and subordination. Building on the urgent need for both analyses of power and for a counternarrative of change addressed in previous chapters, this chapter will take you to the heart of the matter, situating radical practice in the context of our political times. Let's begin this voyage of discovery by considering four dimensions of radical community development.

Four key components of radical community development

Radical community development comprises four vital dimensions that interact to provide a unity of praxis:

(1) Community development is a political activity

The structures of society reach into people's personal lives privileging some social groups and discriminating against others. Neoliberal politics embraces diversity into its well-developed class project using a dominant narrative of stigmatisation of the poor and vulnerable to create fear and hatred that dehumanises marginalised groups, thereby justifying the dominance of the rich and privileged. These are not random acts: they are quite deliberate, considered violations against human rights.

Left unchallenged, these dominant ideas seep into public consciousness so forcibly that they win support for policy changes that structure discrimination into personal lives. So, going back to my point about disconnection, you will see that if people are prevented from reading, meeting together, questioning and organising, they fail to make connections between the overlapping, intersecting forces of power that result in multiple oppressions of class, race and gender acted out through capitalism, imperialism and patriarchy. These critical connections simply cannot be understood without situating local lives in their wider political times.

(2) Community development is an educational activity

Knowledge is the basis of action: without knowledge there is no struggle, no change. Ideas are the tools of struggle because they offer the key to understanding power and disempowerment, and this is vital, for without understanding how power works to silence people into submission, how can we possibly know how to work for change? This is precisely why I have introduced you to key current intellectual activists in Chapter 2. They provide us with the analytic tools to see the political context in more critical ways, and offer suggestions for practice that keep us sharp and current.

Education is power, which is why community development involves releasing the potential for intellectual thought in everyone. People's natural curiosity and the capacity to think critically have often been snuffed out by experience of an education that is not relevant to their culture, or one that demeans, humiliates, silences. Community development is about popular education in community, the sort of education that encourages people to ask thought-provoking questions about their everyday lives and 'to question answers rather than merely to answer questions' (Shor, 1993: 26). In simple ways, defined by Paulo Freire as critical pedagogy or liberating education (see Chapter 4), community development provides the context for people to question the everyday contradictions in life. Our job as critical educators is simply to ask what's happening here? This is the beginning of critical consciousness, a way of seeing local experiences as part of the bigger political picture rather than as disconnected, random acts.

(3) Community development is a theoretical activity

Community development is about thought and action, thinking and doing, theory and practice as a unity, an integrated praxis. If we fail to find the space to think critically, our practice becomes thoughtless, and we do not have the tools to work for change! This is a dangerous path to take. We leave ourselves wide open to working to support the discriminatory *status quo* rather than to change things for the better. Community development has an eclectic theory base which builds on its strong foundations in the revolutionary praxis of Paulo Freire to incorporate new ideas that give added insight into what is going on in current times. Over the years, we have extended community development's body of knowledge as ideas have taken our understanding of discrimination deeper, most particularly by getting to grips with intersectionality. Intersectionality has taken us from binary – this or that, one thing or the other – analyses of oppression into the notion of a complexity of intersecting, overlapping oppressions that conspire to keep power in place, including environmental degradation. In this chapter, I place particular emphasis on the two weaknesses that I identify in community development praxis: the lack of depth of neoliberal critique and the absence of any compelling counternarratives, both so necessary to the process of social change.

(4) Community development is about collective action for change

Without collective action there is no change. Together we can change anything. But, action for action's sake will not bring about sustainable change. If you want to change the world, you have to know how it works! This is why change builds on questioning what is going on, developing critical consciousness, the confidence to think and act to create a different world based on seeing the world differently. Collective action connects groups across community, forms alliances and networks beyond community and unites with social movements.

These four dimensions to practice are interlinked in a very straightforward process, but it is vital that each one is kept in mind as you develop your practice.

This book will provide you with the tools to reclaim the radical agenda by offering profound insights into the way that neoliberalism has weakened humanity's ties with each other and the living planet by choosing to adopt an economic system that 'puts a price on everything and a value on nothing' (Monbiot, 2017: 19). It will also outline the skills needed for practice to develop a critical edge, developed in detail in Chapter 4. Theory and practice come together in a form that develops theory in action and action from theory, placing the tools at your fingertips to work together to change the story, and therefore change the course of history! But, firstly, let's take a look at the emergence of community development's radical agenda.

Tracing the roots of radical community development

In the first edition of this book (Ledwith, 2005), I traced the foundations of community work to Victorian benevolence, the university settlement movement, particularly Toynbee Hall, and the early examples of feminist action and class action. Here, I want to focus more specifically on the roots of *radical* community development with its commitment to social change for the simple reason that I believe this to be more relevant to the challenges that we face today.

Community development is a contested occupation that sits at the interface of reactionary practice and revolutionary practice. By this, I mean that our work is vulnerable to distortion from other agendas if we do not remain vigilant, critiquing the changing political times that provide the context for community life.

In the UK, community work began to emerge as a distinct occupation with a strong educational component in the 1960s, following publication of the Younghusband report (1959), which identified community organisation as a key component of social work, based on the North American model. Community organisation was seen as an approach that supported people to define their own needs and identify ways in which these may be met. Based on Younghusband's definition, Kuenstler (1961) presented the first collection of community work material directly relevant to the British context, in relation to social need and current practice at the time. This was the beginning of British community work as we know it today.

The term 'community development' gradually became applied to community work that was based in local neighbourhoods. In 1968, the Gulbenkian report, informed by research into the role of community work in the UK, located community work at the interface between people and social change (Calouste Gulbenkian Foundation, 1968). It defined community work as a full-time professional practice based in neighbourhoods, helping local people to decide, plan and take action to meet their needs with the help of outside resources. Within that definition, key components were improving the delivery of local services, developing interagency coordination and influencing policy and planning (Calouste Gulbenkian Foundation, 1968). In its broadest sense, the report recommended that community work be a recognised part of professional practice for teachers, social workers, the clergy, health workers, architects, planners, administrators and other community-based services. There was a fundamental split in the recommendations between educationalists who saw community work as essentially adult/community education, and others who placed more emphasis on planning and service delivery. In contrast, Scotland, particularly after the publication of the Alexander report (1975), chose to place much greater emphasis on community development as community learning (Scottish Education Department, 1975). In the end, despite concerns expressed by community workers, the Gulbenkian report chose to gloss over the contradictory and political aspects of the work (Craig et al, 1982; Popple, 1995).

The emergence of radical community development

Social unrest heightened in 1968. It was a time of transition and change: 1968 was the 'year of the barricades': 'a watershed – a turning point in post-war history and a reassertion of the power of popular protest and its ability to change the world … it was a year of mass mobilisations and rebellion that rocked the entire globe', widely acknowledged as a critical juncture in world history (Ferguson and Lavalette, 2017: 3). It was a year when civil disobedience erupted in the form of race riots, student demonstrations, civil rights marches and anti-Vietnam protests, and which witnessed the assassinations of Martin Luther King and Robert Kennedy. At the same time, there were significant developments in community work practice: the Urban Programme was set up in 1968, from which the national Community Development Project (CDP), the largest government-funded action research project, emerged in 1969. The Urban Programme was a Labour government response to social unrest generated by unemployment, immigration and race relations, inflamed by Enoch Powell's 'rivers of blood' speech; and the CDP targeted 12 communities in poverty for interventions based on the pathology-based assumptions of Keith Joseph's (Secretary of State for Health, 1972–74) 'cycle of deprivation' theory (Rutter and Madge, 1976: 3). Participatory action research is a powerful component of community development praxis. The CDP workers developed an insightful analysis of the impact of poverty on people's lives, based on participatory action research, and rejected the pathological analysis of the 'cycle of deprivation' theory in favour of structural analyses of power.

Gary Craig, Emeritus Professor of Social Justice at the Wilberforce Institute for the Study of Slavery and Emancipation, University of Hull, who worked in Newcastle for the Benwell CDP, comments on how this experience was instrumental in defining community development's radical agenda.

 **The Community Development Project, 1968–78**

One of the early struggles for the identity of community development followed the emergence of the very substantial volume of writing of the workers on the national CDP. An influential caucus of CDP workers developed what came to be known as the 'structural analysis' of the decline of inner-city areas (where most of the 12 projects were based), pointing to industrial disinvestment and the rundown of public services as the major reason for poverty and deprivation in these areas, rather than, as the governmental literature would have had people believe, the fecklessness of inner-city residents. Virtually every one of the 100+ workers employed on the local CDP projects was engaged in some form of neighbourhood work: their point was that without an understanding of the structural causes of decline, neighbourhood work could be misdirected and ineffective. The analysis, taken forward by others later on, argued instead for the need for alliances, across neighbourhoods, between community activists and trades unions, between women's groups and what had historically been male-dominated organisations, and across ethnic divides, in order to use the analysis for effective political action at local level.

Source: Craig (2011).

~~~~~~

Ideas change the world

It is no surprise that these times of radical practice were set in times of radical ideas. The translation of Gramsci's *Prison Notebooks* (1971) and Freire's *Pedagogy of the Oppressed* (1972) into English had an immense impact on community development praxis, as did Alinsky's *Reveille for Radicals* (1969), well-thumbed copies of which poked out of the pockets of any community activist. In fact, Gramsci's ideas had a huge impact on Freire. Nothing ever emerges from a vacuum! This is precisely why Sayer (2016) emphasises that all of us benefit from and build on our common inheritance, and we should be aware of it. In this period, the theory and practice of radical community development came together. Community work rose against what it saw as 'the social control functions of both the welfare state and the state-sponsored caring professions. Community work presented itself as a radical alternative to social work, which it caricatured as "soft policing". Similarly, youth work was dismissed as a means of simply keeping working-class kids off the streets. The welfare state, it was suggested, was designed to contain rather than cure poverty' (Jacobs, 1994: 156). It is this commitment to get beyond the symptoms to the root causes of oppression and to work for structural/cultural change that defines radical community development.

This radical perspective on community development was a direct result of a number of dimensions converging at a moment in time. Firstly, the influence of radical new ideas – Freire, Gramsci, feminism, anti-racism – coincided with a historic juncture. Secondly, these ideas resonated with other interests, including that of participatory action research, revolutionary in its capacity to challenge traditional, controlling approaches to research by dislocating the external researcher as expert and putting ordinary people at the heart of co-creating their own knowledge, vital to any form of radical practice. Thirdly, the 1960s generated a context of hope and optimism, a feeling that a better world was possible for all. All of these factors, in turn, triggered new perspectives which ricocheted through grassroots activism and gathered momentum as new social movements. We witnessed theory in the making at grassroots level in community groups by sharing lived experiences to co-create new knowledge and coming together in action to change policies. Alliances transcended boundaries and rose up into movements for change, and in doing so, began to embrace diversity in a more common humanity. In a democratic grassroots process, we decided that community development was not about sticking plasters on the symptoms of injustice; it is about social change for a more just and equal future. Community development came to see itself as a political activity due to the impact of Paulo Freire.

Paulo Freire: how did this man from Brazil make such an impact?

Freire's capacity to connect is astonishing. Here is a man from Latin America speaking as relevantly and coherently across race, class and gender to influence critical educators around the world as much as his own culture. Antonia Darder (2015: 41), for example, like bell hooks (1993), places particular emphasis on the way that Freire is able to connect across culture and identity to inspire 'in activists and educators of color a political clarity and commitment'. Yet, he was the first to acknowledge that what he offers is born from his own experience, it is not a blueprint for a liberating praxis to be superimposed on every identity, culture, time and context. It is an evolving praxis that needs to embrace new ideas and experiences if it is to remain critical. This level of humility seems to me to be the essence of what is required to dismantle the arrogance of a single truth, a dominant way of seeing the world that excludes other ways of knowing. Early on in his practice Freire realised the importance of humility. We can only fail if we try to impose our own culture on others. He discovered that listening is the answer, listening respectfully from the heart, not just with the ears, to the stories people tell.

Paulo Freire: the power of ideas to transform practice

Paulo Freire not only transformed my understanding of power, but at the same time he gave me the tools to transform my practice. In turn, I have worked with thousands of practitioners who are excited by Freire's relevance to their practice today. In 1997, I met Freire in Omaha, Nebraska, with Nita Freire and Augusto Boal. His humility, together with his uncompromising commitment to *liberating education* as the route to becoming fully human, was palpable. His emphasis on *critical praxis* was his launching pad for a challenge: we cannot expect this to be a passive process. We need to work with new ideas, exploring their relevance to the way we see an ever-evolving political context, share these ideas in dialogue and integrate them into practice. Doing this, we build a living praxis, one that has relevance to the local and wider political context.

Freire's belief was that education is a fundamental right for everyone, from cradle to grave, and that this should be a holistic approach to knowledge generation, based on the understanding that learning comes from feelings and experience, not just the intellect, as well as from culture, ethnicity and identity. This is the basis of knowledge democracy, the right for many ways of knowing to be accepted as legitimate knowledge. This claims back epistemologies and ontologies that are subordinated under a dominant ideology and the structures that embed its dominance in society, such as the formal education system that influences the way we see ourselves in the world from the early years. Critical praxis takes a holistic approach to knowing the world, using stories of everyday life as the key to social change. It is founded on freedom of thought and freedom of being, the key to diversity. Freire felt that a profound love for humanity and the world is an essential component for this approach!

Paulo Freire: early experiences that influenced his ideas

Born on 19 September 1921, in Recife, North-East Brazil, Paulo was the younger of two surviving children of four. He had a happy childhood, learning to read with his parents under the shade of the mango tree in their garden. At the age of eight, all this changed. He was 'woken up from his dream when his family lost everything with the 1929 world crisis of capitalism' (Freire, N., 2014). His experience of the way people were silenced by poverty made an impact on him for the rest of his life.

Freire was only 13 when his father died, but memories of the times they shared together lasted all his life. In a dialogue group with Walter de Oliveira in 1996, the year before he died, he talked of the right and responsibility we have to work at becoming who we are, despite the circumstances we face. He told the following story about the lessons of freedom, respect and solidarity he learnt from his father.

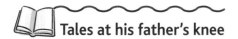 **Tales at his father's knee**

'It is very strange today that I am 75 years old and older than my father at his death. He died in 1934 and I feel his presence almost as if he were here now. Such was his influence and presence in my childhood. In our short experience my father gave me a lot. He gave me a serious testimony of respect for others. For example, he experienced very well his opportunity as father, but he never went beyond a certain level, he always respected our freedom. He helped us to be free, to accept the necessary limits without which freedom gets lost. With him I learned tolerance. For example, he was a Spiritualist, a follower of Allan Kardec, the French philosopher... My mother was Catholic. Of course, he was not a churchgoer ... He did not accept the ways of believing God offered by the Catholic Church. This was in the first part of the century, constituting a fantastic example of his openness and his courage. I remember when I was seven years old there was a one-week mission in the parish we lived in, which I participated in and I was trained for my first communion in the church. I went to him not to ask his permission but to tell him that on the following Sunday I would go to the church to have my first meeting with God. And he said to me "I will go with you". You cannot realise how that speech marked me until now. That was a deep understanding of tolerance, of respect for the different. Here was a father in a very particular society, a very conservative one. He could say, "No, it is a lie, I cannot leave you free to commit a lie, to participate in such a lie." On the contrary, he went to the church and gave me a fantastic example of the absolute and fundamental importance of solidarity, of how respect for the other is absolutely indispensable, how to discuss changes and how to discuss transformation with respect.'

Source: Freire, N. and de Oliveira (2014: 48–9).

~~~~~~

Freire's schooling came to an abrupt halt when his father died and continued only when his brother started work and could put food on the table. As a consequence, Freire's secondary education did not begin until he was 16. It was life on the streets that educated him to make sense of the world, and the ways in which poverty works to silence and dehumanise people. These are the stories that contain the truth of life's reality. This became the foundation for the rest of his life.

He went to Recife University to study law when he was 20. He worked as a lawyer, then as a high school Portuguese language teacher, and finally an adult educator, once he came to realise that liberating education was his passion.

Paulo Freire: his adult life

Freire's meeting with Elza, another teacher, was to change his life: 'My meeting her was one of the most creative meetings in my life' (Gadotti, 1994: 4). Elza encouraged him to study and develop the work that was the foundation for his seminal contribution. They married when he was 23, and she continued to be a huge influence on his life and work until her death 40 years later. They were both involved in the radical Catholic Action Movement, until they identified the contradictions between the church's teaching and its privileged congregation. Freire could see the reluctance of the powerful to give up their privilege, and became aware that change needs to come from grassroots action. Privilege does not willingly hand its power over! His critical consciousness was the result of profound reflection on experience: 'I said many beautiful things, but made no impact. This was because I used my frame of reference, not theirs' (Freire, in Mackie, 1980, pp 3-4). Caring and commitment alone was not enough: he needed to suspend his own way of seeing the world and be open to hearing and empathising with the many truths that emerge from diverse experiences. 'I was taught by them that the right way to think was concrete, real, everyday life with all its connotations, nuances and contradictions ... they are teaching me to *think right'* (cited in Freire, N., 2014). Benevolence is not transformative, it is tokenistic and holds onto power. Real change comes from tolerance, respect for others, a commitment to freedom and the right to think and the right to be. This was a deepening in practice of the 'absolute and fundamental importance of solidarity' that he learnt from his life with his father.

Freire's concept of the *culture of silence* was a direct consequence of his own childhood experience into the way that passive acceptance of injustice comes from people blaming themselves for their own suffering. This formed the foundation of his critical pedagogy. He began to understand the way that literacy is embedded with values of superiority and inferiority, and that teaching people to read and write from a critical perspective exposes the injustices of everyday life. When people see that their circumstances are not due to their own inadequacies, it restores the dignity to act for change.

Freire was an activist in the Movement for Popular Culture, and the practice of democracy became the focus of his doctorate awarded by Recife University in 1959. After this came a Chair in History and Philosophy of Education at the University of Recife until 1964, when he was imprisoned. In 1962, he became director of the government's regional adult literacy programme in the Northeast Region of Brazil, a popular education movement designed to combat massive illiteracy in Brazil. His radical teaching was based on the belief that everyone is capable of engaging in *critical dialogue* once they see its relevance to their lives. Here we see the connection between thought and action emerging as praxis. After this regional appointment, Freire became director of the national literacy programme (Taylor, P., 1993). During this period, there were widespread experiments with his approach to mass literacy. By 1963–64, there were courses for coordinators in all Brazilian states and the plan was to establish 2,000 *culture circles*, community groups that would reach out to involve two million people in critical dialogue (Holst, 2006).

Freire's use of literacy as a vehicle for critical consciousness exposed the links between education and power, and this led him to be seen as an enemy of the state when the multinational-backed military coup took place in Brazil in 1964. He was arrested, stripped of his professorship, and imprisoned. His trial lasted for 75 days, accused by one of the judges as being a 'traitor to Christ and the Brazilian people' (Gadotti, 1994: 35). He was labelled a 'subversive, a threat to the *status quo*' (Mayo, 2004), and these allegations were a direct result of encouraging poor people to read, write and think for themselves! Although the charges were dropped, he accepted political asylum in Bolivia, fearful for his life if he stayed in Brazil. But fifteen days later there was a coup in Bolivia, and he was exiled to Chile from 1964–69, where his work at the Institute for Research and Training in Agrarian Reform gave him the opportunity to re-evaluate his pedagogy in theory and practice from a different cultural and political perspective, to question Brazil from across borders.

During this period, seminars were held on Freire's critical pedagogy at the UN School of Political Sciences. He wrote *Education as the Practice of Freedom* in 1965 based on notes he brought with him from Brazil, but this was more reformist than radical. It was during his time in Chile that he became interested in Marxist thought and involved in strong working-class organisations (Torres, 1993). The impact of the Chilean political context was reflected in *Pedagogy of the Oppressed,* written in 1968, making it one of the most significant books on popular education to this day (Holst, 2006). Freirean pedagogy emphasises both the importance of the social, political and economic context of any transformative practice and the necessity of collective action in social change. Freire felt a deep compassion with the pain of those experiencing poverty. 'To find explanations, he studied Marx, but the historical materialist dialectic didn't give him all the tools to understand what was going on in the most intimate of those beings whose education had been denied ...' (Freire, N., 2014). He turned to a wide range of theorists to help his thinking including Jean-Paul Sartre, Herbert Marcuse, Che Guevara, Fidel Castro, Maurice Merleau-Ponty, the critical theory of the Frankfurt School, and African thinkers Amilcar Cabral, Frantz Fanon and Julius Nyerere. This eclectic approach to ideas, together with lived experiences of working with people in community, deepened his conceptual thought and practice.

In 1969–70, Freire was a visiting professor at Harvard's Center for the Study of Development and Social Change. In 1970, he went to Geneva as an advisor on educational reform with the Department of Education of the World Council of Churches. Freire's influence spread, and his critical pedagogy was welcomed as a practical tool for popular educators engaged in political/cultural projects around the world. He spoke at conferences, acted as consultant to projects and advised governments.

After the amnesty of 1979, he returned to Brazil the following year and began "relearning Brazil" by reading Gramsci and "listening to the *popular Gramsci* in the *favelas*" (cited in Torres, 1993: 135). By this, he means not that the people in the favelas, the shanty towns, had read Gramsci, but that Freire himself, after reading Gramsci, could hear how power was woven into these stories of everyday life. This happened to me after reading Freire: I could hear and see Freire in action everywhere around me. These are the ways in which ideas change the way we make sense of the world: we begin to see in new ways. Freire spent at least two afternoons a week with people in their communities, listening to their experience of life and the way that they made sense of it. This is what he means by creating *critical praxis* out of lived experience; we apply theory in action, and out of that action we, in turn, deepen our theory. Gramsci saw this as a *unity of praxis*: theory and practice become an inseparable part of each other in cycles of action and reflection.

Although his original interest was in the relevance of people's education in developing countries, particularly through literacy, health, agricultural reform and liberation theology, Freire also worked closely with radical educators in North America and Europe, arguing that issues of exploitation and discrimination exist everywhere.

Freire joined the Workers' Party in Sao Paulo and for six years led its adult literacy project. When the Party was elected in 1988, he was appointed Sao Paulo's Secretary of Education. On his 62nd birthday in 1983, Paulo Freire received a letter from 24 children from Gustavo Teixeira School in Sao Pedro, Sao Paulo State, asking him to 'continue loving children for ever'. His reply addressed them as 'Dear Friends from the First Grade', saying that he was 'very happy to see you had such a lot of confidence in me when you asked me to continue loving children' and 'I promise I will never stop loving children. I love life too much. With love from Paulo Freire' (Gadotti, 1994: xx).

This reminds me of Gandhi's words to the angry mill workers of north Lancashire when he came to apologise for his embargo on English-woven cotton. He explained that millions in his country were starving and needed to spin and weave for themselves. At one point, he added 'Please tell them that I love all children of the world as my own' to the man with the microphone, who in turn said 'Mr Gandhi says to tell you that he loves all children of the world'. The microphone picked up Gandhi's softly spoken voice: 'That's not what I said! As my own, I love all children of the world, as my own'. I puzzled over this before working out why those three extra words made so much difference. Then it dawned on me that loving all children of the world *as much as our own* is a political position that counters self-interest and individualism. If we really love all children as our own, we will not support policies that starve the children of poor families. This insight into praxis, not only integrating theory and action but emotions and intellect, was central to the important feminist project on knowledge, difference and power in Belenky's work on women's ways of knowing as connected knowing; it emphasises experience and feelings as legitimate knowledge that underpin action for change (Belenky et al, 1986, 1997). This awareness links Freirean pedagogy with feminist pedagogy, combining theory, politics, experience and feelings to provide us with the possibility of becoming effective agents of change for social justice.

When Elza died in 1986, Freire lost his long-time companion and colleague, and was plunged into deep grief. But, when giving a seminar, he reconnected with Ana Maria Araujo (Nita), a friend of the family and a former student, with whom he developed 'a deep and intimate bond, as lovers of life, political allies and intellectual comrades', and they married in 1987 (Darder, 2018: 19). She continues to travel the world promoting his work today. Freire remained active to the end. In the last 10 years of his life he was Secretary of Education in São Paulo (1989–91) and taught at the Pontifical Catholic University in São Paulo. He also wrote prolifically and gave inspiring talks around the world. I was lucky enough to hear one of his last talks at the Pedagogy of the Oppressed Conference, initiated by Doug Paterson at the University of Omaha at Nebraska in March 1996. Both Freire and Augusto Boal, his Brazilian colleague and author of *Theatre of the Oppressed*, were conferred with honorary doctorates. It was my great pleasure to meet Nita Freire again at the Freire Institute's conference at the University of Central Lancashire, Preston, UK in 2014, not having seen her since her visit to Omaha in 1997 with Paulo. Her work is tireless in promoting his ongoing relevance to the world.

Finally, it is important to mention Myles Horton and the Highlander Folk School in Tennessee. Freire and Horton, from two vastly different cultures, had a similar vision of the role of popular education in the process of empowerment. The idea for Highlander was stimulated by Horton's visit to Denmark to study the Danish Folk High School movement. In the following year, 1932, he started Highlander with Don West, with the broad idea of using popular education for social and economic justice. He was its director until he retired in 1972. In the early 1950s, Highlander focused its attention on racial justice, and from then it played a key reflection and action role in the emerging civil rights movement, forming connections with prominent black activists such as Rosa Parks and Martin Luther King, Junior. A key community initiative was the development of citizenship schools, which concentrated on black literacy as a route to political power. Horton and Freire eventually came together in December 1987, and Freire felt that their meeting brought him through his despair over Elza's death. The talking book they did together, reflecting on their lives and their experience of radical education, united their shared beliefs, and was published as *We Make the Road by Walking* (Horton and Freire, 1990). A week after they met to discuss the manuscript, Horton died. Freire went on to become director of public education in São Paulo.

Ideas do not develop in a vacuum, they develop in relation to life experience and build on ideas that have gone before. Understanding Freire's life offers insight into the way that his ideas were formed from life experience based on his identity, his cultural background and his political times.

(Paulo Freire's life story above is adapted from Ledwith, 2016: 26-33.)

Ideas and action weave together in praxis

Freire's vision was the transformation of humanity to a state of mutual and cooperative participatory democracy through a process of liberating education for critical consciousness and collective action for social change.

Ideas and action are part of the same continuum because the way we *make sense* of the world has a direct impact on our *being*, how we behave in the world. In this respect, Paulo Freire has influenced community development more than any other thinker. He developed his *critical praxis* by listening to the stories people told about their lives. He heard the consequences of *structural power* in their stories, how power reaches into personal lives to privilege some and punish others. He taught community development to listen from the heart to people's stories in order to develop *theory in action* simply by questioning life's unacceptable contradictions.

As a grassroots community worker in the 1980s, I listened to Freire on the streets of Manchester. It brought Freire's ideas to life for me. I learnt what his concepts looked like in reality, expressed in people's everyday stories. And, it opened my mind to the way that injustice is woven into the structures of society. I began to see that the answers to understanding political power and social change are all around us, in the stories people tell about their lived reality!

This process is called *popular education* because it happens in the heart of community, by simply encouraging people to question what's happening in their lives. Everyone involved starts to *see* things differently and to *think* more critically. Collective action for change grows from local projects to campaigns, to alliances, to movements for change. But everything is informed by understanding how power acts in the interests of the privileged against the interests of the poor. In Manchester in the 1980s, we took on international issues of freedom, such as the

Nicaragua Solidarity Campaign, twinning Puerto Cabezas with Manchester, and we took to the streets to voice our dissent: "Free Nelson Mandela", "Maggie, Maggie, Maggie, out, out, out". Miners' Support Groups were everywhere: Lesbians and Gays Support the Miners, Black People Support the Miners, alliances of solidarity with the miners. The imposing Victorian Town Hall opened its doors and offered a critical public space for the people. We organised collectively, from local groups to international movements, meeting in identity groups, forming theory from experience, rising up to be politically conscious and determined to change the world.

It was the time of new social movements: women, black, disability, gay, green and peace protesters rose up to strike out for social change around identity and culture, adding intersectionality to the class struggle. We had a hard time making sense of it all. We needed compartments, fixed boundaries rather than these new intersecting, overlapping, overlaying, fluid complexities that defied understanding an issue in relation to its opposite. This left us stuck when we considered white women's experience in relation to black women's, or disabled people's, or sexuality … let alone dealing with environmental issues and their class component. We often found ourselves ranking each other in terms of multiple, disjointed oppressions or even locking horns or running away from the pain of it all, as we did when we tried to form alliances around women's action, black and white, or where this all intersected with class. We didn't have the benefit of today's insights into white privilege and the role of stigma as a neoliberal class project within the complexity of intersectionality, but just as Paulo Freire transformed our understanding, we paved the way for these ideas to evolve.

Freire's liberating education

Freire, from his early days in Brazil, recognised the vital energy produced by using popular education (or liberating education as he often called it) for critical consciousness, because it has relevance to people's lives:

> People will act on the issues on which they have strong feelings. There is a close link between emotion and the motivation to act. All education and development projects should start by identifying the issues which the local people speak about with excitement, hope, fear, anxiety or anger. (Hope and Timmel, 1984: 8)

People make critical connections when they link cultural, political, social and economic issues with their everyday life experience. This counters the apathy and disaffection symptomatic of a *culture of silence*. Such insights into the nature of oppression, and the ways in which the traditional education system functions to maintain the obedience of paternalism, informed the development of Freire's pedagogy, a form of learning based on questioning answers rather than answering questions, in a process of 'extraordinarily re-experiencing the ordinary' (Shor,

1992: 122). The cornerstone of his theory is that every human being is capable of critically engaging in their world once they begin to question the contradictions that shape their lives.

I witnessed Freire's critical pedagogy in action in Nicaragua in 1985, a living example of participatory democracy in process. The local Nicaraguan people I met in their own communities, often geographically isolated, felt politically engaged in the development of a participatory democracy. Their national literacy campaign, to which Freire acted as consultant, reduced illiteracy from 50%, one of the highest in Latin America, to less than 13% within five months (Hirshon, 1983: xi). Antonia Darder, born in Puerto Rico, talks about the Nicaraguan literacy campaign as one of the Sandinista government's major 'ideological enterprises' (Darder, 2002: 205). She reflects on her own political awareness as a schoolgirl being triggered by some of the most progressive Freirean thinkers in her country. Freire's ideas inspired such radical training texts as Hope and Timmel's *Training for Transformation* series (first published in 1984), developed out of practical experience in Zimbabwe in the 1970s, copies of which were like gold dust to UK community workers of the 1980s. People travelling to Africa would bring copies home, until eventually there was a supplier in the UK. Freire's reach has been global, influencing the practice and analysis of many local projects, from the Adult Learning Project in Edinburgh (Kirkwood and Kirkwood, 1989) to West Bengal, where Freirean approaches to literacy developed by Satyendra Nath Maitra from 1978 onwards brought popular education to adult literacy through folklore, using puppetry, song, short story and popular culture that were all adapted in reading primers. This approach developed across India to have wider influence (Asoke Bhattacharya of the Indian Paulo Freire Institute, Kolkata, in conversation with me in 2011).

Ali Sedaghati Khayaat, is a 70-year-old writer, activist, and self-taught teacher in Iran. Here is the story of how he became a popular educator, now widely known as 'Uncle Khayaat'.

The art of reading and writing in the service of social justice

It all started 10 years ago. One night in my creativity class, Mojib, one of the older pupils, interrupted me to ask if the class could end a little sooner in order to solve a problem. Another one asked, "What problem?" and he answered, "Nothing's the matter! Teacher is capable! He can tackle anything, can't you, sir?"

The class was filled with chattering, chuckling voices. To my surprise, Mojib sat down quietly without saying a word until the end of class. He was a thoughtful, honest and hardworking student. Last year, when I was editing the fifth collection of *When Whales go Mad*, Mojib was the one who noticed my frustration and suggested I needed help. And so it was that a group of them took responsibility for selecting the best works.

For quite a while, I had been running creativity classes in different marginalised districts of Tehran, aiming mostly at the child workers. Using stories, theatrical pieces or other codifications, I tried to evoke their suppressed creativity and encourage them to draw, paint or write their own stories. I had already published a few collections of their works, and now the sixth book was ready.

"Ok, Mojib! You had something to say, go ahead."

He turned red and in a faltering voice started by saying how sorry he was for his years of lying and cheating me. Then, to my astonishment, he went on to say that, firstly, if the book went to print all his stories should carry his elder brother's name as they were actually written by him; secondly, stories of Farshid that I had so much praised were written by a girl in his neighbourhood paid for with boxes of chocolates; thirdly, Javad's .... His confessions were interrupted by the chaos other students made trying to stop him, turning the class into a battlefield. At that point, I was persuaded to leave the room and they continued their warlike play behind doors.

To my surprise, it was a planned play! A theatrical act, very convincing and very well performed. It revealed the truth about the pressures they faced by trying to tackle their illiteracy, with problems of poor handwriting and lack of time to study. They were child workers-turned-to-manual workers, with wasted childhoods and (as Mojib later said) an unspoken fear of returning to complete illiteracy. All of them were yearning for knowledge, and would give anything to find a way to learn to read and write in a short time.

Ever since, thinking of that short cut for these children not in school became my main preoccupation in life.

Reading history, I already knew of some foreign scholars including orientalists, and even spies, who had learned Persian reading and writing in less than two months, and this revealed something about the competency of the language. Seeking explanations from formal pedagogues and adult education experts proved to be disappointing. I had to count on myself, so I began reviewing our language structure with a fresh look, came up with some ideas, and put them to the test. Gradually, a fully-fledged method showed up. Out of my experience with marginalised children, I defined the scope of aural vocabulary for potential learners according to their age groups. Then, the learning materials, including reading broadsheets, were prepared and printed.

Pilot courses indicated that, using the new method, it took only 15 days (45 hours) for adults and 30 days (90 hours) for children below ten to learn the art of reading and writing in Persian language.

Fortunately, this move was well received by university students and academics and a great many soon joined to help. Moreover, some grassroots organisations and independent non-government organisations found it a suitable means of education in the most deprived regions in the country.

One good example is the group of five trained educators who went to Baluchistan province. They settled in the boys' dormitory of Farabi High School in Polan [a Baluch city], and selected a six-class primary school in one of its villages for evaluation. More than one hundred students out of the total 113 turned out to have extremely poor results. They were divided into two groups of below and over ten years old, and the learning process began. A separate group was also made for seven Baluchi- and Jadgali-speaking students who could neither read nor speak Persian. They were to receive learning in their native language, which meant night work for educators to translate and localise the materials. At the end of a 30-day period, all of the under-educated students returned to their classes in school and did well, as declared by the regional education headquarters. The success of the project attracted the contribution of several Baluchi-speaking poets and writers, who later greatly helped in establishing teacher training centres for Baluch people.

The project did not finish there. Immediate requests came from Farabi High School itself, where more than half of the students could not read and write in Persian. Later, we heard about residents of Nohani Bazar, a village north of Polan, who were illiterate Baluchs with no knowledge of Persian. Devastated by storms, the village was more a slum, hardly accessible by outsiders, with no water and no electricity let alone schools. Residents earned their living by pasturing goats and camels of neighbouring villagers. Yet they were extremely hospitable and eager for learning. We started teaching in Baluchi right away, and their ten-year-old children soon began reading and writing in Persian.

Returning to Tehran, we were flooded with requests, so much so that we had no time to analyse our findings. New classes opened every day, new education centres opened every week, and unexpected trips to different cities all around the country happened every month. A very demanding job, despite the increasing number of trained educators, and a never-ending process that would take a lifetime longer than Noah's [the prophet], considering the huge challenge of illiteracy!

Thinking of a solution, I focused my concern on increasing the number of trained educators, which meant teaching learners who would be educators. And recently I've made it a rule: "From now on, anyone who wants to learn 'the art of reading and writing at the service of social justice' should bring along at least two non-readers, and attend the class continually at the specified time for 15 days."

Source: Ali Sedaghati Khayaat, translated from Persian by Manizheh Najm Araghi

Stories are at the heart of social change

Radical practice has a transformative agenda, an intention to bring about social change that is based on a fair, just and sustainable world, and it all starts in the stories of the people. In this respect, it locates the roots of inequality in the structures and processes of society, not in personal or community pathology. In this sense, relations of superiority/inferiority are exposed as discriminatory, subordinating some social groups in the interests of privilege and power. This has implications for practice. Collective action for change has to follow through from local to structural levels in order to make a sustainable difference. Anything less is ameliorative, making life just a little bit better around the edges, but not stemming the flow of discriminatory experiences that create some lives as more important than others. Once we begin to question that everyday taken-for-grantedness, our blinkers are removed and we see life from a more critical perspective.

Community development is never static: its practice is always re-forming in dynamic with current thought, political contexts and lived experience. So, my proposal at this point is that community development is a practice that needs to be constantly re-examined in relation to participatory democracy in order to maintain its integrity and relevance to its commitment to a fair, just and equal world. It is a 'thinking' and 'doing' practice, constantly developing theory in action, and it needs to evidence its contribution to change. Without this necessary vigilance, we leave ourselves open to manipulation from external agendas that may not be operating from the social justice perspective that is central to our purpose.

Freire's exile in Chile gave him a different cultural, ideological and political perspective. The concept of *conscientização* (conscientisation) gave fresh insight into the political nature of popular education as a tool for liberation. And his attention to the importance of the stories people tell of their lived reality was an act of humility, recognition that we need to suspend our own truth in order to hear other truths. In this way, we discover knowledge that has been marginalised and excluded by a dominant ideology.

He gave us confidence to believe that we can develop theory in action, based on the underlying belief that we all have the right to be fully human in the world. In other words, people, when they are thinking critically, are capable of analysing the meaning of their own lives. Freire's great strength is the way that he locates critical pedagogy within an analysis of power and the way that it becomes woven into the structures of society. In this way, Freirean pedagogy is not segregated from life in the false structures of a classroom but is all around us in the places that people live their lives; an engagement with people in context.

Empowerment and the use of story

For Freire, theory and practice is woven through the narratives of the people. He emphasises that transformative theory begins in lived reality, and we can hear it in the stories people tell us in dialogue. Dialogue is much deeper than a chat with someone: it is founded on mutual, reciprocal relations of trust, a sharing of stories that are told from the heart and plumb some of the deepest aspects of our being. This places the use of story at the core of the deeply personal and the profoundly political. Power and empowerment, poverty and privilege, nature and humanity are all inextricably linked by the interdependent web of life on earth, and the beginning of change for a just and sustainable future begins in the personal. It is this personal/political dimension that I want to focus on by linking the use of story to collective action for change.

> A real narrative is a web of alternating possibilities. The imagination is capable of kindness that the mind often lacks because it works naturally from the world of Between; it does not engage things in a cold, clear-cut way but always searches for the hidden worlds that wait at the edge of things. (O'Donohue, 2004: 138)

If the stories of the people are the beginning of the process of transformative change, where does story link to the process of empowerment? Steedman (2000: 72) says that 'The past is re-used through the agency of social information, and that interpretation of it can only be made with what people know of a social world and their place within it.' Life is a fiction. We tell and retell the stories of our lives differently according to our audience, our recollection and our insight; thus stories become shaped by time and space and understanding, and the telling of stories can be, in turn, the vehicles of our understanding. But, for this process to follow through to its collective potential, personal stories need to be set within a theoretical analysis that offers critical insight for action.

In relation to personal empowerment, Mo Griffiths talks about the 'little stories' that link voice to narrative, making that vital connection between the deeply personal and the profoundly political 'by taking the particular perspective of an individual seriously; that is, the individual as situated in particular circumstances in all their complexity [and linking this] to grander concerns like education, social justice and power' (Griffiths, 2003: 81). Voice is an expression of self-esteem; it is rooted in the belief that what we have to say is relevant and of value. If we are not heard with respect, our voices are silenced. My point is that the simple act of listening to people's stories, respectfully giving one's full attention, is an act of personal empowerment, but to bring about change for social justice this process needs to be collective and needs to be located within wider structures.

There was a revival in the ancient tradition of storytelling linked to the political activism of the late 1960s, emerging from the civil rights and anti-Vietnam struggles (Little and Froggett, 2010), and it was also at the heart of the women's movement, where the myriad of little stories captured understanding of difference and diversity and formed the basis of building theory in action as collective narratives for change. The telling of stories is the articulation of experience, which in its articulation presents possibilities for reflection and analysis. In this process, personal stories link to collective experiences which become capable of challenging dominant ideology. Storytelling, used in these ways, can be seen as a democratic force embodying a radical agenda. Chris Cavanagh talks about the way in which story is so much a part of our lives that we overlook its significance and power, and its potential for imagining counternarratives:

> Stories define societies, cultures, communities … Popular education is a practice that … enable[s] people to tell new and better stories – recovering personal and community histories that have disappeared or were subjugated and subordinated to the dominant (or hegemonic) narratives. It also develops our collective capacities to imagine different stories about where we might be going in the decades we might yet have to live – assuming we survive the imminent crises of peak oil, global warming, extreme neoliberalism and the ever-present militarization of our beleaguered world. (Cavanagh, 2007: 45)

Storytelling is central to the process of community development, encouraging participation through listening and understanding. Belonging and confidence grow as people are listened to, valued and taken seriously. Autonomy and action gather strength in a collective process of change for equality and justice. In this sense, storytelling has many parallels with forum theatre, where an individual experience is acted out and audience participants change the experience to give possibilities for practising that change in the world (Boal, 2008). In discussing the use of storytelling around the world, Little and Froggett (2010) note that the West's preoccupation with identity and the self is not so central to non-Western narratives, where culture and community come before self. This observation helps us to understand story as a possibility for reconnecting Western people to a fractured whole, with community as the key connection.

Stories offer the basis of analysis for critical consciousness and social change. Sharing stories embodies mutuality, respect, dignity and all the other qualities that frame this approach to practice, and out of the process, trusting relationships are formed. The act of listening from the heart is the foundation of dialogue:

> Paulo somehow connected his whole being, his reason and emotion, to the whole being of another.… His ability to listen, not just to hear the other person, but that way of listening mentioned in the [*Pedagogy of Freedom*] – also noticeable in his look signaled the moment when he accepted and gathered within himself what he was hearing from the other.… In Paulo, to touch, to look and to listen become moments of me and you in dialogue about something which he and the other person wanted to know. (Nita Freire, 1998: 3–5, cited in Mayo, 2004: 80)

Stories across culture, class and difference

Feminist pedagogy, like Freirean pedagogy, is rooted in everyday stories as the beginning of a process of personal empowerment leading to a critical understanding of the nature of structural oppression. This is based on the notion that the deeply personal is profoundly political. But feminist pedagogy emphasises difference, and the complex interlinking, overlapping matrix of oppressions that shape us all according to race, class, gender, age, ethnicity, sexuality, disability, religion, and so on, rather than a simplistic dichotomous analysis of oppressor/oppressed.

> Radical visionary feminism encourages all of us to courageously examine our lives from the standpoint of gender, race and class so that we can accurately understand our position within the imperialist white supremacist capitalist patriarchy.' (hooks, 2000: 116)

From a feminist perspective, any form of emancipatory practice needs to examine the power relationship in the collaboration. For example, I continually ask myself whether I am focusing my middle-class, white, female, heterosexual, Northern English, Quaker gaze across difference and putting my interpretation on other lives as an outsider looking in (Weiler, 1994, 2001).

Let me give you an example of what I mean in relation to my own practice. Wendy and I found our lives woven together in 1985 when I began work as the community development team leader and community centre manager in Hattersley, Wendy's community. Wendy, who had been a community activist for a number of years, was elected chair of Hattersley Forum at the same time. This was the beginning of a seven-year partnership, and our friendship continues across the 100-mile divide that was created when I moved to Lancaster. The idea of using story in the process of empowerment being useful to emancipatory practice is captured in the following story, and in its fragile conception, when Wendy powerfully and immediately identified my 'outsider' gaze.

 In the beginning, the idea ...

The summer sunshine beamed on us. I drove, Wendy by my side, Celia and Mary in the rear, out for the day in the rugged Derbyshire countryside. Our reunions, this little group of women who had pioneered Hattersley Women for Change in the 1980s, happened at irregular intervals out of a shared history and a fondness for each other. This would be the last, the end of an era, as we were destined to find out a few months later, when Celia died. Today, my head was full of ideas for a partnership with Wendy, based on collaborative action research, a continuation of the political activism we had shared. We stumbled down the slope together to the wishing well, to witness where baskets of provisions had been left for plague victims several centuries before, Mary and Celia too infirm to make the little detour from the car.

While we were alone, I gingerly broached the subject, trying to inject it with enthusiasm. 'I've got an idea for some important work we could do together ...' Wendy looked ill, drawn, preoccupied, and inwardly I had nagging doubts. Was this really an opportunity for a reciprocal venture, or was I using my friendship with her to further my own academic interests? At that stage, I was acutely aware that the experiences we shared in common as women had vastly different outcomes, some of which led to her being so unwell. I had tried to avoid pre-formulating my ideas, asking Wendy to climb aboard my wagon, on my terms, and I stuttered, trying to communicate my good ideas in the face of her lukewarm response. She'd give it some thought, she said.

Some weeks later, we strolled over the miniature wooden bridge in dimmed light to the sound of running water and found a secluded table where we could talk. This theme pub, built at the end of the new motorway that led to Hattersley, was a landmark for passing motorists, a sign of consumerist luxury never dreamt of in my days there. Tentatively, I revisited my ideas. In my mind, this research would focus on the story of Wendy's life. It didn't occur to me that, in my intention to call the research collaborative, I had clearly perceived the collaboration to be in the product; I failed to notice that I was levelling my middle-class gaze at her working-class story. She looked at me, "Are you suggesting that I should be the one left standing in my underwear in public? I don't think so! You join me, and we'll stand in our underwear together." In those words, she located the inherent contradiction in my ideas. I, in turn, felt exposed! This was Wendy, identifying and dislocating my power in relation to her, and presenting me with a critical insight into my own assumptions. I was shocked into silence!

~~~~~~

Wendy's challenge located and named power and privilege acted out within our relationship. In Freire's terms this comes into the concept of 'denunciation and annunciation', naming power in order to dislocate and change relations. From that time on, Wendy's challenge to my consciousness and my openness to reflect on it resulted in a much more mutual, comparative approach to our life stories in order to identify the power structures that have shaped our different experience of the world.

There is an oral tradition in many subordinated cultures that are valued as wisdom and knowledge. I talk more about the subordination of indigenous and minority and women's ways of knowing in relation to knowledge democracy in Chapter 4. Here, in relation to the use of story in the process of empowerment and action for change, I want to remark on the need to understand the value placed on oral expression. Take communities with an African heritage in which the 'person of words' commands the highest form of respect, 'be he or she preacher, poet, philosopher, huckster, or rap song creator ... the verbal adroitness, the cogent and quick wit, the brilliant use of metaphorical language, the facility in rhythm and rhyme, evident in the language' (Delpit, 2009: 329) of prominent black orators, rappers, singers, intellectuals ... But most important of all, this survives in the communities in the people, despite subordination under the weight of dominant ways of knowing, and is waiting to be liberated.

Lisa Delpit (2009: 329) talks about the children who come to school with a richness of language, 'from communities with very sophisticated knowledge about storytelling, and a special way of saying a great deal with a few words', like many of the indigenous cultures. Not only is story a way of personally empowering subordinated groups by celebrating the cultures they carry within, but it is an act of democratic liberation, a political act that elevates a diversity of knowledge and frees us all from domination. As Delpit nails it: 'we will then all be enriched'!

A sense of who we are in the world

If story has a powerful potential in the process of critical practice, it is important to have a theoretical understanding that explains how it might work most effectively. Griffiths (2003) supports the idea that 'little stories' restore self-respect through dignity, mutuality and conviviality, but stresses that this is not transformative until it becomes a collective process. Darder talks about the way she provides learning contexts in which she resists giving answers, but encourages people 'to reach into themselves and back to their histories' (2002, p 233). Using reflective writing to explore the inner depths of memory and history, she works with her students to analyse their stories from theoretical perspectives. The focus of each reflection moves in a connected way to excavate the deepest life experiences. Take, for example, Darder's idea of *problematising* 'reading' with her students. Reflections begin with the first memory of hearing stories told by people who love us, extending by degrees to reflections on learning to read in school. By reaching inside themselves and their histories, she uses this approach with her students to develop reflection and story as a discovery of who they are and what has shaped them in their world in relation to the stories they have been told. This is the beginning of *critical consciousness*. These stories are critical pedagogy in action, leading to personal autonomy and a collective will to act together for change.

In these ways, we begin to build theory and practice around the role of story in developing the self-esteem that leads to autonomy and the confidence to act. Most importantly, we understand the significance of beginning in the deeply personal stories that have constructed people's reality in the overall process of collective action for social justice. Stories give voice to experience, and in turn provide a structure for reflection on the world. The insight gained from this reflection reveals the political nature of personal experience and leads to critical consciousness and critical action. More than this, the sense of identity that emerges leads to personal autonomy.

Doyal and Gough (1991) suggest that autonomy of agency is a basic human need that leads to critical autonomy, and they see this as the prerequisite to critical participation in society, the basis of collective action. This fits with Freire's concept of becoming more fully human, that we all have a drive to be the person we have come to be. Expressed diagrammatically, this offers a clear structure to the development of critical practice (see Figure 3.1). It suggests that identity politics plays a vital part in discovering the pride and confidence in who we are that is so necessary for community activism. But, for personal empowerment to become a liberating force, our consciousness must be critical; we need to understand ourselves in relation to the structural forces that shape us if we are to empathise with others and act collectively for a fair and just world. These theoretical insights link the practical strategy of reflection as story, with a political discovery of who we are in the world.

Figure 3.1: Critical autonomy and collective action

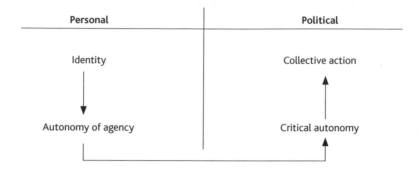

Richard Winter, in his work on patchwork texts, remarks that story often starts from a personal interpretation, an 'exploring inwards':

> ... but if fiction is to be the basis for a process of reflection that is to be sustained, we need a format where questioning and exploring beyond one's initial set of ideas is made explicit and is built into the writing process itself, as well as into the discussion of the writing.... In order to sustain the reflective process, a format is needed which is flexible enough to allow different ways of writing to be combined, a format which allows the writer to move easily between description, imaginative creation and analytical commentary. (Winter et al, 1999: 65)

He suggests that we can create a plurality of voices without false claims to a single truth: that we can present a unity of narrative out of this diversity if we are explicit about uncertainty and present conceivable, plural truths. In other words, it is possible to link the personal and the collective without reducing or silencing the diversity of different experiences. It is also possible to engage with paradox and contradiction as a more complex 'truth', a counterforce to positivism, as suggested by O'Donohue (2004).

BOX 3.1: Practical ideas for using story with community groups

1. Start with your own stories to put everyone at ease, keeping them relevant and focused, embodying the values of Freirean ways of working: trust, mutuality, reciprocity, respect, dignity, empathy.

2. Learn to listen respectfully from the heart to the stories of others.

3. Begin in a spontaneous, unstructured way, building on critical incidents from everyday life, developing listening as part of the dialogical process. Use one story to build on another, building trust and confidence in the group, leading to 'multiple paths of exploration' (Treleaven, 2001: 268). Do not analyse unless it evolves spontaneously from within the group.

4. Choose a relevant issue, so that no one feels daunted and everyone has something to say: a conflict, a misunderstanding, a missed opportunity, a moment of joy, compassion, hope, fear, anxiety, inspiration, danger, a new beginning, and so on (Bolton, 2005).

5. Notice the extraordinary re-experiencing of the ordinary (Shor and Freire, 1987: 93), feminist claiming of feelings and emotions as legitimate knowledge, exploring whiteness and maleness as assumed power ...

6. Gradually develop a more structured approach, as people offer their stories. Develop skills of respectful questioning and sensitive feedback in the group, together with the idea of connected knowing – profound empathy with experiences and ideas that are different from our own (Belenky et al, 1986).

7. Make critical connections with the bigger picture, identify common themes, make critical links with historical, cultural, political and social structures, identify experiences of power relations linked to dominant narratives as you move from the personal to the political.

8. Use story as reflection, as *problematising,* as noticing, as fiction, as a skill for training community workers.

9. Experiment with writing fictional counternarratives, reconstruct the original story in new ways. Pay attention to values as the basis of a new story.

10. Share these counternarratives and explore how they could influence new directions, new futures. Turn to the provocations set out in Chapter 9 to stimulate ideas. What action needs to be taken to sustain change – projects, alliances, networks, movements for change?

'Little stories' connect to bigger pictures, and the personal is then understood as political.

> You can begin to trace the pattern of story as a reaching inwards to explore the self under the microscope of a self-reflexive narrative, to discover the ways in which 'the social is embedded in ... skin and bones'. (Berger and Quinney, 2005: 265)

As Giroux et al (1996) say, counternarratives not only counter grand narratives, but they also challenge the hegemonic narratives of everyday life that manipulate people to think and behave according to a dominant set of cultural beliefs.

This model encapsulates the ideology, theory and action of community development in a framework that moves from the deeply personal story through to collective action for change. Freire understood the power of lived stories in the construction of knowledge and saw that revisiting this lived history is an inner resource that is vital to deepening consciousness:

> The more I return to my distant childhood, the more I realize there is always more worth knowing. I continue to learn from my childhood and difficult adolescence. I do not return to my early years as someone who is sentimentally moved by a ridiculous nostalgia or as someone who presents his not-so-easy childhood and adolescence as revolutionary credentials. (Freire, 1996 *Letters from Cristina*, cited in Darder, 2018: 3)

This is precisely why starting with Freire's lived stories and ending with the relevance of story to empowerment in the process of social change is the focus of this chapter. My introduction to story as the basis of both critique of the political context and imagining counternarratives of change lays the foundation for developing a Freirean toolkit, which forms the substance of the next chapter.

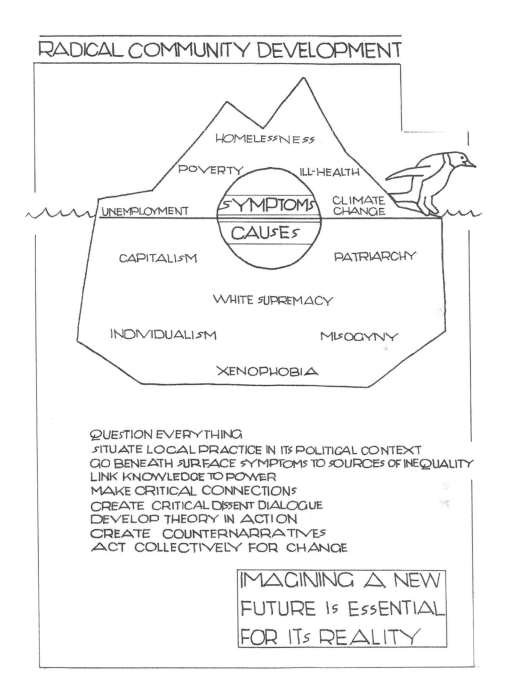

RADICAL COMMUNITY DEVELOPMENT

HOMELESSNESS

POVERTY   ILL-HEALTH

UNEMPLOYMENT   SYMPTOMS   CLIMATE CHANGE
CAUSES

CAPITALISM   PATRIARCHY

WHITE SUPREMACY

INDIVIDUALISM   MISOGYNY

XENOPHOBIA

QUESTION EVERYTHING
SITUATE LOCAL PRACTICE IN ITS POLITICAL CONTEXT
GO BENEATH SURFACE SYMPTOMS TO SOURCES OF INEQUALITY
LINK KNOWLEDGE TO POWER
MAKE CRITICAL CONNECTIONS
CREATE CRITICAL DISSENT DIALOGUE
DEVELOP THEORY IN ACTION
CREATE COUNTERNARRATIVES
ACT COLLECTIVELY FOR CHANGE

IMAGINING A NEW
FUTURE IS ESSENTIAL
FOR ITS REALITY

4

Radical community development in action

Here, I concentrate on putting Freire into practice. I introduced Paulo Freire's life story in the previous chapter, as an important aspect of understanding the context for the emergence of his ideas. Freire felt that the stories people tell about their everyday lives expose the paradoxical, unjust nature of experience and contain both the theory and practice to bring about change. The power of personal stories was evident in the new social movements, particularly the way that second-wave feminism emerged as a political movement simply from women meeting together in community groups to share their stories and form a common theory from shared experience that triggered collective action for change. I was part of that movement, and remember the power of critical consciousness, the realisation that as we shared our experiences of life together, it released the confidence and energy to organise collectively for change.

I will now move on to introduce some of Freire's key concepts in a simple, structured way as a precursor for putting Freire into practice. Familiarise yourself with Freirean terminology (see Glossary). Although it may sound rather strange in places, once understood it is simple to grasp and opens up a journey of critical discovery, freeing minds from internalised, controlling ideas to become aware of the way that power works. The first act in the process of transformative change is seeing the world through a different lens of infinite possibilities. Freire's concepts are the key to the richness of his insight and open up a knowing that is beyond the written word. You will find just as I did that, equipped with this understanding, complex concepts come alive out of the taken-for-grantedness of everyday life, and you see the world in ways that you have never noticed before!

By the end of this chapter, you will be able to understand how Freire's concepts fit into what the outstanding Freirean scholar Paula Allman called 'an integral whole' – a unity of praxis that simply does not work if used in a random, fragmented way. Keep this in mind!

Moving on with Freire's key concepts

As a jumping-off point, let's contextualise Freire's key concepts within the rich imagination of his thinking. This avoids any sense of them being an eclectic, disconnected, rather random set of ideas, but presents them as essential dimensions of an integrated whole that provides radical community development with the potential to bring about change.

At the heart of this approach is *conscientisation*, the process of becoming critical in order to see beyond the contradictions of life that we take for granted, unquestioningly accepting life as it is. Conscientisation is about questioning everything, seeing situations with fresh eyes, removing the blinkers to see the stark reality of power permeating the essence of our being. Once those blinkers have been lifted, an exciting journey of transformation begins.

> Freire's pedagogy of the oppressed must be first and foremost understood as revolutionary praxis that counters capitalist relations of production and colonialism, in that it is committed to a larger political project of societal liberation. (Darder, 2018: 104)

Darder's point is that Freirean pedagogy may begin in the lives of local people, but to be a complete transformative endeavour it both needs to engage with critiquing power at the level of society in order to understand how structural power reaches into communities and to follow through to collective action in order to bring about change.

By sharing the lives of the people, Freire came to recognise and name concepts that expose political domination in everyday lives. Freire's identification of a *culture of silence*, the way in which structural discrimination leads to passive acceptance in those who are subordinated, in turn, gave me a deep understanding of the impact of *dehumanisation*. Rather than being mystified by the absence of people in public spaces in the early communities of my practice, I understood that whereas anger has an energy to fight back, hopelessness can create an apathy that lacks the energy for action. I began to see that the value base of Freirean praxis – dignity, respect, mutuality, reciprocity, trust, cooperation – not only offers a frame for the quality of every interaction in practice, but it begins the process of healing the psychological wounds of political violence, a necessary precursor to problem-posing *dialogue* as the route to *critical consciousness* (Ledwith, 2018a).

Critical pedagogy

> Critical pedagogy has failed to articulate a vision for self-empowerment and social transformation; consequently, the term 'critical pedagogy' needs to have its meaning specified in more precise terms. (McLaren, 1995: 34)

Critical pedagogy involves questioning, naming, reflecting, analysing and collectively acting in the world. It is a form of education that liberates rather than controls, in which relations are reciprocal rather than dominant, and where the humility of the educator enables a co-educator/co-learner relationship to flourish, which is precisely why Freire would often refer to it as 'liberating education'. Critical pedagogy is the democratic process of education that takes place in community groups and forms the basis of transformation. It is founded on *conscientisation*, the process of becoming critically conscious. By *problematising* local issues, *critical dialogue* exposes socially constructed identities that have been silenced:

> ... in this respect, a postcolonial narratology encourages the oppressed to contest the stories fabricated for them by 'outsiders' and to construct counterstories that give shape and direction to the practice of hope and the struggle for an emancipatory politics of everyday life. It is a pedagogy that attempts to exorcise from the social body the invading pathologies of racism, sexism, and class privilege. (McLaren, 1995: 105)

In other words, the community worker is a popular educator who, in the process of dealing with everyday issues, poses questions that encourage us to see our world from a critical perspective, and in turn we pose our own questions, going deeper into the nature of oppression. In so doing we:

> ... free ourselves from the dead weight of dominant corporate consumer narratives. We can do this by crossing cultural boundaries and negotiating new, hybrid identities. (McLaren, 1995: 104)

In rediscovering our histories, we reconstruct our cultural identities and, in the process, we collectively identify the values we hold dear as the basis of counternarratives, stories of a different future based on social and environmental flourishing. In these ways, critical pedagogy, locating itself both within community and within larger contexts of global capitalism, enables people to identify other possibilities that are based on a more just, participatory democracy 'that promotes sustainable, people-centred development, equal opportunities and social justice' (Craig and Mayo, 1995: 1). But for this to be effective, we need theories that are capable of critiquing our current times as the bedrock for the process of change. Freire was insistent that he handed us a critical praxis developed from his own experience in its culture and times, but we need to work to develop this foundation if it's to be relevant to our here and now. Let's take a deeper look at key Freirean concepts in this respect.

Digging deeper into Freirean concepts

> The insistence that the oppressed engage in reflection on their concrete situation is not a call to armchair revolution. On the contrary, reflection – true reflection – leads to action. On the other hand, when the situation calls for action, that action will constitute an authentic praxis only if its consequences become the object of critical reflection.... Otherwise, action is pure activism. (Freire, 1972: 41)

Freire achieves theoretical coherence because his work unites a philosophy of hope with a pedagogy of liberation; in other words, thought and action become part of the same process. The basic belief underpinning this is that human beings are capable *subjects*, able to think and reflect for themselves, and in doing so transcend and recreate their world. This is set in juxtaposition to the dominant neoliberal dehumanisation of people as *objects*, unthinkingly and unquestioningly bound to their world in systems of power and control. Constant reference to dehumanising stereotypes in politics and the media – for example repeatedly stigmatising marginalised social groups as worthless wasters – means the story sells itself as a given truth in popular imagination. Freire's quest was to identify a process of critical discovery through which oppressed people could free their minds and become aware that they hold the key to transformative change (Ledwith, 2018b).

Culture of silence and dehumanisation

Freire identified the way in which perceptions of powerlessness are not only external forces, but become internalised and erode hope, creating a *culture of silence*. In the struggle for freedom and justice, critical pedagogy aims to restore people's full human potential:

> This struggle is only possible because dehumanization, although a concrete historical fact, is *not* a given destiny but the result of an unjust order that engenders violence in the oppressors, which in turn dehumanizes the oppressed.... In order for this struggle to have meaning, the oppressed must not, in seeking to regain their humanity (which is a way to create it), become in turn oppressors of the oppressors, but rather restorers of the humanity of both. (Freire, 1972: 21)

Freire's belief was that silencing the people is a violent act of *dehumanisation*. 'The *problem of humanization*, ... he regards as *an inescapable concern* of those committed to a just world' (Darder, 2018: 95,emphasis in original). The structures of society reach into people's being and embed dominant ideology– the stories of whose lives count – into everyday lived reality. It is an extremely effective way of maintaining control, as we see from Imogen Tyler's research into the way that stories based on stigma marginalise and dehumanise a wide range of social groups – the poor, migrants, travellers, disabled people ... – generating the hatred and fear externally that internalises worthlessness. We witness this in today's society with extreme social divisions in rich countries, resulting homelessness, food banks, hungry children, violence ... Tyler's ongoing research is important in helping us to understand that this is not simply a binary, class-based analysis, but a clever and conscious intersectional project to maintain power (see stigmachine.com).

Labelling people worthless internalises a sense of worthlessness which Freire describes as fatalism, hopelessness and despair. He put great emphasis on the importance of finding hope, even from the depths of despair, as vital in the process of claiming back the right to be fully human. Without hope, he sees dialogue as impossible: people are alienated and unable to reflect on the realities of their exploitation. The struggle for freedom is impossible without hope: 'without hope fatalism can overcome us, disintegrating our dreams' (Darder, 2018: 124). Hope releases energy from apathy, the will to enter the struggle for change. The optimistic note here is that when taking a Freirean approach in practice, I have seen hope generated in a single encounter by simply listening from the heart to hear, to value and to care about what people have to say. This generates trusting relations, the basis of true dialogue.

Three levels of conscientisation

'Conscientisation is the deepening of the coming of consciousness.' But Freire continues with a warning that 'not all coming to consciousness extends necessarily into conscientisation'; without curiosity, critical reflection, rigour and humility, it is not possible to reveal the 'truths hidden by ideologies' (Freire, 1993: 109). Consciousness may remain partial. The process of becoming critically aware is seen by Freire to have three levels:

- *Magical consciousness* refers to the level at which people are passive and unquestioning about the injustices they experience. The harshness of their lives tends to be passively accepted, and their explanations are often based on fatalism, such as that suffering in the present is paying for past sins.
- *Naive consciousness* involves a degree of insight into the nature of individual problems but does not connect these with structural discrimination. At this level of consciousness, people are likely to blame themselves, and say, for example, that they are not clever enough, or they should have worked harder, or studied better at school. This individualisation of problems plays into the neoliberal hegemonic blaming of victims, which is integral to maintaining the domination of those in power.
- *Critical consciousness* is the stage at which connections are made with the discriminatory structures of society, that not only reach into communities but penetrate the very essence of people's being with their destructive messages of worthlessness. Seeing from a critical perspective lifts the passive silence of hopelessness. It restores the confidence to claim a rightful place in the world, to join with others at the helm of the world's destiny. The process is rooted in critical reflection and collective struggle.

Conscientisation is founded on Freire's problem-posing approach as a method for co-creating knowledge and will be discussed in Chapter 5 in relation to knowledge democracy and emancipatory action research.

False generosity and false consciousness

False generosity is a term originally coined by Engels. It influenced Freire's thinking about the empty gestures that give the appearance of equality without changing the underlying structural conditions that create discrimination.

It is also linked to Marxism's *false consciousness,* the ways in which marginalised social groups are persuaded to accept their lot by pathologising them, making them passive and pessimistic. It may be worth revisiting Chapter 2 and re-reading Imogen Tyler's theoretical development of social abjection theory, deepening the ways in which we understand how stigma is used with great effect as an intentional component of the neoliberal class project to maintain relations of domination and subordination.

False generosity is seen by Freire as an attempt to soften perceptions of the power of the oppressor through charitable practices, benevolence, tokenism .... Freire sees false generosity as a form of violence that perpetuates hopelessness, despair and poverty to keep the necessity of oppressed masses in place for neoliberal capitalism to justify enormous social inequalities and create the unacceptable human suffering that Philip Alston (2018) names and shames as human rights violations in his report to the United Nations (detailed in Opening Thoughts). For Freire, false generosity is a necessary component of hegemony, a smokescreen that blurs the impact of discrimination by giving the false impression of justice at the same time as maintaining power and control by keeping the mass of people in poverty. Violence, as he sees it, lies in the fact that false generosity acts as a barrier to the struggle for freedom by deepening dependency on the oppressor and keeping power and privilege in place in the hands of the few, who ' see their wealth as an inalienable right, which they've earned through their wherewithal and intelligence. Meanwhile, the *have-nots* are seen through a victim–blaming lens, where they are deemed incompetent, and lazy, and worst of all is their unjustifiable ingratitude towards the "generous gestures" of the dominant class.' (Freire, quoted in Darder, 2018: 100–1).

As Bregman (2018) puts it so well, most wealth is not created at the top, just devoured there! If we get to grips with the way that 'austerity' has violated human rights under the neoliberals in Britain, that it has been unnecessary and violent (Alston, 2018), we touch the edges of exposing the neoliberal dominant ideology as greedy and self-interested as well as damaging to the fabric of society. This opens up the process of conscientisation. *True generosity,* in Freire's eyes, is based on the right of everyone to dignity and respect, freedom to be more fully human in relations of cooperation and kindness ... and this is where we once again see the power and relevance of the values that underpin every dimension of Freirean pedagogy.

Education as the practice of freedom

Pedagogy of the Oppressed remains the most important of all Freire's extensive published work because it contains not only his most fully developed philosophy but also his revolutionary strategy. This is why it is still the foundation of transformative thought and action, a critical praxis for our times.

Freire sees transformative change as having two stages: *cultural action* and *cultural revolution. Cultural action* is any project which enables people to develop a critical insight into the ways in which power and disempowerment dehumanise their lives as a precursor to involvement in collective action for change. *Cultural revolution* refers to sustainable change, 'a permanent process in which conscientized people engage in the continuous creation and recreation of their society' (Allman, 2009: 427).

The opposite of this is *cultural invasion*, or *anti-dialogue*, which involves the imposition of a dominant group's assumptions, values and perceptions of the world on others, silencing and disempowering. This is a form of dominance that permeates within and between cultures.

Freire stresses the political nature of education. Education is never neutral. It is either *domesticating* or *liberating*. In its domesticating form, the *banking* approach is used. The educator is seen as powerful and all-knowing, pouring information into the unquestioning minds of learners, who are seen as malleable and controllable *objects*. The educator is active and the learners passive. This is the traditional, hierarchical model of education, which transmits knowledge based on dominant interests in society.

Hall and Tandon (see Chapter 2) in their research into knowledge democracy, the subordination of other ways of knowing under the weight of a dominant truth, argue the case for cognitive injustice to sit alongside social injustice and environmental injustice as interlinked and necessary for a radical, transformative agenda. They provide insight into the way that dominant knowledge has now been commodified and sold in a profit-making enterprise by universities, which neglect their role in the pursuit of truth to become tools of the neoliberal project in reinforcing the inequalities in society.

Animateurs and culture circles

Animateurs are popular educators who create the context for questioning lived experience in community groups. It is a term we are not widely familiar with, but for Freire it captures the essence of an educator committed to working in a mutual, reciprocal way with participants in a *culture circle,* or community group. The horizontal nature of this relationship challenges the traditional top-down, vertical relations of teachers and learners in traditional education. It is a fundamental relationship of equals, with the *educator-learner* and *learner-educator* being interchangeable. It calls on us to be open to learn as much as we are to teach. Popular educators, or animateurs, provide opportunities for marginalised groups of people to value their experience, history and culture in curious, creative and questioning ways, thereby restoring confidence and giving voice. This can be achieved by using *generative themes* in a *problematising* way.

A *culture circle* is a community group that, in dialogue, questions an issue that is relevant to everyday life. This is the critical space for creating dialogue. It may happen in a group that has come together for any purpose at all. The important dimension is that the community worker sets the scene for the values that form the basis of the experience – respect, dignity, mutuality, reciprocity, equality, trust. Each person must feel that they are active participants, that they have a voice, that they are listened to and are taken seriously. *Listening from the heart* reflects high regard, builds mutual respect, trust and self-esteem. This is the threshold of a journey into critical consciousness.

Generative theme

A *generative theme* is a relevant issue or concern which emerges from stories people tell about their everyday lives. They are 'generative' because they generate a passion from their relevance to people's experiences, and that releases energy from the apathy of hopelessness that comes from having little control over life's circumstances. You can identify these themes because they repeatedly come up in the stories you hear, and they are spoken about passionately. A theme could be anything from unemployment to play facilities to violence to parenting to public transport, or it may be a crisis that has erupted or even something you would never have anticipated! This is captured from people's experience and presented to the group in a form that encourages them to see it critically. The form in which this is presented as a decontextualised life experience is called a *codification*.

Problematising

A problem-posing approach, or *problematising* – whether using theatre, literacy or any other medium – is based on a horizontal model, that of equality between the *educator-learner* and the *learner-educator*. This co-learner relationship is the basis of *dialogue* and is fundamental to the process of liberation. It 'strives for the *emergence* of consciousness and *critical intervention* in reality' (Freire, 1972: 54; emphasis in original) by placing educators and participants together in a mutual educator–learner relationship. It is more than just a technique; it requires a belief and trust in the potential of people to be intellectuals, with the capacity for *action and reflection*. It is a process that creates critical, inquiring and responsible citizens who 'carry both the seeds of radical change and the burden of oppression' (Popple, 1995: 64). The role of the educator in critical pedagogy is to provide the context in which shared problems can be critically questioned and analysed. It is a mutual process founded on reciprocity and humility that gets beyond the power imbalance of the traditional teacher–student relationship. The roles of educator and learner become interchangeable because the educator is open to learning as much as teaching.

This is the interface of praxis at which the knowledge and theory of the educator come together with the everyday experience of the people.

Let's be more specific. For instance, a group of people may come together motivated initially by the need for safer play facilities in the community. Freire would term this community group a *culture circle*. The community worker may choose to focus the group by providing overhead slides of the play areas that already exist. This would be termed a *codification*. The secret to success lies in using an appropriate form of codification that the participants will relate to, one that is capable of engaging the group in a way that expands consciousness. In context, everyday experience is too familiar to be questioned. Taking the reality out of context and capturing it in another form enables people to see the issue from a less taken-for-granted perspective, and to begin the process of questioning. As questions are raised, the community worker responds with questions rather than answers, taking the questioning to a more critical level. Why? Where? When? How? Who? What? In whose interests? ... Why are those swings rusty and broken? Why are broken bottles lying around? Why is it so dangerous? Why is it open to the road? Successive questions probe deeper towards the source of the problem. It is a process that liberates the thinking of the group members as they become confident, analytic and creative in investigating the issue. They move towards a solution that is likely to be closer to the root of the problem, and as they are active in the process of reflecting on the issue, they are more likely to engage in action to tackle it. Of course, this process is not uniform; it develops at many different levels, both within the group and within the lives of the individuals of that group. But, once the questioning has begun, it continues; like water flowing through a valve, it is propelled forwards. As Freire says, '*starting* with the "knowledge of experience had" in order to get beyond it is not *staying* in that knowledge' (Freire, 1995: 70; emphasis in original).

Codifications

The process involves codifications (stories, photographs, poetry, drama, and so on) that capture the essence of an issue relevant to local life, one that people readily relate to (a *generative theme*), one that will naturally stimulate interest: Where's this? What's going on? When did it happen? Who's involved? How are they affected? The critical educator uses these prompts to encourage questioning, but never dictates the answers.

Originally Freire used line drawings, but equally photographs, drama, video, story, poetry and music are effective forms of codification, depending on their relevance to the group. The term *codification* simply means the medium that is used to capture the essence of everyday issues and to present them to the group. Taking an experience out of its context enables people to see it with fresh eyes, rather than from the taken-for-grantedness of everyday life. When the experience is seen in a different light, it is more likely to generate the emotion that motivates action. To be effective, it must be *coded* in a form that is relevant to the culture of the people concerned, drawing on their experience and encouraging them to question.

One outstanding example is the way in which a Brazilian colleague of Freire, Augusto Boal, developed Theatre of the Oppressed as a medium for *conscientisation*, influencing radical theatre on an international level (Boal, 1994, 2008; Schutzman and Cohen-Cruz, 1995). In Brazil, until his death on International Workers' Day, 1 May 2009, Boal was still involved in popular theatre as a vehicle for consciousness and a collective force for influencing national policy decisions. Boal's forum theatre is an interactive theatre form that begins in a specific lived experience of discrimination. This could be racism or violence or anything that has been a diminishing experience. The audience participates by discussing the performance, and this is facilitated by the Joker. When the play is restarted, a member of the audience known as a 'spect-actor' (Boal, 2008) freezes the scene and without dialogue, swaps with the protagonist to change the experience. 'The act of transforming is, in itself, transforming' (Boal, 2008: xxi). This process of participation continues with other 'spect-actors' until it feels appropriate to debate the learning generated by these changes to the original experience. The Lawnmowers Independent Theatre Company, founded in 1986, based in Gateshead, North East England, worked with Augusto Boal to develop these methods. The Lawnmowers is a 'theatre for change' company run by and for people with learning difficulties (www.thelawnmowers.co.uk).

Dialogue

Dialogue and *praxis* lie at the heart of the process of humanisation. 'Only dialogue, which requires critical thinking, is also capable of generating critical thinking. Without dialogue there is no communication, and without communication there can be no true education' (Freire, 1972: 65). Dialogue embodies values of dignity and respect, encouraging people to relate to each other in ways that are mutual, reciprocal, trusting and cooperative. For Freire, this is an encounter to name the world and, and as such, is a precondition for true humanisation.

Dialogue is not easy; it is at the heart of transforming relations of domination and subordination that mark the dominant culture. It is a crucial skill that calls for critical reflection on the internalised attitudes we have absorbed from the dominant culture in order to fully live the values that are at the heart of a kinder and more just world. It is critical praxis in action: 'In dialogue, teachers and learners learn to relate differently to each other by relating differently to knowledge' (Allman, 2009: 426). Allman points to how Freire contrasts dialogue with *banking education* where 'people enter into discussions in order to articulate what they already know or think' (Allman, 2009: 426). She continues:

> Dialogue … involves the critical investigation of knowledge or thinking. Rather than focusing only on what we think, dialogue requires us to ask of each other and ourselves why we think what we

do. In other words, it requires us to 'problematize' knowledge (Freire, 1972: Ch 3). This means all sorts of knowledge, academic and personal knowledge as well as how we have come to a subjective knowledge or 'feeling' about some issue. (Allman, 2009: 426-7)

Praxis

Praxis is a unity of theory and practice, the interweaving of action and reflection, of theory informing action and action generating theory. It is not about theory that is detached from action, but theory that is rooted in everyday life, and deepened in action as we work together to co-create the sort of knowledge that comes from experience, from culture, from lived histories. Reflection and action are part of this process. All of those involved, no matter who, are called on to investigate the nooks and crannies of our inner being, those places where unconscious attitudes and assumptions lurk. Bringing them into consciousness, we are able to name them and challenge them. Freire urges us to question our ideological beliefs in these ways, and this links to the work of Reni Eddo-Lodge on white people's reluctance to question internalised assumptions on white privilege (discussed in Chapters 2 and 8). It is only by questioning our innermost attitudes that we are able to alter the way we make sense of the world, to make space for new stories that embody the world we want to create for the future. This is a changed epistemology, a different way of making sense of the world, which changes the way we act in the world. The two go together. Reading the world in these ways locates knowledge as power in relation to our histories, to the present and to change the future. It brings into consciousness silenced ways of knowing and creates the space for a diversity of knowledges rather than one dominant knowledge.

Freire argues that critical consciousness and action for change are a living praxis, a unity, and that it is impossible to separate the two. These dialectical opposites, theory and action, become an integral whole. It is only as a unity of praxis that our thinking becomes critical and our action become relevant. A unity of praxis becomes a way of being, a critical, living praxis, as Freire describes it, a shortening of the distance between what we say and what we do (Freire, 1997: 83).

At all stages of their liberation, the oppressed must see themselves as people engaged in the vocation of becoming more fully human. Reflection and action become essential. True reflection leads to action but that action will only be a genuine praxis if there is critical reflection on its consequences. To achieve this praxis it is necessary to trust in the oppressed and their ability to reason. Whoever lacks this trust will fail to bring about, or will abandon, dialogue, reflection and communication ... (Freire, 1972: 41)

Collective action

Freire insisted that liberation is never personal, it is a collective experience. True freedom involves the commitment to transform all society (Freire, in Shor and Freire, 1987). This is why empowerment is never a personal freedom; it is only when it becomes part of a collective movement that it can be seen as a true process of liberation. Personal empowerment is only the beginning of a process of critical, collective action, from local projects to movements for change through campaigns, alliances and networks. Freire urges critical educators to build communities of solidarity, hubs for critical consciousness and change, for problematising neoliberal globalisation and the extreme inequalities it has created in its wake (Darder, 2009: 574). But where do we find the collective component when public spaces have been privatised, colonised and controlled? Some social movement theorists feel that new technology is no substitute for more interpersonal connections of identity, community and protest. Think of the Arab Spring and the Occupy Movement here. Victoria Carty (2015: 184) suggests that initial weak ties established through Facebook, Twitter, YouTube, and so on, can transform into strong ties as the link from community to campaigns, protests and movements for change builds solidarity though a digital media platform: 'virtual information sharing can politicize new areas of social life and help translate personal troubles (shared in cyberspace) into social issues that ultimately lead to local organizing in concrete communities'.

Critical pedagogy is a process that begins in personal empowerment and extends to critical consciousness which energises collective action, from local projects to movements for change. The collective action stage is a vital part of the process; it is about people in movement, transforming their world for a better future.

Culture circles in action: the Adult Learning Project

When I was a student of David Alexander's, in 1982–83 at the University of Edinburgh, I had the great pleasure of meeting Gerri Kirkwood who came to talk about her pioneering work, knocking on doors to involve people in setting up the Adult Learning Project (ALP) 'Freire in action' in Gorgie-Dalry, Edinburgh, in 1979 (Kirkwood and Kirkwood, 1989). At this time, the political context was about to plunge into dramatic change with the rise of neoliberalism on a global scale, taking hold as the Thatcher revolution in the UK. The ALP survived its first decade as the rhetoric of the 'welfare scrounger' paved the way for the dismantling of the welfare state at the same time as unemployment escalated. We witnessed a massive transference of wealth from the poor to the rich, and were told to tighten our belts, there would be a 'trickle-down effect', social divisions widened and Scottish feelings ran high. Despite Scotland returning no Conservative MPs to the Westminster Parliament in 1992, it had nevertheless been governed from London by the Conservative government since 1979. Then, Margaret Thatcher had the audacity to test out her Poll Tax on the people of Scotland in 1989, and the riots that erupted as a consequence contributed to her eventual political decline. The resentment in Scotland fuelled a growing movement to demand a Scottish Parliament, and the ALP was active in identifying a range of generative themes:

- power, control and democracy
- culture and identity
- democratic education
- women in Scotland
- land and environment.

This formed the basis of the 1989 ALP co-investigation which responded to popular protest to build a Freirean pedagogy of hope through cultural action and reflection. The Scottish Parliament was established in 1998. The ALP continues its political and cultural relevance today, run by the democratic body at its heart. It is one of a global network of Freire-based initiatives widening through the Freire Institutes and organisations that act as hubs for the ongoing development of Freire's work in the world: in the UK, Ireland, Brazil, Canada, the US, South Africa, India, Finland, Germany, Spain and Portugal, to date. I see this as a vital link between the local and the global, a network linking grassroots action to global movements for change. Freire Institutes are emerging from fertile ground the world over, generated by a hunger for a practice that can make an impact on the social and environment atrocities we witness in our world. (Check them out at www.freire.org which lists publications, courses and connections with those working for education that is critical, empowering and transformative.) This collective energy of people in movement opens a space for change to be possible: once people see things differently it becomes much harder for politicians to tell the same old stories and get away with it!

The ALP is celebrated in Scotland and internationally as a prime example of the transformative potential of Freirean pedagogy. Here is a story from Barbara Munro and Luke Campbell, who set the scene for their work with the Aye Write group at the Adult Learning Project.

 ## Aye Write

Currently celebrating its 40th anniversary, the Adult Learning Project (ALP) is 'a sustained experiment in applying the principles of the Brazilian adult educationist, Paulo Freire, in a Western European post-industrial urban environment' (Brown, 2011). Based in Tollcross (central Edinburgh), the organisation supports adult learners through a varied programme of activity encompassing art, democracy, literacy, and community activism (ALP, 2017). Established more than 15 years ago, Aye Write is one of the longest-running groups at ALP. Operating out of the Tollcross Community Centre, members meet every Friday afternoon to cultivate their artistic talents through dialogue, writing, and performance.

With a core body of 10 to 12 regular attendees – two of whom have attended Aye Write almost since the group's inception – this member-led group incorporates Freirean approaches through democratic decision-making processes whereby participants shape the curriculum each semester. Freire (1996: 73–4) contested that 'without dialogue there is no communication, and without communication there can be no true education'. Given their dialogue-centred approach, Aye Write members engage in a creative process of action and reflection, expressing their ways of seeing the world through artistic expression. Aye Write remains one of ALP's most popular groups, with a fully subscribed membership list and continues to attract new interest. Members co-facilitate regular closed performances and socials during which participants have the opportunity to showcase their work and receive constructive feedback in an intimate and deeply personal setting.

As observed by Kirkwood and Kirkwood (2011), this educational method is extended throughout the ALP's programme of activities (for example The Democracy Group, Fayre for Women, Glory & Dismay, The Local Economy Group, and Art Space for Women). Members of all groups remain committed in terms of attendance, but also in their desire to actively participate – demonstrating both Freire's (1972) belief in 'preoccupation' with learning and commitment to 'reflection … upon their world in order to transform it' through art (Freire, 1998). Crowther and Martin (2011: xviii) note that 'through its pedagogy and curriculum ALP has made a significant contribution to enabling the often marginalised voices of Scottish communities to be heard'. In the context of an increasingly qualification-orientated global trend in adult education (see Biesta, 2011; O'Brien, 2018; Fraser, 2018), the supportive and inclusive environment offered by Aye Write ensures creative spaces remain open to those wishing to participate.

~~~~~~~~~~~~~~~~~~~~~~~~~~~~~

And here are two remarkable poems that capture the work of the Aye Write group:

POEM #1
'A Woman's Place'
Anne Milne

Aye – A Man's a Man for a' that!
That Donald Trump
Would ge ye the hump
– To think his mother was a Scot!
She's got a lot tae answer for!
Naw. He must hae taen efter his faither.

A new fiver features a wummin.
What are things cummin tae?
Well, in Scotland, we ken.
A'll tell ye again
Aboot a Wummin's Place.

'A Woman's place is at the sink.'
That's what you think!
'A wife should do as she is told.'
Aye! Those were the days.
We've changed our ways.
We've broken the mould!

Kezia Dugdale, Ruth Davidson and Nicola Sturgeon –
ALL WOMEN – bearing the burden
Of leading their parties in the Scottish Parliament.
BUT – when I went to school, the rule was
That boys were superior – and girls inferior

But WOW! Look at them now.
THEY'VE BROKEN THE MOULD!

And what about WOMEN Chancellors, Prime Ministers
and Presidents – the world over?

There's nae goin' back.
They've got the knack.
You never thought you'd see the day.
What would our beloved Rabbie say?
'A wummin's a wummin for a' that!'

POEM #2
'Sediment of War'
Barbara Munro

Nothing.
Nothing to do with me;
I'm not involved.
All those half dead souls adrift
floating aimlessly across the seas
in a no man's land, going nowhere,
and no future other than uncertainty,
no right to live as human beings
where they come from
or where they're going.
Nothing.
They carry nothing;

nothing at all.
No luggage other than their sorrows,
their past, their memories;
memories of dear daughters, raped, then sold in slave markets,
nightmares of abuse, starvation, war.
And after palm is crossed with silver, and gold tooth glints,
nothing is left; but, goaded on by a half-remembered map,
remnant of long forgotten school days,
they'll take any chance, for they have nothing to lose.

Think of these people and know
we want for nothing,
Nothing at all.

Here, Selma Augestad and Orlaith McAree tell the story of the ALP's Art Space for Women, an explicitly intersectional feminist Freirean pedagogy. As you read through their story, pay attention to frequent references to the theories and concepts that inform their praxis: feminism, intersectionality, multiple truths, white privilege co-learners/co-teachers, reflection and action ... to name but a few.

The Adult Learning Project's Art Space for Women

> Feminist education - the feminist classroom – is and should be a place where there is a sense of struggle, where there is visible acknowledgement of the union of theory and practice, where we work together as teachers and students to overcome the estrangement and alienation that have become so much the norm. (bell hooks, 1989: 51)

'Art Space for Women is a place for theory, reflection and action!' read the first ad for the group in late 2016.

> 'I came to the group because it sounded like a different way of learning.'

> 'I think she (the tutor) had particular themes in mind in the beginning, but the group evolved according to what we discussed and the different experiences of women in the group.'

> 'It felt like there was an absence of hierarchy, but we did need Selma (the tutor) there to structure the sessions.'

Art Space for Women explores the role of women in the world of art, and the world more generally, as both creators and subjects. The group provides a space to reflect on these topics, on the personal and collective experiences of women in the group, and on feminist theories that have helped to frame many of the issues and experiences that the co-learners/co-teachers have brought. Rooted in an explicitly intersectional feminist Freirean pedagogy, the group focuses on reflection, questioning, re-naming and re-framing personal and collective experiences of different women in society.

> 'It became clear to me that problems I've had as a woman weren't just in my head, that it's not just me.'

> 'Selma (the tutor) would introduce a particular theory to the group. Then we'd all be discussing with the same basic theoretical knowledge but all bringing our own experiences too.'

> 'It helped me learn the jargon – the language – in English. The group was about going back through my personal history and understanding it better. It gave me another frame to read things.'

As well as providing a space for an exploration for theory, the group has an explicit focus on action, generating art around the subjects of capitalism, gender, race, sexuality, health, disability, class and age. There was a search, in the group, for multiple truths and also a focus on how all oppression is connected.

> 'There's such depth and so many layers of oppression. When you peel off a layer, there's a whole other load of layers underneath, but I think that what always gets lost is class.'

> 'I had a very white, privileged notion of feminism before I came to the group.'

The journey taken by the group is reflected in weekly 'journey maps' (see Figures 4.1a and 4.1b) which illustrate the subjects, theory and action taken in each group. Every week, new knowledge is used to take action for change through the creation of art in different media, but learners also take personal and collective action outside the group using art and other means.

Speaking about trying to change the structures that function to perpetuate the oppression of women, one learner said: 'I've been involved in activism before, and I feel it is often groups of people from the same backgrounds that get together, it fails to reach further. But, coming to this group has helped me to question that and I've been trying to change this. I'm tired of what I'm seeing ... Not everybody can do direct action – I can't get arrested for example – so I've set up a group which makes art to support direct action and invite new people to activism.'

Over the course of a year, Art Space for Women created a space for reflection and action, exhibiting their work and delivering educational activities for over 60 self-identified women and non-binary people aged 20 to 70 from a range of backgrounds.

Figures 4.1a and 4.1b: 'Journey maps'

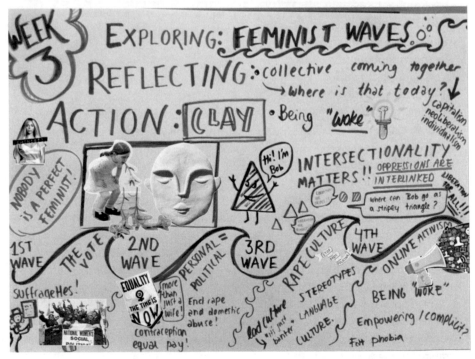

The Adult Learning Project Association grants Margaret Ledwith usage rights for photos produced as part of the Art Space for Women group. The images are products of the Art Space for Women group at the Adult Learning Project.

And, in Figures 4.1a and 4.1b, are two wonderfully graphic examples of the way that Art Space for Women works with the process of conscientisation in relation to women's ways of knowing.

In these ways, culture circles set the context for dialogue between equals, people mutually engaged in a process of critical inquiry, co-learners and co-educators in consciousness. By listening to the *narratives of the people* and engaging in *dialogue*, the critical educator is able to establish strong relationships based on an understanding of local culture; in turn, local people develop a sense of confidence and trust and the process expands from the personal to the political.

Local–global action

Here, my emphasis is on reaching from the personal to the group, from to the project to the community, and beyond the community through alliances and networks to movements for change.

Women in movement

My first port of call is to explore women in action from a local to a global level through the Women's Forum at the Beijing Conference. In 1995, in Beijing, at the United Nations (UN) intergovernmental conference, the NGO (non-governmental organisation) meeting runs in parallel, and this year it was attended by 30,000 women from all over the world, many of whom had suffered persecution and violence trying to get to the conference. The Women's Forum played a key role in evidencing women's common concerns across the globe. Women united across age, class, nationality, ethnicity, race, ability and sexual identity to influence the recommendation of the Global Platform for Action. This document defines women's demands for justice and was signed by the governments of the 189 countries represented at the conference to follow it through to implementation at national levels (Ledwith and Asgill, 2007). The important realisation is the amount of grassroots action that made this global action possible. Preparation for Beijing concentrated on campaigns to develop public awareness of human rights abuses against women. Success was based on strategies that linked grassroots activism through networks and alliances in a 'two or three year preparatory process of negotiation and consensus building to produce a programme of action, a declaration, and recommendations for implementation to demonstrate that "women's concerns" must be placed at the centre of economic, social and political agendas, and can no longer be considered in isolation' (Page, 1997: vi).

Grassroots organisations were the bedrock for the regional organisation, which, in turn, sustained the process through to a global level. In the UK, women were active at local, national and international levels across difference, involving grassroots women in the preparatory process by raising awareness about the relevance of the Conference to campaigning work.

There has been a concerted effort to keep the Platform for Action current. After Beijing it was resolved to review progress on a five-yearly basis, to keep gender equality as a human right at the heart of the pressing challenges of our times – economic crises, climate change, health care, violence against women and escalating conflicts – all especially affecting women, not only holding back women, but holding back the world because it's women who have the ideas and leadership to solve these problems. At the 20-year stage, in 2015, *The Beijing Declaration and the Platform for Action turns 20*, was published (available at www.unwomen.org), with a review of the implementation of the Beijing Declaration and Platform for Action and the achievement of gender equality and the empowerment of women over the 20 years, as well as opportunities for strengthening gender equality and the empowerment of women in the post-2015 development agenda through the integration of a gender perspective. Similarly, the UN 2030 Agenda for Sustainable Development with its 17 Sustainable Development Goals adopted by world leaders in 2015, has gender equality and women's empowerment integral to each of the goals, with the realisation that by ensuring the rights of women and girls across all goals not only will women's rights be met but economies will work and environmental sustainability will be resolved. The UN Women's 2018 flagship report, 'Turning promises into action: Gender equality in the 2030 Agenda' has not only data, but stories, videos and publications that are useful for working on these issues (see www.unwomen.org).

Finally, at this point, with reference to Sayer's ideas on common inheritance (see Chapter 2): without the bravery of the Suffragettes, led by Emmeline Pankhurst, many of whom were subjected to violence, imprisonment, force-feeding and ridicule, we would not be at this point in history, even though there is a long way to go. Visit the Pankhurst Centre in Manchester which presents a reconstruction of the Pankhursts' living room where the ideas that led to the action were nurtured, and honour your gratitude to those who suffered for our generations to have the vote. Manchester City Council have constructed a statue to Emmeline Pankhurst after the action group Womanchester noted that, apart from Queen Victoria, every public statue was male!

The Occupy Movement

The Occupy Movement is an international action against global social and economic inequalities. It is part of the global justice movement and is testament to the power of new technology to trigger immediate global action and collective strength. The Occupy slogan, 'We are the 99%', brought neoliberalism's intention to unjustly reward the rich at the expense of the poor into public consciousness: 'On January 21st, 2012, *The Economist* magazine asked "*Who exactly are the 1%?*" ... It was only in that year that many came to fully realise just how much more the very best-off had taken' (Dorling, 2018: 23).

Inspired by the Arab Spring, Occupy started in Kuala Lumpur in July 2011. However, the first Occupy protest to be widely covered in the world's media was

Occupy Wall Street in New York on 17 September 2011. Within three weeks, Occupy protests had taken place in over 95 cities across 82 countries, and in the US 600 communities were occupied. By 1 December, there were 2,686 Occupy communities worldwide. Edinburgh's Occupy community was even given official sanction by the city council. The movement was described as a 'democratic awakening' by Cornel West, activist and Princeton University professor, in the *Occupied Wall Street Journal* on 18 November 2011:

> We the people of the global Occupy movement embody and enact a
> deep democratic awakening with genuine joy and fierce determination.
> Our movement – leaderless and leaderful – is a soulful expression of
> a moral outrage at the ugly corporate greed that pushes our society
> and world to the brink of catastrophe. (West, 2011)

Only months before the first Occupy protest, riots had erupted across England in areas with the greatest inequalities. In the wake of these riots, the Archbishop of Canterbury warned us to either give our children hope or expect more riots as high levels of anger and despair were reported in young people. A YouGov poll conducted for the Prince's Trust in 2014 found that one in every 10 young people in Britain feel they have nothing to live for, often expressed as self-loathing and panic attacks over the future. On a global scale, it is the younger generations who are bearing the brunt of the fall-out of the 2007–08 economic crash, the crisis of capitalism (Hyland, 2014), and now 'austerity' measures, coupled with the British nervous breakdown that is Brexit, a total failure of government to act

in the interests of the people. 'In highly connected complex systems, such as the world today … the multiplying connections of our world offer an unprecedented opportunity for the rise and spread of leaderless movements' (Ross, 2018). Ross raises the successes of the #MeToo movement in action on gender relations across the globe, but cautions that Occupy found that whilst it 'succeeded in inserting inequality and economic injustice into the mainstream political conversation … it couldn't articulate a specific political programme to reform the system … leaderless movements have largely proved incapable of such complicated decision-making' (Ross, 2018). At this point, consider whether you agree with Ross, and reflect on the need for a counternarrative which embeds values as the basis of policies for a new politics.

Extinction Rebellion, the latest British leaderless movement on reducing carbon emissions to net zero – a goal directly opposed by France's 'gilets jaunes' whose action targets fuel tax rises that threaten to hit the poorest hardest – is a current example of the paradoxical nature of the beast. A change in the system itself calls for leadership in mass action to resolve the major world crises of environment and inequality when the injustices we face are so interconnected and contradictory. Carty (2015: 183) raises the issue of strong and weak ties, suggesting that with Occupy 'it was their mobilizing and tenting on the streets that transformed weak ties into strong ties. This exhibits the relationship between information sharing and protest activity in local communities – the spillover effect – and new ways of creating solidarity that digital media platforms enable.'

In the UK we have largely dislocated the connection between community development and politics, and in doing so, disconnected politics from the everyday lives of people. It is precisely because resources are allocated unjustly that the key to understanding injustice lies in everyday life – and it is the analytical awareness of this injustice that is the process of *conscientisation*. Therefore at the heart of action for change is the notion of *politicisation*, that through becoming critical we identify the contradictions: 'power asymmetries become visible which at the level of the state and everyday life, generate the exclusionary logics which doom millions to poverty, inequality and subjugation unless they act on them. Community development is deeply political, because for communities to "develop" they need to grasp these power logics and realize that they can be changed' (Pearce et al, 2010: 270).

Budd Hall describes Occupy as: 'a movement that takes Paulo Freire's admonition to "Read the World" to a mass scale. It is also a movement that blurs the lines between education that is consciously focused within the movement and education that is designed for the broader public. And like the principles of anarchism that have deeply influenced the movement itself, there is a spirit of support for autonomous learning, for the self-organisation of learning and the open and transgressive that might bring revolutionary change closer' (Hall, 2012: 134). The motto of Tent City University is 'anyone can teach, everyone can learn' and acknowledges the work of Paulo Freire in this regard (Hall, 2012: 136).

Tent City University was prominent in Occupy London, its educational division attempting to provide a radical platform for challenging the way that power works in society. Three challenges for radical education programmes were identified:

1. *Breaking down communication barriers between people and a new pedagogy of place.* At Tent City University open dialogue happened spontaneously with a diversity of passers-by, visiting speakers and the occupiers, opening up new debates about alternatives to neoliberalism.
2. *Overcoming a divided society, especially one at peak inequality* (Dorling, 2018), where learning is controlled by those who have power. In Tent City University, migrant workers, bicycle mechanics, former bankers and the homeless shared the same space, learned to listen in new ways and to build new learning communities. This is linked to the knowledge democracy movement (see Hall and Tandon in Chapter 2)
3. *Refuting the right of the state to exclude people from public spaces.* Tent City University challenged the privatisation of the commons in the heart of our cities and opened up spaces for free debate and discussion and offering workshops, lectures, debates, films, games, praxis and action, 'creating a vibrant new chapter in a rich tradition of social movement learning' (Hall, 2012: 137).

The Occupy Movement claims to be, in 2019, in a stronger position than it has been for years (www.occupy.com). And Jocey Quinn, a professor at the University of Plymouth, is working on research into the significance and survival of the Tent City University, a project that is of interest to anyone thinking about what a university is and what role it plays in society. The Tent City University reveals how protest and activism are not just transitory moments but create new learning opportunities that can influence the future.

Summarising Freire's liberating education

Education can be liberating or domesticating. Freire's liberating education is based on praxis as a fusion of experience, on a past–present–future continuum, involving reflection, dialogue and social action. In this way, theory informs practice and practice informs theory, never separating knowledge from action and action from knowledge. It is a critical lens for reading the word and reading the world. By these means we question lived experience, expose the contradictions we live by and evolve a critical consciousness capable of transforming the unacceptable present for a future based on a common good. Framed by values of human dignity, spaces are created for people to come together to question the conditions of their everyday lives. This may be triggered by a crisis, such as a suicide or street violence or a fire (as we witnessed with Grenfell Tower in London), issues that draw people together instantly in solidarity and caring. Or it may be a slower process that builds over time, linking people together in a social group.

Freirean praxis is all about mutual discovery, a *liberating education* based on questioning, rather than traditional forms of education that pour ideas into unquestioning minds, what Freire calls *banking education*. In my practice, people who had been bruised by formal education became autonomous learners and confident activists using Freire's approach. Simply questioning the taken-for-grantedness of everyday life removes blinkers from the eyes to reveal the contradictions we live by, outrageous contradictions that have become normalised by the dominant ideology. This generates critical consciousness, making theory in action and action from theory that leads to the collective potential for social movements.

> In the process of understanding the world, we deepen our consciousness precisely through our actions in and on the world that enable us not only to grasp our positionality in the world but also to transform the totality of social relations that constitute the contradictory character of our existence. (McLaren, 2015: 24)

Paula Allman argued long and hard in her lifetime that Freirean critical pedagogy be understood as a complete process: 'it is an indivisible totality based on assumptions and principles which are inter-related and coherent ... we cannot take hints from Freire or use bits of Freire; we must embrace the philosophy as an integral whole and attempt to apply it accordingly' (Allman and Wallis, 1997: 113; see further discussion in Chapter 7). Attempting to use Freire partially will achieve partial success! Freire offers a distinct process, and to fragment it leaves it incomplete, falling short of its potential.

It is often Freire's revolutionary critique of capitalism and the linking of education to the class struggle that have been under-emphasised to leave a diluted, incomplete version of his critical praxis (Darder, 2015: 39). Darder's argument is that Freire is one of the few theorists who understood 'racism as inextricably tied to the imperatives of social class formation and material exclusion' (2015: 40). In other words, understanding the ways in which social class and poverty intersect with racism to systematically destroy communities, societies and nations by domination, exploitation, colonialism and empire is contained within the racialised culture of class to erode belonging, identity and language 'from poor working-class communities of color, while stripping us of our history, cultural knowledge and language' (2015: 41). Darder says: 'the struggle was not foremost about "celebrating diversity" or cultural identity or even the acknowledgment of our cultural legitimacy, but rather a struggle for our humanity and our survival' (2015: 40). The engagement with Freire, she emphasises, was as much about a personal process of decolonising our hearts, bodies and minds as about the political decolonisation of our communities. This applies to gender and other forms of discrimination, and also links with the work of Budd Hall and Rajesh Tandon on the need for knowledge justice – the wisdom of marginalised peoples to co-create knowledges – to sit alongside social justice and environmental justice in the fight for diversity/biodiversity for healing people and planet.

Allman warns that those 'engaged in local struggle need to understand the global significance of what they do … otherwise victories won are used to defuse and depoliticize the significance of the local effort' (Allman, 1999: 5-6). If we fix our gaze on the local, we reinforce this exploitative system by celebrating small-scale successes that give the illusion of change, but fail to challenge the wider structures that perpetuate oppressions. Critical praxis is necessary for social transformation, and Freire and Gramsci in powerful combination offer insight into the role of education in politics, and politics in education: their potential is reduced if they are used partially or fragmented (Allman, 1988, 1999).

Freire talked of love as a love for all humanity: 'Love is an act of courage, not fear … a commitment to others … [and] to the cause of liberation' (1972: 78). His belief was that the process of dialogue, so central to the transformative project, could not exist 'in the absence of a profound love for the world and for people' (1993: 70).

LOVE IS AN ACT OF COURAGE

WE ARE WORKING FOR A POLITICS OF LOVE FOR THE WORLD AND ITS PEOPLE RATHER THAN HATRED

DIALOGUE ... is nourished by love, humility, hope, faith and trust. When two 'poles' of the dialogue are thus linked by love, hope and mutual trust, they can join in a critical search for something.

5

Researching with the community

> Education, or the act of knowing as Freire calls it, is an ongoing research programme into aspects of people's experience and its relationship to wider social, economic and political factors. (Kirkwood, 1991: 103)

An integrated praxis grows through the ongoing dynamic of research, critical education and community action in symbiotic relation. It is a process of *conscientisation* through *dialogue* (Freire, 1972) that engages with the symptoms of structural violence in daily lives, and builds resistance through critique, imaginative counternarratives and collective action for change for a kinder and more just tomorrow.

Dominant ideology is absorbed into the very fabric of people's being, influencing the way we see the world and engage with it, creating a *false consciousness* that fails to question reality. Community development works on a principle of becoming critical, and this begins by teaching people to question the contradictions of lived reality that are a consequence of inequality. This practice emerges from a strong value base founded on an ideology of equality: a respect for all humanity leads to trust in other people, and it is this trust that, in turn, restores people's faith in themselves. In order to be a critical practitioner, it is necessary to be self-reflective and reflective, an inner and outer process of research. In the inner process, we need to be *reflexive*: to question our reflections, and take them to a deeper level. This is the way we are able to identify and challenge our own internalised attitudes and prejudices. In the outer process, we need to create critical spaces where we can engage in reflective questioning, in dialogue with others, making critical connections with the consequences of inequality on people's lives, building a body of knowledge that takes our collective understanding to more complex analytic levels as the basis of action for change.

Critical thought is discouraged in this neoliberal world; it gets in the way of the interests of the powerful that are served by the subservience of the many. Marcuse talks about false consciousness being the conceptual repression of understanding life experience: 'a restriction of meaning' (Marcuse,1991: 208). In this chapter, I look at the process of co-creating knowledges capable of challenging the dominant neoliberal ideology through critical consciousness in a process of *emancipatory action research* (EAR).

Emancipatory action research: the glue that binds critical praxis

Research is essential to the community development process. It develops knowledge in action, and keeps practice relevant to the changing political context. But the approach to research that community development adopts must fit with its value base. I call this approach 'emancipatory action research' because of its overt commitment to social change. Michelle Fine (2018) calls it 'critical participatory action research'. We are talking about the same process, but emphasising the fact that participatory action research has become diluted over time, not always remaining conscious of its radical, emancipatory intention to situate practice in its political context and to bring about change for social justice (Ledwith, 2018b).

I am suggesting to you that EAR is the glue that binds community development theory and practice as a unity of praxis, keeping it critical. By this, I mean that EAR is relevant to building theory in action and action from theory, intertwined and inseparable. Stephen Kemmis (2009/10) talks about a 'unitary praxis' as an approach to life in which we 'aim to live well by speaking and thinking well, and relating well to others and the world.... If we accept this view, then we might say that action research should aim not just at achieving knowledge of the world, but achieving a better world.' This is precisely our intention: change for a better world, no less!

For EAR to work in this way there are some important issues to consider. Most importantly, in order to reach a transformative potential, we have to be critical at every stage of the process. First, EAR is a process of participation where all people involved come together as co-researchers in action for social change. This, as you can see, involves dismantling the controlling power relations associated with traditional research based on the researcher as an external expert in favour of a mutual, reciprocal inquiry of equals. For work of this calibre to develop, we need to create critical public spaces for dialogue, involving all participants in co-creating knowledge for our times.

> These critical spaces are where 'the cross-cutting blades of exclusion grow visible, and the sweet counter-hegemonic spaces of care, love, and radical possibility come to light'. (Fine, 2018: 95)

Counter-hegemonic critical spaces are where power relationships are deconstructed in order to imagine counternarratives based on human and environmental flourishing. These counternarratives then become the blueprint for a new reality. The concept of a democratic public space is a vital context for community development as a site for bringing people together in critical dialogue to deepen consciousness and act for change (Habermas, 1989). This is a space which is open to all, from a loose connection of strangers to a connection between groups, a weaving together of a diversity of people with a shared intention to reconnect this world of disconnection in the quest for a common good.

Community centres have often served this function. But the community development teams of the past have been targeted by funding cuts and public spaces have been privatised, so there is an urgent need to identify new spaces, including the virtual spaces offered by social networking, in which we can engage in critique and dissent, identifying new truths, and developing the courage to 'tell unwelcome truths' in the wider world as part of our action (Kemmis, 2006). This is what Freire had in mind when he talked about *denunciation* and *annunciation*, critiquing the present opens the space to transform it into a better future. It is a space where counternarratives of hope and possibility are imagined, a vital stage in creating a new reality. In these ways, EAR contextualises personal lives within the political, social and economic structures of our times (Kemmis, 2006). And, to have a sustainable impact on social change, it needs to extend beyond individuals and groups 'to build systemic pictures of what is going on, and systemic intervention strategies, developing multiple inquiries that engage whole systems in ongoing cycles of inquiry' (Burns, 2007: 18).

For too long, I have talked about the divide between theory and practice in community development. It not only leads to inadequate practice, but also leaves us vulnerable to misappropriation. Inadequate practice in this sense refers to that which has no capacity for change based on social justice. I have often drawn on Rennie Johnston's concept of 'thoughtless action' (cited in Shaw, 2004) in relation to this. If our action is 'thoughtless', how can we claim to be contributing to the process of social justice? This is a bold commitment, and practice of this quality needs to be accountable, vigilant and analytic. In order to ensure a critical and systematic approach to practice for social justice, we need to develop a living praxis, one in which theory in action and action from theory are in symbiotic relation in our everyday lives. This is what is meant by a unity of praxis in Gramscian theory, what Kemmis (2009) refers to as 'action that comes together and coheres in the context of a way of life'.

Community development is a cyclic process of action and reflection, one informing the other. Imagine the juxtaposition of epistemology and ontology, that is, the way we see our world, the way we make sense of it, directly relates to the way we act in the world. This is precisely why inciting fear of immigrants has led to the Brexit crisis. A wise approach to practice is to engage with curiosity and questioning, constantly asking what is going on, who is being affected and why. And in relation to our practice interventions, we similarly ask questions that help us to elicit evidence of change, that is, if we claim that our purpose is social justice and environmental sustainability, what evidence is there that we are making a difference? Having stated my position, I now want to look at what this means in relation to becoming more critical in everyday practice. The aim to create a 'better world' (Kemmis, 2009) seems to me to fit into our claims for principled practice based on social justice and environmental sustainability. It imagines a world in which our intention is to live a good life by relating well to others and the world – a life based on connection with people and planet as a life well lived.

Paulo Freire's thinking was instrumental in the participatory action research movement, which challenged the controlling assumptions of traditional research and its role in reinforcing the dominant interests in society. The pioneering work of the new paradigm research movement came to fruition with the publication of *Human Inquiry* (Reason and Rowan, 1981), bringing together an eclectic range of methods within an action research approach based on working *with* people in reciprocal, mutual relationships to co-create knowledge in cycles of action and reflection. In this sense, it is a liberatory practice in its own right that fits well with community development.

KEY INFORMATION: Emancipatory action research

EAR is overtly committed to social and environmental justice:

• grounded in an ideology of equality, with values of mutuality, reciprocity, human dignity, respect and trust woven through every stage;

• adopting a methodology that is emancipatory not controlling, working *with* not *on* people, and that changes power relations;

• using non-controlling methods, open to diverse ways of knowing, where experience is explored beyond the written word through dialogue, story, music, drama, poetry, drawings and photographs in a search for multiple truths and a life in harmony with people and planet;

• where action for change emerges from new knowledge, new ways of seeing possibilities for a different world, leading to new ways of being.

This approach to research involves the seven stages in the process of transformational practice that I explore in more detail in Chapter 9:

1. voicing values
2. making critical connections
3. critiquing and dissenting
4. imagining alternatives
5. creating counternarratives
6. connecting and acting
7. cooperating for a common good.

This is an evolving praxis, a living process of co-creating knowledge in action and action as knowledge.

Co-creating knowledge

Based on the idea that 'every idea has an owner and that the owner's identity matters' (Hill Collins, 1990: 218), we all become agents of knowledge, seeking truths that emerge from dialogue based on lived reality. Hill Collins notes that dialogue has its roots in cultures of an oral tradition and is the antithesis of Western dichotomous thought which makes sense of life by creating power relations based on subject/object. She sees an African worldview as much more holistic in search of becoming fully human, with dialogue as central to that process. This links to the African concept of *Ubuntu*, a connectedness that leads us to behave well to each other, to be fully human and compassionate, which, in turn, links to Belenky et al (1986) on dialogue as connectedness rather than separation, and also to bell hooks' comment on dialogue as talk between two subjects, rather than subject and object: 'It is a humanizing speech, one that challenges and resists domination' (hooks, 1989: 1312).

EAR offers an approach to co-creating knowledge in the interests of everyone as a mutual and equal endeavour committed to a fair and just world. Within this approach, education and action, the investigation of social reality with critical consciousness, in cycles of action and reflection become 'prerequisites for participation' (Tandon, 2008: 288).

Traditional approaches to research with people give power to the researcher as an external expert carrying out research *on* people rather than *with* people. One of the key concepts here is *cultural invasion*: the 'imposition of the values, belief systems, ideology, cultural norms and practices of an imperialist culture on those it has colonized and oppressed' (Southgate and Randall, 1981: 53). It is ideological hypocrisy for community development to resort to research methods that are based on unequal, culturally invasive relationships.

One of the most formative contributions to my thinking was Rowan's 'Dialectical paradigm for research' (Rowan, 1981). In his attempt to define old and new paradigm research, he analyses three concepts: *alienation*; *social change*; and *the research cycle*. 'Alienation' refers to the treating of people as fragments, as a result of which they are not perceived as an essential part of a whole. In other words, studying the way people behave without relating it to the whole person, let alone their social and political context, is a dehumanising act. People function as whole beings within a context, and we need to understand the context in order to understand people. I am, therefore, suggesting that research that is taken on without critical, ethical analysis is likely to be incomplete, oppressive and alienating. It is likely to be based on assumptions that reinforce discrimination. If we are seeking a style of research that is compatible with anti-discriminatory ideology, we need to be sure that it contributes to the process of liberation from oppression. EAR involves everyone in the process of change, demanding 'that the investigator be as open to change as the "subjects" are encouraged to be – only they are now more like co-researchers than like conventional subjects' (Rowan, 1981: 97). This is a model of research that is based on collective action, with all participants acting in the interests of the whole. It begins as a response to the experience of the oppressed and becomes a mutual, reciprocal process of discovery 'where the researcher and the researched both contribute to the expansion of the other's knowledge' (Opie, 1992: 66).

Emancipatory action research is about democratising knowledge (see Hall and Tandon, discussed in Chapter 2). It is located profoundly at the heart of critical praxis, co-creating knowledges from the bottom up. It begins in stories. Stories hold the manifestations of structural violence, make critical connections with the political dimensions of personal lives and release both the fury of injustice and the imagination for counternarratives of possibility for a kinder and more just tomorrow. EAR embodies values of reciprocity and cooperation, horizontal values that fly in the face of current political times in which top-down values justify dispossession of the poor in the interests of the rich, an ideology that is destroying both humanity and the planet. This is precisely why values matter. They lie at the very heart of the process, framing the lens through which we see the world, so need to be understood and named. EAR is a process of mutual discovery in communities, building critical consciousness, co-creating knowledges for a diversity of ways of being, imagining counternarratives of change and making them the reality of a better future. EAR projects:

> reveal the systematic forces of structural injustice, flexible levers for change, and exceptional spaces mobilized against dominant flows, as irresistible as they may seem … When we work both *in* and *across places,* the sharp blades of oppression and the coarse ties of resistance grow apparent, but so do the delicious alternatives that represent vibrant possibility of what might be. (Michelle Fine, 2018: 96)

The cycle model

I am proposing that research is an integral and essential part of the process of change, and that EAR is the approach that is consonant with community development ideology. The cycle model structures our often chaotic and tangled practice in clear, diagrammatic form, representing balance and directional flow. This does not mean to say that it denies any of the complexity of the process; quite the opposite. It is of great value in offering structures within which to contain and disentangle the knots. For the community worker, I feel it represents stages of the process in relation to the whole. It reminds busy workers that practice is only effective when it is part of a balanced process of reflection, action, inquiry and communication: 'seeing research as a set of phases can also help make clearer some of the problems facing community development in its work of developing alternative ways of doing research' (Graham and Jones, 1992: 236).

Rowan's research cycle model, which I have adapted in Figure 5.1, offers a clear diagrammatic structure for stages of community development, taking an EAR approach that is central to critical praxis.

Figure 5.1: The cycle model

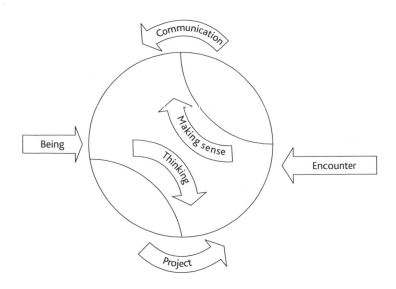

Source: Adapted from Rowan (1981).

The cycle model is particularly useful in integrating reflection and action in the process of community development. Although it is possible to enter the cycle at any stage, for ease of explanation I will begin at *Being*, the stage at which we become aware of a need for change. Perhaps an issue has arisen that calls for new thinking. The cycle has an inner and outer flow. As we move into the stage of *Thinking*, the arc indicates an inward process of seeking. It is a collective process that gathers people together, sharing ideas and experience, and finding out relevant information. At some point, thinking is not enough and we need to move outwards to the stage of *Project*, involving others as the process moves on. At this stage, we formulate a plan of action, which moves from the contradiction of the existing situation towards new practice. Continuing the outer movement, we move towards *Encounter*, the stage at which we engage in action with the wider community. The model is flexible: it is possible to flow back and forth between stages, until we are satisfied with the relevance of our work. But there is a point at which action needs to move inwards from *Encounter* to a stage of *Making sense*. This is the stage at which 'experience turns into meaning and knowledge' (Rowan, 1981: 100) and where a balance between achieving understandable simplicity and complex connections has to be reached. Following the arc outwards to the stage of *Communication* with new understanding emerging from practice, we are generating knowledge in action and need to share it so that others can learn from the experience. Community workers need to share experience by writing up projects for publication in books and journals; having dialogue with other communities; sharing ideas and experience at conferences and meetings; and using the media, including social media, more effectively. In doing so, we collectively contribute to an increasing body of community development knowledge.

The cycle does not remain isolated. It becomes part of multiple cycles in an interlocking model. These can be used sequentially to go deeper into an issue, producing a spiral, or they can be used concurrently so that the same issue is developed from diverse perspectives. An example of a spiral from my own practice would be the way that a group of women writers got involved in Hattersley Women for Change, which in turn developed Hattersley Women's Room, a critical public space for women. An example of a concurrent model would be the way that Keeping Hattersley Warm, a home insulation project, had sideways links with the precinct action group, the residents' association, and a gardening/allotments project, connecting groups across the community, all of which focused on different aspects of improving the quality of the environment. When developed in conjunction with critical questioning, the cycle model becomes more rigorous, and at each stage we are reminded of the anti-discriminatory, reciprocal and empowering essence of this approach. 'By making each cycle fully rigorous in its own terms, we can achieve a recursive validity of a cumulative nature – yielding a deeper and more extensive truth than that given by a linear approach' (Rowan, 1981: 105).

At each point in the cycle I have adapted categories of questions (influenced by Rowan, 1981; and Reason and Bradbury, 2001) that check the quality and validity of the process, helping it to become more rigorous and insightful, and also to check that we are doing what we claim to be doing. This is a collaborative process, and these questions should be decided on by all those involved:

1. *Methodology and methods:* What is the approach to this research? How is information gathered and by whom? How does it fit with the value base of community development?
2. *Process questions:* Who has initiated the research? Who has defined the issue? Who is involved? How is the power and decision-making shared?
3. *Power questions:* Is the social/political/economic context being taken into account? How is this research representative of the diversity of the community? Who has control?
4. *Dialectical questions:* Is just one answer being sought? Is the situation being explored from more than one angle, based on multiple truths?
5. *Legitimacy questions:* Is there pressure to avoid certain issues? Who is funding the research? Are there preconceived outcomes?
6. *Relevance questions:* How will this research benefit people? Will it benefit some people more than others? Is it relevant to the people who took part? How does it contribute to social and environmental justice? How does it address race, class, gender issues and intersectionality?

In practice, I found my adaptation of Rowan's cycle model useful in the way that it focused my mind on important stages of the community development process, and helped me to see the complementary connections between different projects and to ground them in their wider political context. In turn, it is a model that capable of structuring the diversity of social struggles fighting neoliberalism across global spaces as a 'transnational political project' (de Sousa Santos, 2014).

Researching black and white women working in alliance

> Consciousness doesn't come automatically; it comes through being alive, awake, curious, and often furious. (Maxine Greene, 2008: 17, cited in Fine 2018: 113)

There are widely held assumptions that women come together 'naturally' in action for social justice. Paula and I, as a black woman and a white woman, both with many years' experience of working in community in Manchester, told a different story. When we found ourselves working as colleagues in the same university department, our common experience as grassroots community workers brought us together. But when we touched those tender edges of friendship, the curious led us into the often furious, as Maxine Greene expresses above. An enduring story I tell in this respect is of our shared working trip to Chicago.

 Alive, awake, curious and furious

Atlanta, in a hotel over dinner. Paula, head held high and proud, had been visibly ten feet tall as she mingled amongst the black commuters during the day, wearing the signs of status rather than poverty, her own people accepted as mainstream. In our conversation, we talked of our histories. Feeling confident to go deeper, I mentioned both my young sons getting violently attacked in Manchester, expressing my guilt at them not being streetwise, I asked her whether I had the right to choose to live in a diverse area and for them to suffer because of my commitment to social justice. Her eyes flashed: "You think you're so **** great, don't you? You have the choice, my people don't." Shocked, I cried! Then, I was furious. It took me several days to relate to her again, cautiously, not letting her under my skin. In these ways, our friendship stumbled along: 'Alive, awake, curious, and often furious' (Greene in Fine, 2018: 113).

There were those in Paula's black sisterhood who frowned on our friendship in the early days: 'Why would you want to be friends with a white woman?', a comment from one of her closest Manchester friends expressed with curled lips and a frown! I was both mortified and scared witless. But we persevered with our friendship and with our research. We could not recollect instances in all our years of practice where alliances between black and white women were sustained over time, but we had many experiences of where they had collapsed in rage or fear. As friends and colleagues, we wanted to delve deeper into understanding the issues at stake. The concerns that drove our research were founded on the way that feminism without an analysis of racism denied the barriers that white privilege inevitably presents to black and white women's alliances for social action.

Black rage and white fear are the emotions that characterise the breakdown of alliances. Often white women assume the power to set the agenda and invite black women to join them. Immediately, this creates a power imbalance in the relationship. Fine et al (1997) identify the importance of understanding whiteness within an anti-discriminatory analysis, otherwise, while we may have a greater understanding of the nature of black oppression, we remain ignorant of the insidious and unconscious ways in which white power works to advantage white women, which is the essence of Reni Eddo-Lodge's argument (see Chapters 2 and 8 for further extensive discussion on this point).

We found the courage to engage in sensitive dialogue with each other initially, before inviting 16 (eight black and eight white) women from across England who had experience of community activism to take part in this inquiry. In order to structure our thoughts, we developed a model based on stages that span from personal empowerment to collective action.

Our research model

To structure our thinking, we adapted Rowan's cycle model (see Figure 5.1 on p 141), an excellent model for a complex process which gave us a greater insight into the flow from the personal to the collective, and helped us to identify the importance of personal autonomy as a prerequisite for collective action.

There are five distinct stages in this process: (i) being, (ii) seeking, (iii) separateness, (iv) autonomy and (v) critical alliance.

Being is the stage at which we begin to question our experience. Our difference becomes apparent. We begin to recognise that our blackness or whiteness, or age, or sexuality, or class, or culture all interact in complex ways to shape our identity. Think about this in relation to Gramsci's concept of *hegemony* (see Chapter 6), which helps us to understand the complex ways in which the structures of society filter into our minds and the power that these ideas have to construct our worldview.

This awareness causes dissonance. We can no longer carry on with the old way of seeing ourselves; it pushes us into a stage of **seeking** new ways of seeing ourselves in relation to our world.

Following this we identify a need for **separateness**, a withdrawal into relationships where we feel at ease with those who are similar so that we can share ideas and make sense of our personal experience:

> Every once in a while there is the need for people to ... bar the doors.... It gets too hard to stay out in society all the time.... You come together to see what you can do about shouldering up all your energies so that you and your kind can survive ... that space should

be nurturing space where you sift out what people are saying about you and decide who you are. (Reagon, 1983: 357-8)

Autonomy is the stage at which we are able to name who we are, feel confident and proud of who we are, and gain a sense of personal empowerment. Our identity is strong enough not to fear dilution. This involves unlearning internalised oppression and internalised superiority (Pheterson, 1990).

The potential for **critical alliance** emerges from this personal *autonomy*, a clearer sense of who we are in the world. From greater confidence in our own identity, we have the humility and compassion needed to understand difference not as a division, but as a strength. This is the basis for joining together in sustainable alliances across difference in action for a more fair and just society.

The importance of emotion and experience as legitimate knowledge (refer to Weiler, 1994, 2001, discussed in Chapter 8) is a theoretical link that is crucial to understanding the experience of black rage and white fear and the way that they hinder alliances. Without this, we react with fight/flight behaviour that limits the sustainability of the collective process.

Our conclusions from the research

Our research as a whole supported the evidence that, despite popular beliefs in community development about women uniting across difference, there is little to prove that this is found in practice in any sustainable way. Our model provided useful ways in which to structure experience in community and offered possibilities for shifts in understanding. Based on our experience together and the evidence of the black and white women activists, we concluded that clear strategies are needed for the development of sustainable alliances. *Critical alliance* depends on the personal autonomy of black and white women to reach out to each other with confidence and respect, and this process needs to begin in separate groups where critical consciousness emerges from reflection on shared experiences. Pride in who we are in the world, in our separate identities, leads to more equal alliances where issues of power have been addressed.

Sustainable critical alliance as a form of collective action offers an alternative to the unifying aspects of class solidarity, while retaining class as a major structural oppressive force, alongside patriarchy and racism. Clearly, there is a need for work on identity and autonomy in community development, despite the fact that this has largely fallen off the agenda.

Our five defined stages – (i) being, (ii) seeking, (iii) separateness, (iv) autonomy and (v) critical alliance – offer a structure to community workers that helps to make sense of the staged development of work that needs to take place at a local level as the basis of collective action. Paula and I were co-creating knowledge that involved a complex range of emotions and experience. As we deepened our friendship, we were able to acknowledge the invisible white privilege that she helped me to recognise and name, and I became able to prove my friendship when she became seriously ill.

Co-creating a community profile using the cycle model

Perhaps the next step with your dialogue group is a community profile. This calls for you to develop skills in all participants, skills that involve listening from the heart, valuing and respecting others and creating critical dialogue, just as they have experienced in *culture circles*. What do you collectively know about your community, its diversity, its history? Perhaps you could provide your participants with cameras so that they begin with themselves, photographing what's significant around and about the community to their own daily lives. You could work with a writing group to capture community life in story, poetry and drama (see the work of the Adult Learning Project on p 120 for inspiration). Your team could develop research skills through the discipline of noticing, using journals to record events, encounters and conversations as they happen (Mason, 2002). Maybe you could develop a display of photographs, poetry, archive material, stories to engage people in passing, encouraging them to get involved in the research. This could be the first step to expanding the process of conscientisation by getting people involved in the life of their community. For instance, we had a reminiscence group of older residents who worked together with local children for a radio programme. The children began with their favourite playground games, and this stimulated cross-generational dialogue about local life and its similarities and differences over time.

How will you motivate people to act together? How will they perceive a community profile as relevant to their lives? Who will you contact and where will you find them? Are there any existing groups? Should you hold a public meeting? How will you ensure the people who join in are representative of the diversity of the community?

The important questions can be elicited through problem-posing. This is done by capturing an aspect of community life in drawing, photography, film, drama, music or writing, as I discussed in the previous chapter. This focuses the group and stimulates dialogue. The community worker facilitates the process by asking questions rather than giving answers. In other words, you create a learning context in which the group can explore its ideas about its own community more critically. Here are some ideas.

Problem-posing to produce a community profile

(1) The individual

As community workers, we listen to the deepest feelings of the local community. Freirean pedagogy involves listening with compassion to people's fears, worries, hopes, resentments and joys. What are their deepest concerns? What most affects their lives? These emotions are the key to the motivation to act. The act of listening, of giving people your full attention, is empowering in itself. It takes people's experience seriously, creating a respectful and dignified encounter.

(2) The group

What unites people in their current experience? What are the different interests represented between groups? How active are groups in the community? What are the successes people have achieved by uniting in groups? We should always build on the strengths and value the experience of the community.

(3) The community

What makes people feel a sense of belonging to the community? How do people feel about living here? What has united people in their history and culture? What diversity is there within local culture? Are differences celebrated? What are the skills that people have? What is the local economic base? Has this changed? Who does the unpaid work in the community? What are the resources that exist in the community? What are the resources that are, or could be, available to the community from outside? What are the collective concerns for the community? How positive or confident is the community to act on its own behalf?

(4) A structural analysis

How do community statistics compare with the local authority, region, country or even the world? How do diversity and difference in your community compare with the country as a whole? To what extent are the issues affecting your community in line with wider social trends? In what way do current policies benefit/discriminate against local people? How relevant and efficient is service delivery? What plans are in place for developments? How might these benefit or act against the interests of the local community? Do local people feel that they are taken seriously? What environmental policies and issues impact on the community?

(5) The wider society

In this section, think local to global. Who represents local people in local and national government? Are there other leaders who act on behalf of the community to influence decisions? What changes are there in dominant ideology, and how is it affecting the local community? What wider social trends are reflected in the community? What links does the community have with other communities, networks, social movements? What environmental policies and issues affect the local community? Are people making connections with structural discrimination?

Presenting the profile

However you present your profile, the community must feel that it belongs to them, that it represents them in the most accurate way possible, that it is empowering and that they are proud of it. How will you make it compelling, relevant and readable? Will you have a community launch to celebrate its findings? Will this include a video, photograph or graphic display of the findings as part of a social event? Could part of it be displayed on a community noticeboard for a wider audience? How will you use it to stimulate action in the community? How will you use it to provoke critical thinking in the community? How will you integrate theory and practice?

The process of constructing the profile, once you have established a working group, will be life-changing for the people involved and will form the basis of further community development practice.

Model of critical praxis

Always keep in mind the links between the individual, the group, the community and the wider society. Reflections on my own practice led me to develop a model of critical praxis which helped me to see the relationships between the internal and external forces in community.

The model aims to locate power and domination within a social and political framework, and gives an idea of the way in which subordination is reinforced. In juxtaposition to this is *critical consciousness*.

The two come together at the interface of *community* and *praxis*. The model indicates two major circuits: one I have labelled *hegemony* to denote the ways in which ideological persuasion leads us to unquestioningly accept the *status quo*, absorbing dominant attitudes and values into the core of our being; the other I have labelled *critical consciousness* to indicate an alternative way of seeing life based on equity and justice. These two circuits overlap in *community*. Let's follow my journey round the model.

Starting in ideology, I developed certain beliefs and values that were based on my experience and perceptions of the world (*epistemology*). These are always in process and have reformed many times. They are constantly re-examined in relation to my engagement with the world (*ontology*). As a community worker, I cannot make sense of my practice without having conceptual tools of analysis. Of these there are many, but I have chosen to name Freire, Gramsci, class, feminism, whiteness, neoliberalism and the critiques and counternarratives offered by my 14 key thinkers (see Chapter 2) as prime areas of thought which have profoundly influenced me in my search for a theory of transformative change. In much the same way, these theories would make little sense without my experience.

Practice includes the stages of development in community, so here I have included *action*, *development* and *organisation* as reminders that community development adopts different approaches at different stages. These come together in *praxis*, the

Figure 5.2: Model of critical praxis

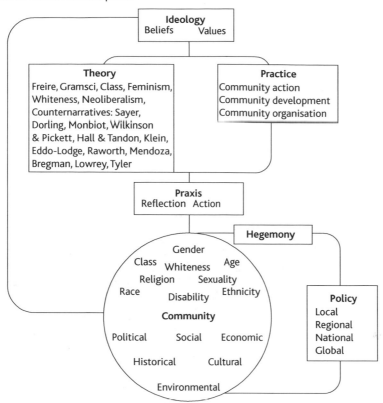

synthesis of *action* and *reflection*. Here, it is important to mention that this journey is not carried out in isolation. In *praxis*, my journey comes together with others in the quest for *critical consciousness*: making sense of the world in order to transform it is a collective experience. I share my thinking and ideas in dialogue with people in *community* as we move forwards in mutual inquiry and action. The dynamic between ideas and experience takes us deeper into the process of *conscientisation*. It locates understanding in experience, rather than as an abstract, decontexualised, intellectual activity, and this is the basis of collective action.

Hegemony is flexible and in constant reformation in relation to its context. On the model, the impact of local, national and global changes is seen in relation to *community*. If my praxis had developed in relation to community alone, failing to recognise the impact of outside forces, it would have been incomplete and much more likely to follow a self-help rather than a critical approach to practice. *Critical consciousness* is not possible without an analysis of *hegemony*. The two come together in *community* and form the basis of *critical praxis*. In this way, the journey towards critical consciousness is rooted in an analysis of the lived experience of people in their communities, within society.

Knowledge democracy

Knowledge democracy is about intentionally linking values of justice, fairness and action to the process of creating and using knowledge. It is inextricably intertwined with social justice and environmental justice, an important insight into the interconnectedness of neoliberal hegemony. Freire identified the banking system of education as serving a function of power by pouring knowledge as a commodity into the minds of unthinking students. Whose knowledge counts? Whose lives matter? Everyone's knowledge needs to be seen as relevant and legitimate. If a dominant ideology is elevated as a real truth, only the chosen are given access to that knowledge. The filtering starts early in life with young children in school being offered a knowledge that may or may not resonate with their cultural origins and ways of seeing the world. In classrooms our children are a rich and wonderful source of diversity. University may offer a possibility to the ones who stay the course. But David Lammy (Adams and Barr, 2018) has recently been exposing the proportionately low number of black students who get accepted into the University of Oxford, the shaming fact being that those who get the same high grades as their white counterparts are more likely to be rejected at interview. For a long time, universities have been talking about widening participation, but in reality this has very little to do with whose knowledge counts. Even when those termed 'non-traditional' students manage to storm the barricades, the rules are that you leave your indigenous, gendered, subordinated knowledges at home and play the rules of the dominant game. This is not knowledge democracy.

Budd Hall and Rajesh Tandon (introduced in Chapter 2) have played a key role in developing the concept of knowledge democracy, understanding that it is much more than the fair access to existing resources; deepening democracy demands that we engage with the questions 'whose knowledge counts?' and 'whose knowledge is creating the world we live in?'. In other words, what is the relationship between knowledge and privilege?

> Knowledge is the star of each drama. Knowledge is dynamic, active, engaged and linked to social, political, cultural or sustainable changes. (Hall and Tandon, 2017)

Hall and Tandon refer to De Sousa Santos's (2007) work on global injustice being intimately linked to global cognitive injustice, and so the struggle for both becomes one and the same thing. Therefore we cannot begin to address these crises in a disconnected way, but need to understand how dominant knowledge has been elevated as a commodity to benefit an elite by colonising, subordinating and even killing other knowledge systems (*epistemicide*).

The knowledge democracy movement is engaging with universities as existing recognised centres of knowledge production which could play an important role in promoting knowledge democracy. But widening participation is much more than opening doors on condition of a dominant truth being the only knowledge on offer. As Tandon has argued:

> ... different voices represent different forms and expressions of knowledge – different modes and articulations of knowledge from diverse experiences, locations and perspectives. This is the essence of 'knowledge democracy' – a movement that respects multiple modes, forms, sources and idioms of knowledge production, representation and dissemination.' (2013)

I heard a female professor on the radio lodge her right to retain her working-class cultural origins *and* to be a professor, a working-class professor. This assumption that once you fight your way into a high-status job, there is a requirement that you leave behind your working-class culture fascinated me. I was drawn into the same battle being fought admirably by Alethea (Ali) Melling, when I was invited to attend her inaugural professorial lecture at the University of Central Lancashire. I sat amongst the Asian community of Burnley who formed the majority of Ali's audience with pride to hear about her own life story and experience as a 'non-traditional' student and her pioneering role not only in opening the doors of the academy to others but her essential work in changing perceptions of the relevance of the university in the eyes of the black community.

The University of Central Lancashire is part of Advance HE, a UK universities consortium set up to explore issues regarding access to higher education. The aim of the national project is to create a picture that will help inform policy and practice. Here, Ali Melling and her colleague Paul Wilkinson tell a story of their work in prising open the gates of the University of Central Lancashire to welcome South Asian communities, Eastern Europeans and white British young men from low participation backgrounds in Pennine Lancashire and peripheral areas. In the Advance HE project, they collaborated with community stakeholders and families in developing interventions that challenge dominantly perceived views of higher education, towards creating a culture where this is viewed in terms of benefits rather than barriers.

Knowledge democracy in the radical university

Paulo Freire told us that 'education is an act of love, and thus an act of courage'. The ethos that drives this project is grounded within Freire's statement. We must therefore address the significance of 'love and courage' for both students struggling to access education, and those who continue to challenge the structural barriers that prevent this. Love, in this context, is the love of humanity, and therefore social justice.

Education is a human right, as without it, people struggle to become socially integrated[1] egalitarian agents of change. The freedom to access a meaningful empowering education therefore becomes a social justice issue, with implications for democracy. Social integration is not only a British issue, but a global issue, symptomatic of what Bone (2015) refers to as '... increasingly widening inequality and, potentially, stark socio-economic exclusion'. However, the issue of access to higher education is not simple. Caroline Kelly, from Noble's Pritzker College in the United States, stated '... the challenges faced (by students from low income backgrounds) can be categorized into five different "buckets". One is financial, one is motivation, one is family, one is academics, and one is social integration' (Riggs, 2014).

Courage is needed by everyone involved in the process of widening access to higher education. Students face negative challenges in their personal lives as well as institutional barriers. As part of this project, our participants shared stories about their challenges. These have included domestic violence and emotional abuse. Ostracisation is frequently gender biased towards women and girls. A female participant who was denied access to education for cultural reasons, in turn, challenged us: 'Just by writing about these case studies is not enough, you have to act on it to ensure that girls receive an education'. We therefore, as facilitators of learning, need to show courage, integrity and resolve in meeting this challenge.

For the purposes of this study, we chose EAR as our methodology. These principles were applied in several contexts to engage participating communities in problematising barriers to education in order to create a theory of change. EAR principles were employed innovatively through several engagement projects, such as 'Barrier Football', where we utilised football coaching techniques to engage young people in problematising the barriers they faced in accessing both further and higher education.[2] We used an EAR methodology, delivered by peer researchers or 'animateurs' (Ravangai, 1995). The research process is influenced by Freirean critical pedagogy based on dialogical, horizontal relationships between people, and the importance of stories shared empathetically in a democratic safe space (Freire, 2007a). Margaret Ledwith in her work on 'Emancipatory Action Research as Living Praxis', discusses the role of the dominant narrative in shaping thinking and attitudes (Ledwith, 2016b). Within this context, we seek to give voice to a counternarrative to change the story; therefore co-creating knowledge in action in partnership with marginalised people, knowledge that is relevant to the changing political context (Ravangai, 1995; Ledwith, 2016b).

We have referenced Moore's (1988) original definition of 'Barriers to Higher Education', which continues to have resonance today. The first barrier is *situational*, whereby the individual faces personal 'limit situations' relating to family or carer dynamics. Juxtaposed is employment, financial debt, and the simple logistics of getting to and from university whilst negotiating other external pressures. For instance, Moore notes that unsupportive employers make accessing any form of learning problematic, particularly if they do not see the value of it in relation to the work role (Moore, 1988).

As many students from lower socio-economic backgrounds face *economic* challenges, income generation whilst studying is necessary; therefore, earning whilst learning becomes a barrier. This is further compounded by institutional structures and procedures that fail to accommodate the needs of such students. Examples of institutional barriers range from unhelpful timetabling that fails to take into consideration domestic responsibilities, prohibitive administrative procedures, an exclusive rather than inclusive pedagogy, and rigid entry requirements that do not recognise experiential learning and alternative qualifications. These barriers may be further obfuscated by bias from academic and administrative staff.[3] Institutional structures, attitudes and behaviours impact on *dispositional* barriers, where an individual's attitude to learning is often shaped by poor past and present experiences. Dispositional barriers are compounded by factors such as peer pressure, poor confidence, low self-worth, often experiencing 'imposter syndrome', whereby the individual has no concept of their own merit and believes that they shouldn't really be in higher education. This latter point is particularly pertinent to female students already facing cultural barriers relating to traditional gender roles and expectations.

The facilitators worked with 397 people from across the target groups. Moore's definitions around dispositional, situational and economic barriers are reflected clearly in the participants' answers to questions around perceptions of higher education. Following the EAR process (Ledwith, 2016b), three key themes emerged, each linked to Moore's definitions.

Economic barriers were the most dominant throughout all the target groups:

> "*Financial problems and childcare*" (South Asian, most dominant answer)

> "*Many bills to pay, family back home rely on me working.*" (Eastern European, most dominant answer)

> "*Debt was what made me decide not to do higher education.*" (White British)

> "*Investment in education always gives a return*" / "*Culture still stands – engineers have respect [due to] wage security.*" / "*[Therefore] Asian parents want their children to be doctors and engineers nothing in between.*" (South Asian Community)

Economic and status value influenced course choice. Programmes with a strong vocational element were a key factor, particularly if the vocation 'signalled' success. For students from the target groups who have entered the University of Central Lancashire, the choice of study was dominantly vocational, South Asian students favouring high-status professions such as law, business, and engineering, whilst the white working-class students inclined towards caring professions, such as nursing and social work.[4]

The facilitators investigated the significance of parental views on higher education, as this can have a bearing on what, and whether, their children study.

> "*Our parents was scared of education [for girls]. What if our kids get educated there is not a cat in hell's chance they're gonna get married in Pakistan; we're not gonna get that praise label; we're not gonna be able to make our sister comfortable; we're not gonna make our brothers comfortable; we're gonna be frowned upon; what kind*

of parents are you ..., letting your children take over there, over your head? You have lost your kids. That's why parents fear education." (South Asian Community)

"Not bothered about education"; "my son will not go university he will come work in factory with me and earn money for back home"; "our skills we have from back home is our education." (Eastern European Community)

"Me and my parents have different views on higher education, they say what is the point"; "my parents never really took interest and didn't see the benefits"; "what an absolute waste of time, my children will be working 9–5 earning real money not wasting time in a classroom." (White British Community)

The facilitators were also interested to see what dispositional barriers emerged once in higher education. The third most dominant theme overall, and the most pertinent once in higher education, was low self-esteem and confidence, usually augmented by lack of family and external peer support.

"No aspirations" ; "People putting me down saying I wouldn't go far in life" ; "I was always told I would amount to nothing from parents."

This research is coming to an end and we are ready to work on solutions to identified issues. Initial findings have demonstrated that barriers to education continue to exist, as do barriers to social integration. The barriers that Moore identified in 1988 will continue unless social equality and integration improve, creating a classic cycle of disadvantage: barriers to education = limits to social integration = barriers to education. This must be addressed through institutional change in terms of expectation bias, starting in primary school, and cultural change in perceptions around higher education.

Statistically, although more marginalised students are entering higher education, the barriers along the journey remain, and until we address these issues, no matter how many come through the door, their attainment and social integration may well be limited. The *National Strategy for Access and Success for Students in Higher Education* acknowledges that 'considerable progress has been made in widening access and achieving student success in recent years. But there is still a long way to go' (Department for Business Innovation and Skills, 2014). We, as educators, need to facilitate more mature women students and marginalised groups into meaningful learning to go on to create change in society if we want to make a contribution to social justice. In addition, marginalised students entering higher education, need curricula with the breadth and scope to positively challenge perceptions of self and of others.

[1] Access to education is often labelled as an enabler of 'social mobility'. We prefer to use the term 'socially integrated' as a more egalitarian definition. 'Socially mobile', as a descriptor, can be confused with the neoliberal concept of 'upwardly mobile', thus transcending the social class framework for capital gain.

[2] A film has been produced which highlights key findings, as well as the process involved within the Barrier Football project.

[3] Unconscious bias may be social and follow a specific group or community through mainstream education and into higher education.

[4] Due to the relatively small number of Eastern European students from the target group studying at UCLan, evaluating this group in detail would contravene GDPR (2018) legislation.

Acknowledgement: Thank you to the University of Central Lancashire as an institution committed to community and inclusion for supporting our work. Also, to our community partners Access Alpha, Marsden Heights Community College, Saima Zeb, and our wonderful Community Leadership Students, who never fail to inspire.

Source: Alethea Melling and Paul Wilkinson, University of Central Lancashire, January 2018.

~~~~~~

UNESCO is exhorting universities to re-examine their research and teaching practices in light of 'preparing the next generation of ethical global citizens' (Tandon, 2014a: 5). This requires an enormous change of consciousness in universities. The production of new knowledge and its learning by students is possible through engagement with communities; such an engagement may also produce socially relevant knowledge. It may open up the possibility that knowledge acquired by students is based on a deeper understanding of their local contexts and a respect for knowledge residing within the communities. It is this process of *co-construction of knowledge* that may enhance the contributions of universities as sites for the practice of knowledge democracy (Tandon, 2014a: 4).

> Knowledge is defined in several ways: the facts, feelings or experiences of a person or a group of people, a state of knowing or awareness, and/or the consciousness or the familiarity gained by experience or learning. Knowledge is created through research, through the experience of the wise, through the act of surviving in the world, and is represented in text, poetry, music, political discourse, social media, speeches, drama and storytelling. Knowledge is linked to practical skills, to our working lives and to universal and abstract thought. Knowledge is created every day by each one of us and is central to who we are as human beings. (Escrigas et al, 2014: xxxiii)

Freire (1972) rejected knowledge as a gift bestowed by those who consider themselves knowledgeable upon those they perceive as ignorant; a view that fundamentally challenges the role of teacher with its false status.

Knowledge democracy is based on a counternarrative fuelled by 'a democratic imagination with a non-market, non-competitive view of the world, where conversations, reciprocity, translation create knowledges not guarded by elite experts but as cooperation between ordinary people who take both power and knowledge into their own hands' (Visvanathan, 2009).

Knowledge democracy demands celebrating a diversity of knowledges as legitimate and accepting that knowledge is not only about thinking, but about experience of the world, about being and doing and acting in the world and about feeling in and about the world. This is why Freire was so insistent that stories hold the answer: if I see more critically, I feel, and if I feel, I act to change the world. In this way human beings restore themselves to an integrated thinking-feeling-doing wholeness, claiming the right to be more fully human. This is why accepting knowledges rather than a dominant knowledge is a precursor to change in the struggle for a fairer and healthier world.

> At this juncture of humanity, as we stand at a crossroads, we seek to ask: What should be the nature of human thought, emotion and action? Should we continue on this path forever? Or should we pause to discover another? The human mind, its knowledge and capacity to dream can provide seeds for re-discovery. In taking steps towards such re-discovery, we need to look around the world at institutions of higher education. (Tandon et al, 2016: 1)

Boaventura de Sousa Santos said: 'There will be no global social justice until there is global cognitive justice' (2007: 10). His statement indicates the interrelated whole that is social justice/environmental justice/knowledge justice, which cannot be understood in parts.

Freire and emancipatory action research

> One of the radical promises of critical research is the possibility that we can tell a different story. (Fine, 2018: 11)

Freire's liberatory methodology is rooted in the lived reality of everyday people. He gives us direction on using *generative themes* to begin the research process with a community. The lived histories of the people are the starting point for Freire's work in community: educational projects must respect the local people's view of the world. This reduces any form of research that falls short of this level of respect for people and participation to *false generosity,* perpetuating the interests of the *status quo,* or *cultural invasion,* a superimposing of the dominant ideology on marginalised people's lives. The methodology of *conscientisation* is at the basis of knowledge democracy, it is for the people to claim their own knowledge through their cultural histories and lived experiences, and this begins with the practical use of generative themes. These ideas have had a huge impact on understanding how traditional approaches to research with people act in invasive, controlling ways and this insight triggered the participatory action research movement.

But conscientisation is more than a concept, it is:

> a methodology by which people's generative themes are critically engaged through a dialogical praxis of participation. Just as problem-posing education counters the lifelessness of banking education, a problem–posing approach to research with the people constitutes a life-affirming praxis founded in love, faith, and trust in the people's capacity to generate those themes that are truly meaningful with respect to their world. (Darder, 2018: 132)

This collaborative approach to research sits well with community development practice and plays a key role in critical praxis by uniting theory and practice in emancipatory action. It calls for an ideological change of consciousness on the part of the researcher, where the skills involve being fully present to 'suspend thinking and to stay aware of your experience in the ever-flowing present' (Reason and Rowan, 1981: 122). Rather than the claimed neutrality of the traditional researcher, the emancipatory action researcher is involved in the process as a co-researcher in partnership with the community. To be fully present is not as simple as it sounds. It requires the community worker to operate at critical and self-critical levels of awareness, otherwise 'all we are doing is opening ourselves to our most unthought-out prejudices and emotional reactions' (Rowan and Reason, 1981: 123).

One of the most challenging concepts to emerge from this approach to research is that described by Heron (1981) as a state where there is full interpersonal reciprocity at each stage of the research action – where the researcher becomes co-subject and the subject becomes co-researcher in a truly Freirean way. This not only integrates the researcher in the process, letting go of any delusions of neutrality, but it also relinquishes power over the process and the product to achieve a more participatory experience in partnership with the community. Traditional research is epitomised by the researcher having full control and the subject having no control and often very little idea of the purpose: a model that can be invasive, exploitative and harmful. An emancipatory approach expects subjects to share control appropriately at every stage of the process, and for researchers to be co-participants in the research. Of course, there are many intermediate points where participants may be more involved in some stages of the research process than others. True endogenous research is that which is generated and conducted from within the culture by people who are of that culture according to their own knowledge and values (Maruyama, 1981: 230). This, in its strict sense, is free from cultural invasion and hegemonic exploitation but may, nevertheless, contain prejudice and discrimination internal to that culture.

The new paradigm researchers of the 1980s were profoundly influenced by Freirean pedagogy. An overt example is that of Randall and Southgate's approach to dialogical research using a *problematising* approach with community groups in a community centre (Randall and Southgate, 1981: 349). The situation is a familiar one in community development: conflict was raging between groups who disagreed on the purpose of the centre, and they, in turn, were blaming the community workers. Using cartoons as codifications, they identified major contradictions that emerged in dialogue, de-personalising the anger and diverting the energy into forming new alliances. Emancipatory approaches to action research often start from a position of *problematising* or problem-posing – the Freirean approach to identifying an issue, which also questions the underlying causes. In developing a critical understanding of social problems and their structural causes, the possibilities for overcoming them become part of the whole. It calls for *dialogue*: a horizontal interaction between researchers and those with whom the research is conducted, embracing both action and reflection. In other words, it is committed not to abstract external knowledge, but to active, democratic participation in the process of change.

In these ways, pioneers in the participatory action research movement were inspired to use Freire's thought as the basis for a new paradigm. This is vital for community development inasmuch as: (1) it makes a clear break with alienating methods based on scientific research; (2) it offers a method that moves us towards the wholeness that is necessary to heal alienating experience in everyday life; (3) it offers a holism within which to contain fragmented thought; (4) it supports a critical pedagogy that is founded in collective action; and (5) it offers a language and structure of research that 'yield a deeper and more extensive truth' (Rowan, 1981: 105). *Knowledge in action* is used by Reason as the term to denote a transcending of the chasm between intellect and experience in which Western consciousness has placed value on 'thinkers' at the expense of 'doers', dividing theory from practice. Knowledge in action is, therefore, engaged in the world rather than alienated from it.

> To heal means to make whole: we can only understand our world as a whole if we are part of it; as soon as we attempt to stand outside, we divide and separate. In contrast, making whole necessarily implies participation: one characteristic of a participative world-view is that the individual person is restored to the circle of community and the human community to the context of the wider natural world. To make whole also means to make holy; another characteristic of a participatory world-view is that meaning and mystery are restored to human experience, so that the world is once again experienced as a sacred place. (Reason, 1994b: 10)

Michelle Fine identifies two questions that repeatedly get raised in her research, teaching and activism in schools, communities, prison, and youth and social movements:

- 'Where in the body, the family, the culture, the nation and in the globe do bodies of sadness swell and fester in the shadow of progress?
- And, then, where lies the missing discourse of desire?' (Fine, 2018:5)

> Early in my biography, I look back and identify in 'the folds in my own skin and the touchpoints where my skin, desires, pain grow intimate with others'; to tell, re-tell, and trouble already settled stories from a critical perspective of those who have paid the greatest price for 'normalized' injustice; to seek out those spaces where the light doesn't shine; to document the long shadow of exclusion and humiliation cast by national policies designed to protect 'us', and to ask who is (and is not) 'us'. And to engage this work as critical, public science. (Fine, 2018: 9–10)

As I think about this, I am minded of Wilkinson and Pickett's input to the ideas in this book with their identification of the mental suffering that is directly triggered by income inequality in rich countries. The ranking of personal worth by status markers of social superiority and inferiority, and the resultant anxiety epidemic that gives rise to stress, mental illness and a lack of wellbeing is linked to a plethora of symptoms identified in their detailed chart in Chapter 2. This is a revelation of the multiple ways that status anxiety gets under the surface of our skin to create widespread mental and physical ill health, in children and young people as well as adults. If we deal with fragmented symptoms, we fail to see the whole as systematically linked to the violence of structural discrimination. Fine from her research identifies the internalisation of environmental degradation and its correlation with low self-worth as well as physiological and psychological environmental stressors not only on academic achievement but inducing negativity and anger in young people. Complex, systemic discrimination permeates all the nooks and crannies of everyday life to dehumanise and to destroy lives, some more than others.

> Little did I know that in the late 1980s mass incarceration was seeping aggressively into the darkest neighborhoods of New York State. The state coffers were quietly realigning budgets and transferring monies and bodies of color from schools to prisons. (Fine, 2018: 15)

Questioning the role the universities have taken on as they have become neoliberalised as profit-generating institutions is vital. Once seen as sites of critical debate and knowledge generation, they are not only commodifying knowledge for sale on market demand and impoverishing students who have to buy their education as a lifetime debt, but recent news headlines raise concerns about their restrictions on free speech by banning external speakers who are seen as engaging with challenging ideas – amongst them highly respected academics like Germaine Greer and human rights activists like Peter Tatchell (2 February 2018, www.guardian.com). The knowledge democracy movement is also restricted by the neoliberal university censoring research that focuses on inequality: 'The state is increasingly abdicating its responsibility to fund research in the public interest and public education as well. Thus, democracy as academic freedom in research and other educational practices is highly constrained' (Torres and Reyes, 2011: 2). Research as praxis is doubly confounded by the continuing divide between knowing and doing. Torres and Reyes point out that it is not only traditional research that separates research and social action, but it is also common in other qualitative methodologies, which 'weakens the urgency of organizing for social change, fragments organizations, and holds back the political vision of liberation and emancipation by considering them as impossible and illusive' (Torres and Reyes, 2011: 3), leaving critique severed from transformative action.

The free-market mantra has become a new 'common sense' for success and prosperity. Yet the 'austerity' smokescreen that has led to 'peak inequality' (Dorling, 2018a) still serves to advance this Far Right agenda by concealing the damage that poverty is doing, not only to our social, economic and cultural wellbeing, but also penetrating the surface of our skins to dehumanise, diminish and destroy our emotional and physical wellbeing. Emancipatory action research is not just a research paradigm, but a philosophy of life committed to human and environmental flourishing which is founded in praxis: not just interpreting the world but changing it. In this sense, grounded in radical participatory democracy, it rehumanises local people to become co-researchers in making sense of what is to bring about change for the better through social action. It begins in dialogical encounters in which 'popular and academic knowledge meet and become mutually enhanced' (Torres and Reyes, 2011: 4), with the ultimate intention of changing the course of history, bringing about transformation for a better world. Take this forward with you as a tool of praxis as we revisit Gramsci's analysis of power in the next chapter as a stepping-stone to intersectionality.

WHITE PRIVILEGE

AN INVISIBLE KNAPSACK

PEGGY MCINTOSH'S INVISIBLE KNAPSACK CONTAINS
UNEARNED PRIVILEGES - INVISIBLE, ASSUMED ASSETS:
I SEE POSITIVE IMAGES OF PEOPLE LIKE ME ON TV
I CAN REMAIN OBLIVIOUS OF BLACK LANGUAGES + CULTURE
I CAN ALWAYS BE IN THE COMPANY OF PEOPLE LIKE ME
I CAN GO SHOPPING ALONE FEELING SAFE
I EXPECT MY NEIGHBOURS TO BE PLEASANT TO ME
I DO NOT EXPECT TO FEEL ISOLATED, OUT OF PLACE,
OUTNUMBERED, UNHEARD, HELD AT A DISTANCE
OR FEARED

LISTEN!

YOU ARE IN DENIAL
YOU ALWAYS SPEAK
BUT YOU NEVER LISTEN
I ALWAYS HAVE TO TIPTOE
AROUND YOUR SENSITIVITIES
YOU DON'T KNOW HOW TO EMBRACE
ME AS A TRUE EQUAL
YOU LEAVE ME TO WORK AT ANALYSING
STRUCTURAL RACISM
YOU ALWAYS SET THE AGENDA
WHY DON'T YOU THINK YOU
HAVE A RACIAL IDENTITY?
BE HUMBLE! LISTEN! BE OPEN TO CHALLENGE!

6

The power of ideas

The crisis consists precisely in the fact that the old is dying and the new cannot be born; in this interregnum a great variety of morbid symptoms appear' (Gramsci, 1971: 276)

This chapter demonstrates the power of ideas in the processes of both domination and liberation, exploring the usefulness of Gramsci's concepts of *hegemony* and the role of *the intellectuals* to radical community development praxis. Linking this to Thompson's (2016) PCS model offers insight into the way that the Personal, Cultural and Structural (PCS) contexts interact in the interests of power and privilege, in turn, locating key sites of intervention for change.

Introducing Antonio Gramsci

Antonio Gramsci was pivotal to my understanding of the way that power works in society to maintain relations of domination and subordination. Within minutes, as a student of community learning and development at Edinburgh University, David Alexander's explanation of Gramsci's concept of *hegemony* changed my consciousness forever. The blinkers were lifted; I saw power acted out around me in everyday situations in sharp definition! Gramsci is essential to community development in today's political context. His expansion of the concept of *hegemony* provides a profound understanding of politics, the complex ways in which the power of the state reaches into the lives of local people to elevate some as more important and relegate others to the margins. In addition, his analysis of the role of *the intellectuals* in the process of social change enables us to locate community development as a site of resistance.

Gramscian/Freirean theorist Paula Allman claims:

> A socially and economically just and an authentically democratic alternative to capitalism is possible, but … it can only be created by people who understand why capitalism invariably leads to crisis and why of necessity it is driven to produce wealth for a minority and either endemic insecurity or perpetual poverty and scarcity for the vast majority, and by people who also understand why its remedies for environmental destruction must be inextricably linked to profit margins. (Allman, 2001: 2-3)

Understanding hegemony is vital for critical practice. It offers profound insight into the way that economic, social and political forms of domination weave through our lives and minds, and locates critical education at the heart of the struggle for social justice. At this point, I am mindful of the way the new social movements that emerged from grassroots practice from 1968 onwards were transformative, or so we thought. As I sit here now, reflecting on the dramatic emergence of the Far Right on a xenophobic, misogynistic, white supremacist populist ticket, I wonder how much of what we achieved was reformism that did not follow through to fully transformative social change based on altered consciousness. Myles Horton talks about the way that Freire, influenced by Gramsci's thinking, placed critical education at the heart of the struggle. Highlander Folk School (now the Highlander Research and Education Center), in the early days, concluded that 'reform within the system *reinforced* the system, or was co-opted by the system. Reformers didn't change the system, they made it more palatable and justified it, made it more humane, more intelligent … so I think when Highlander was first recognized to the extent that we were invited to talk about education was after Paulo [Freire] made this kind of education respectable by being a professor at Harvard' (Horton and Freire, 1990: 200–2).

Gramsci, from his own experience, felt that the unions offered a corporate stage of consciousness, but that this was based on a limited sector of the economy that could, therefore, achieve nothing more than reformism (Forgacs, 1988). Reforms begin the process of change, but this does not become transformative unless a more collective form of revolutionary change creates an alternative possibility for the better. Gramsci saw critical education as the key to transformative change. With this in mind, let's explore Gramsci's relevance to the crisis of inequality that we face today.

Gramsci's relevance needs to be understood in relation to his historic times and cultural context. Nairn suggests that lessons from Gramsci can only be understood in the specific light of the Sardinian and Italian historical context (Nairn, 1982: 159). Added to this are his personal struggles. Gramsci's life was epitomised by loneliness, poverty and ill health: 'the struggle against material hardship and poverty, the struggle against political adversaries and finally the psychological struggle for survival in prison' (Ransome, 1992: 54). Out of this context emerged Gramsci's profound intellectual thought. His insight into power relations elevates him as '*the* Marxist thinker for our times' (Eaton, 2018).

Who was Antonio Gramsci?

Gramsci was born on 22 January 1891, in Ales, Sardinia, the fourth of seven children. His father, Francesco Gramsci, was a civil servant from mainland Italy, and his mother, Giuseppina Macias, came from a moderately wealthy family by Sardinian standards. But, Sardinian living conditions were harsh in comparison with mainland Italy, a contrast that was to form the basis of Gramsci's ideas on injustice. He did not have an easy childhood. At the age of four, he developed a back deformity, which, at the time, was attributed to falling downstairs, but this is now refuted. It is considered likely that his condition, which subsequently developed into a spinal curvature and restricted his height, was a result of tuberculosis of the spine, 'a condition known as Pott's Disease, with which he was diagnosed in 1933' (Kenway, 2001: 48). His parents wanted to hide this due to the superstitious beliefs that were so much part of Sardinian culture (Mayo, 1999), in which werewolves, ghosts and witches were feared (Davidson, 1977). Gramsci resented the fact that the power of popular superstition, which cast disabled people as possessed by evil spirits, had prevented his parents from getting the right treatment to overcome the condition in its early stages (Mayo, 1999). On the advice of a specialist, he was suspended from the ceiling in a leather corset for long periods of time in an attempt to straighten his back by traction. His disability persisted and, as a result, he became a solitary child.

When he was six, his father was imprisoned for over five years, accused of fraud and embezzlement, but it is more likely that it was an act of political retribution. The family was reduced to a state of bare survival and returned to Ghilarza, where his mother's strength and hard work saved the family from destitution. This was a significant turning point in Gramsci's early life. Until then, he had been cushioned by his parents' relatively privileged position in local society. Due to his poor health and his mother's desire to protect him, he started school late, at the age of seven. His disability and his family's reduced status left him wide open to bullying and rejection from other children. This was a formative experience and led to his empathy with all those who suffer injustice (Davidson, 1977). His schooling became fragmented, he suffered from malnutrition, and by the age of 11 his father returned home and forced him to leave school to help support the family. He worked 10 hours a day for six-and-a-half days a week, carrying heavy ledgers around the Land Registry Office, 'many a night I wept in secret because my whole body was aching' (Gramsci, 1988: 238).

This marked the start of feelings of great resentment towards his father. His schooling resumed once his father considered that the family was sufficiently back on its feet, and he was boarded out 11 miles away to receive what he considered an inadequate education based on principles of 'intellectual dishonesty'. His solitary nature led to a great passion for reading. Gennaro, his older brother, away in Turin on military service, started sending him *Avanti!*, the Italian Socialist Party (PSI) paper. At this time, Sardinia began to erupt in the face of the rising discontent of the poor. Fiori (1990) describes Gramsci's cultural and political times – widespread malnutrition and premature death from chronic diseases and work accidents – together with his political reading as having changed Gramsci's political perspective. His dream was of action that would lead to social justice.

His move to the lycée at Cagliari saw the dawn of his active political life. He lived with Gennaro, who introduced him to the socialist movement, and he started reading Marx. Sardinia increasingly rebelled under the weight of the abject oppression of the poor, and Gramsci's identification and involvement with the socialist movement deepened his critical consciousness.

Eventually, he was offered a scholarship in Turin, where the combination of a large, industrial, working-class city and the stimulation of critical thinkers was to influence his philosophical thought. However, the transition from Sardism to socialism was lengthy and protracted. The image is one of extreme unhappiness, a man who was 'too appallingly miserable for people even to want to approach him' (Davidson, 1977: 70). The liberal intellectual Piero Gobetti saw him as 'seething with resentment' and described his socialism as 'first of all a reply to the offences of society against a lonely Sard emigrant' (Nairn, 1982: 161). Gramsci found solace, once again, in excessive study, which, combined with poverty, increasingly damaged his health.

A turning point came in 1916. He abandoned his degree in linguistics, and his long-term ambition to become a good teacher, to work full-time on the political paper *Avanti!*. Turning his back on academic life, Gramsci the revolutionary political activist emerged. A simultaneous change in his personality took place. He became happier and more sociable. 'He was in the process of remaking himself in what Marxists call praxis. By engaging in a practical and active rather than a contemplative life, he was purging himself of the emotional and ideological incrustation of [his] past' (Davidson, 1977: 72). As a political journalist, he put into practice his belief in bringing theory to the workers. He saw this as the route to self-knowledge for the industrial proletariat, liberation of the mind. In a process of reflection on history, he saw the beginnings of emancipation of the masses.

By early 1917, the time of the Russian Revolution, his ideology expressed through his journalism synthesised with a vision of practice located in the factory councils to offer a critical praxis with transformative potential. He was central to the development of the factory council movement in Turin and became increasingly involved in political journalism, helping to found the socialist paper *L'Ordine Nuovo* in 1919, as a tool of consciousness. Its motto was: 'Pessimism of the intellect, optimism of the will'. I interpret this as: see the world as it really is and have the optimism to change it. The factory council, for Gramsci, was the initial context of praxis, the point of contact with the workers: workers' democracy organised through workers' and peasants' councils, which he saw as an educational force that would put ordinary people in touch with their own potential political leadership.

The factory council movement spread rapidly between 1919 and 1920. The moment of crisis came when 600,000 workers from the Italian industrial cities occupied their factories. Gramsci and his friends closed the offices of *L'Ordine Nuovo* and went to live in the factories with the workers. However, as a revolution it was doomed to failure. Gramsci believed that the moment of conflict had been determined by capitalism, and that the workers were unprepared. The result was that the whole movement was premature and uncoordinated. He blamed himself for failing to understand the need for parallel growth in both theory and practice in order to achieve a *unity of praxis*. It was his belief that, had the process been critical and the timing right, it would have enabled the workers to run the new society and the party to play its key role in taking over the bourgeois state.

After the collapse of the factory council movement, Gramsci became actively involved in the formation of the Communist Party of Italy (PCI). These years saw, once again, his emotional withdrawal into a life governed by the intellect. In May 1922, he was a Communist Party delegate on the Executive Committee of the Communist Third International in Moscow. His health deteriorated while he was there, and he was sent to a sanatorium near the Black Sea where he met Giulia Schucht. She was of Russian Jewish ethnicity, and a music teacher who had studied violin in Rome (Kenway, 2001: 48). They married in 1923.

It was only over time that Gramsci realised the significance of the growth of fascism. His analysis was founded on the idea that fascism was a rural phenomenon that released suppressed passions and hatred in the masses. Politically, he saw fascism as separate from the bourgeois state because of its decadence: an uncontrollable cross-class movement dominated by the petit bourgeoisie, the lower middle class, and characterised by legitimate violence. In 1922, Mussolini took power with his March on Rome, which marked the final death throes of the Italian proletariat drive for a Soviet-style revolution. It became apparent that fear and a politics of hatred generated among the masses created the space for a fascist dictator to occupy. By early 1923, communist leaders were being arrested and Gramsci sought to unite the working classes against this wave of fascism.

The volatile political climate made it unsafe for Gramsci to return to Rome until 1924, and he did so without Giulia. In the general election of April 1924, he was elected to parliament and subsequently became the general secretary of the PCI. He travelled the country, addressing meetings and organising the party on the basis of workplace cells. May 1924 saw Gramsci's inaugural speech in parliament. His fearlessness was a constant threat to the fascists who determined to circumvent his parliamentary immunity and silence him. He was constantly followed around the country and eventually arrested on charges of conspiracy, agitation, inciting class war, insurrection and alteration of the Constitution and the form of the state through violence. Davidson considers his chief threat to the fascists to have been his awareness 'that the main battle to overthrow fascism lay among the peasantry' (Davidson, 1977: 118).

Gramsci returned to Moscow briefly following the birth of Delio, his first son. Between October 1925 and July 1926, Giulia joined him in Rome with Delio. She left because of the deteriorating political climate in Italy, just two months before Gramsci was arrested. Their second son, Giuliano, was born in Moscow in August 1926. Gramsci never saw him. Giulia remained the romantic love of Gramsci's life, but she suffered badly from depression, and eventually had a breakdown, never to return to Italy.

From 1926, the international political climate deteriorated and the situation 'demanded a new analysis of the political and ideological resources of capitalist societies, the sources of their extraordinary resilience' (Forgacs, 1988: 189). It was this analysis that occupied Gramsci's thoughts throughout his prison years. In November 1926, he was arrested, along with other communist members of parliament. He was moved from Rome to exile on the island of Ustica, and then to

Milan to await trial. His first plan for his *Prison Notebooks* was formed in this period. Tatiana Schucht, Giulia's elder sister, devoted her life to supporting Gramsci in the difficult years of his imprisonment, and Gramsci became dependent on her for emotional sustenance. (It is Tatiana who would ensure that the Gramscian legacy was preserved by smuggling his letters and prison notebooks past the prison censor into the public domain.) She passed a letter on to his old student friend, Piero Sraffa, who was now a Marxist economist at Cambridge, outlining the subject of his notebooks. Sraffa brought Gramsci's plight to public attention in an article in the *Guardian* on 21 October 1927, but to no avail. Gramsci was transferred to Rome in May 1928. On 4 June, the prosecuting attorney, Michele Isgro, echoed Mussolini's personal instructions in declaring a need to stop Gramsci's brain from functioning for 20 years, such is the threat of powerful ideas to the *status quo* (Milne, undated; Davidson, 1977). Mussolini's enforcement of the 'long Calvary of Antonio Gramsci' had begun (Fiori, 1990). 'His active political practice had finished. He now had four and a half thousand days to think on its theoretical implications for Marxism and revolutionary socialism' (Davidson, 1977: 231).

In July 1928, Gramsci was transferred to a special prison in Turi, in the South, because of his ill health. Not until early 1929 was he given permission to write, and he started work on the first prison notebook in a school exercise book. As part of the amnesty programme for the 10th anniversary of the fascist 'revolution', his sentence was commuted to 12 years and four months. By this time his health was deteriorating rapidly. After he collapsed in his cell in March 1933, his doctor recommended that he be transferred to a clinic. This was supported by Sraffa who, as well as paying for Gramsci's supply of books, worked endlessly to help him over the years by putting moral pressure on the fascist regime. Gramsci's writing continued from the clinic at Formia until 1935, when illness forced him to stop. There were by then 2,848 tightly packed pages of his writing in 33 prison notebooks, an achievement that signifies what Henderson calls 'a prodigy of will, intellect and indomitable staying power' (H. Henderson, quoted in Gramsci, 1988: 10). Gramsci saw this period of his life as 'a time of waiting, a pause and preparation' (Lawner, 1979: 39).

Not prepared to compromise his political position, Gramsci suffered an arduous 10-year confinement under the fascist regime in Italy, while his health slowly disintegrated. 'In 1937, having long been refused adequate health care (his teeth fell out and he was unable to digest solid foods), Gramsci died, aged 46' (Eaton, 2018). A cerebral haemorrhage killed him on 27 April 1937, six days after his freedom had been granted. Tatiana, in a letter to Sraffa on 12 May 1937, describes how, on the very day she brought him news of his freedom, he collapsed. She stayed with him over the two days it took him to die. 'I kept watch over him doing whatever I thought best, wetting his lips, trying to help him get his breath back artificially when it seemed to stop. But then he took a last deep breath and sunk [sic] into a silence that could never change' (quoted in Lawner, 1979: 280). Tatiana saw that all his work was safely deposited at the Banca Commerciale in Rome, from where it was transferred to Moscow, and then to his friend, Togliatti.

Since then, his writing continues to be analysed and published, challenging the thought and the practice of those who read it to this day.

Gramsci's contribution to critical pedagogy

> ... the relationship between teacher and pupil is active and reciprocal so that every teacher is always a pupil and every pupil a teacher. (Gramsci, 1971: 350)

Gramsci recognised the inadequacy of Marxist economic determinism to offer sufficient analysis for the increasing complexity of power relations in the 20th century. He reconceptualised the moral, cultural and political influences in society to offer profound insight into the pervasive nature of these forces of power in everyday life. Of particular relevance to critical pedagogy are his concepts of the nature of hegemony and the role of the intellectuals. Education and culture were two themes that were of constant interest to Gramsci. Much of his early thinking was preoccupied with the problem of achieving working-class intellectual autonomy. His belief was that everyone is innately cultured and capable of intellectual thought, but that this is undisciplined and incoherent without critical education. By placing emphasis on the learner, not the teacher, a learning process can be stimulated that moves through self-knowledge to liberation (Forgacs, 1988).

Gramsci's influence on Freire can be seen in these ideas. Ideology, according to Marx and Engels, assumes that the class with the power to control the material forces of society also controls the dominant ideas in society, which are passively absorbed into working-class minds as the *false consciousness* of *common sense*. So, 'not only does the ruling class produce the ruling ideas, in view of its control over the means of intellectual production, but the dominated classes produce ideas that do not necessarily serve their interests' (Mayo, 2004: 41). This can be seen in the UK and the US today with the rise of the Far Right supported by some of the poorest and most marginalised communities. Although Marx and Engels introduced the role of ideology as an instrument of class struggle, their emphasis was on the role of the party in developing consciousness. Gramsci developed a revolutionary ideology, 'a theory of popular, as well as working-class, ideology of protest' to a much more sophisticated degree (Rude, 1980: 22).

Fundamental to Gramsci's thinking is the notion of revolution as process. He rejects cataclysmic change in favour of progressive revolution through critical education. His belief was that society could only be transformed by the systematic construction and consolidation of new social relationships. The capacity of the people to play key roles in their own destiny is central to this process. Intellectual and moral reform is Gramsci's term for what Freire would call *conscientisation* (see Chapter 4): the process whereby people critically reconceptualise their roles in society from their *false consciousness*. 'The philosophy of praxis is the crowning point of this entire movement of intellectual and moral reformation, made dialectical in the contrast between popular culture and high culture' (Forgacs, 1988: 351).

Gramsci's writings offer an originality of thought and a practical base, a praxis that reflects his experience as an activist.

According to Gramsci, Lenin's belief that there can be no revolutionary movement without a revolutionary theory is of fundamental importance to understanding the function of critical education. Examining traditional working-class organisation and leadership, which had proved so ineffective in conquering capitalism while at the same time existing within it, he developed insight into the dynamics of social, political and economic relations that had never been achieved before. His vision of progressive revolutionary change was based on the role of critical education in achieving mass political consciousness with a democratic, grassroots base rather than an elite leadership. 'Classical Marxism, by emphasising the coercive nature of politics, has been correspondingly weak in analysing the problem of consent' (Hoffman, 1984: 1). Gramsci's substantial contribution is found in his analysis of consent in relation to hegemony.

The concept of hegemony

Gramsci's analysis of the concept of *hegemony* is profound. Hegemony is the means by which one class assumes dominance over the masses in society. Traditional Marxism emphasised that this was achieved through coercion, the way in which the state exercised control through the law, the police and the armed forces. Gramsci extended this understanding by identifying the way in which dominant ideology, as a form of ideological persuasion, permeates our lives through the institutions of civil society. By these means, dominant attitudes are internalised and accepted as *common sense*, and this is the point at which marginalised people are persuaded to consent to their own oppression. Not only did he develop the notion of *consent* within a Marxist framework, but he analysed *hegemony* as 'the entire complex of practical and theoretical activities with which the ruling class not only justifies and maintains its dominance, but manages to win the active consent of those over whom it rules' (Gramsci, 1971: 244).

This development of the cultural and moral aspects of hegemony challenges the entire Marxist conceptual analysis of the state as an instrument of coercion (Hoffman, 1984). Gramsci's notion of the *historical bloc*, a term that encompasses the interrelationships of the economic, cultural and political alliances in society, is bound together by the cohesion of hegemony. He believed that hegemonic dominance established through an intellectual and moral bloc is likely to be much more stable than power achieved through coercion. In other words, if we can be persuaded to internalise the stories told by a dominant hegemony, our consent leads to much more effective subordination than that which comes from force. 'Gramsci is very specific about this object, which is not successfully fulfilled by all parties – the establishment of an integral State, a State which has a fully developed hegemony in civil society encompassing the mass of the population and thereby cementing together a strong historical bloc' (Showstack Sassoon, 1987a: 150).

Think about this in relation to the current work of Imogen Tyler on the use of social abjection under neoliberalism, introduced in Chapter 2.

But hegemony is not a system, it is a process of constant struggle to maintain dominance over subordinate classes, which is actively maintained and modified by agents of the state – in itself a form of praxis (Ransome, 1992). So, having achieved dominance, a ruling class has a continuing need to maintain hegemonic control. The complexity of the concept of hegemony is that its structure is open to constant analysis, challenge and modification (Entwistle, 1979). It is not likely that hegemonic dominance can be maintained effectively without the collective will of the people – therefore the development of a counter-hegemony plays an essential part in the process of change. Reflect on this in relation to the points raised by several of the intellectual activists I introduce in Chapter 2 concerning our failure to imagine a counternarrative capable of offering an alternative to the neoliberal dominant narrative. This is where Gramsci saw the importance of critical education. He also transcended the dichotomous class divide of previous Marxist thinkers by identifying potential alliances between many social groups in the process of collective action, one of those being the role of traditional and organic intellectuals in the process of social change. Hegemony is 'characterised by its non-static nature (it is constantly open to negotiation and re-negotiation, therefore being renewed and recreated) ... there exist moments in which cracks can be detected' (Mayo, 2010, 24). Such a crack where the light shines in has appeared in this current period of political crisis, and in this moment there is an opportunity for transformative change.

Gramsci saw the embodiment of social equilibrium in the interrelationship between coercion and consent. Also of central importance in this respect is the flexibility of hegemony, the way in which peripheral criticisms can be absorbed as acts of compromise. In this way, reformist measures can be negated before they threaten the bedrock of the dominant ideology. By offering such palliatives, the *status quo* can be maintained without resorting to the use of coercion, which is both expensive and difficult to maintain. In a similar vein, Freire refers to *false generosity*, or tokenism (see Chapter 4). *False generosity* is used within the process of *hegemony* to create an illusion of democracy and justice. Think about the tokenistic way that the hegemonic education system allows individuals from some oppressed groups to flourish, while the groups as a whole remain disadvantaged. This individualises educational failure and success, creating a smokescreen for the hegemonic function of schools.

One extreme example of the use of ideological persuasion to cement cracks in a crumbling *status quo* could be seen in Margaret Thatcher's use of the Falklands War to unite the UK in the face of the threat from an outside enemy, namely Argentina. On the other hand, state reversion to coercion during the 1984–85 Miners' Strike, as well as ideological persuasion, aimed at the rest of civil society, that the miners were the 'enemy within' (Milne, 1994), demonstrates the might of the state when the full force of coercion and consent is used in combination. Gramsci provides community workers with insights into the way in which community groups can begin the process of transforming society for the common good. His analysis offers critical insight into the power of ideas to infiltrate the inner recesses of our being to persuade us to accept the dominant order of things unquestioningly as *common sense*. Whereas coercion is exercised overtly through the armed forces, the police, the courts and prisons, consent is subtly woven through the institutions of civil society – the family, schools, the media, political parties, unions, religious organisations, cultural, charitable and community groups – in a way that permeates our social being reinforcing hegemonic control by influencing our ideas. The struggles against oppression around issues of *difference* and *diversity* are located in civil society. This places the community worker at the heart of the process. The values, attitudes, morality and beliefs that are internalised as *common sense* by the masses but serve the interests of dominant groups have to be challenged at a local as well as a structural level. In order for this to happen in a critical way, Gramsci believed that the *false consciousness* of the subordinated classes needed to be transformed to release full potential for participation in the process of social action. This is why both Freire and Gramsci locate critical education at the heart of the process of transformative change.

Based on his own political activism, Gramsci recognised that *hegemony* is a resilient and flexible force. He believed that the critical consciousness of ordinary people is vital in any effective intervention, but that this will not erupt spontaneously. External agents need to act as catalysts in this process, and he conceptualised these as *traditional intellectuals*.

Gramsci as *the* thinker for our current political crises

Gramsci's comment on the 1930s – 'The crisis consists precisely in the fact that the old is dying and the new cannot be born; in this interregnum a great variety of morbid symptoms appear' – is as apt today as it was then.

Eaton (2018) offers an interesting perspective on Gramsci in relation to current neoliberal times and our failure to prevent the ascendance of the Far Right. With reference to hegemony as the defining Gramscian concept, Eaton's emphasis is on the way that political domination extends beyond the coercion of a state or parliament into the very essence of culture and ideas, the arena of persuasion and consent. He talks about right-wing commentators warning that the Left is engaged in a *war of position* trying to bring about cultural change. But the weakness of New Labour was its centrist position, claiming the end of class and condoning wealth at the same time as condemning poverty. Despite its liberal agenda with such movements as gay rights, and its boldness in wanting to end child poverty, it failed. There was no understanding of power, and so there was no challenge to Thatcher's skilful use of hegemony to further the interests of neoliberalism.

In Jeremy Corbyn, however, the Conservatives face the first sustained challenge to their intellectual domination. The Labour Party is now presenting society with a revolutionary counternarrative, a story with people and planet at its heart, sustained by renationalisation, good housing, dignified incomes and decent jobs, good health, social welfare and free education – all funded by responsible taxation of the top 5%. Like the New Right before them, the New Left aspire not simply to defeat their opponents at elections but to overturn their most cherished ideals. When Corbyn and his allies refer to themselves as 'the new political mainstream', they are, in Gramscian terms, seeking to redefine 'common sense'.

Eaton feels that Gramsci would have admired the activist group Momentum and its festival The World Transformed (which has included sessions on such Gramscian themes as lifelong education and political theatre, and a Stuart Hall reading group). As the *Prison Notebooks* advocated, Momentum engages at the level of civil society and popular culture (Eaton, 2018).

> As Thatcher herself remarked in 1981: 'Economics are the method; the object is to change the soul'. (Eaton, 2018)

Revisit Kate Raworth's Doughnut model (Figure 2.3 on p 66), and consider the change in 'soul' that is implicit in this approach to economics.

The role of the intellectuals

Central to Gramsci's thought was how to raise the consciousness of oppressed people without simultaneously destroying their innate energy. He believed that without emphasis on intellectual understanding, the consciousness of oppressed people is likely to be fragmented, manifesting itself in a simple form of anti-authoritarianism – a generic hatred of the state rather than a critical analysis of power and domination. We can certainly see the impact of this idea in today's eruptions of anarchy. Gramsci recognised that critical consciousness could only come about through a political understanding of the illegitimate foundations of class domination. *False consciousness* is powerful and the questioning needed to reach a more critical awareness does not usually happen without external intervention.

Gramsci saw every person as having intellectual capacities for thinking and reasoning. He used the term *intellectual* to refer to people who occupy a wide range of organisational or ideological/cultural roles in society, not simply academics. Within this concept, *organic intellectuals* are those who emerge from their culture of origin. Every social group produces individuals who possess 'the capacity to be an organiser of society in general, including all its complex organism of services, right up to the state organism, because of the need to create the conditions most favourable to the expansion of their own class' (Forgacs, 1988: 301). Gramsci saw *traditional intellectuals* as the product of a previous historical period, whose role has continued to exist in the present, and who are not deeply committed to a class. He particularly had in mind the Catholic Church, which at that time in Italian history had a monopoly not only on religious ideology but on education, morality and justice. *Traditional intellectuals* have an important preliminary role in challenging hegemony by acting as a catalyst in the process of transformation, unlocking mass consciousness (Boggs, 1980). They bridge the divide between theory and practice by becoming committed to action for social justice, and begin the process of liberation by creating the context for questioning the legitimacy of everyday experience.

Gramsci felt it ultimately essential that intellectuals should be generated from the very heart of the working class, but he saw the role of the *traditional intellectual* as having empathy with subordinated people and a commitment to social justice. This is where he identified the external intervention so vital in setting the wheels of change in motion. He was sceptical that their loyalty would be sustained; activists who do not emerge from the people, according to historical analysis, are prone to defect in the face of persecution. But, having cut the ties to their own class, *traditional intellectuals* could play a vital role as catalysts for change. The most important function falls to the working–class *organic intellectual*, a person of ideas, a person with a passion for the people that transcends the dichotomy between *knowing* and *feeling*. Without this unity of praxis, the struggle will remain peripheral. (The knowing–feeling divide is addressed in Chapters 7 and 8 in relation to feminism.)

Organic intellectuals remain committed to their cultural roots. They articulate new values, pose critical questions and invite new ways of thinking about the world. They are more likely to remain committed to their class of origin, sharing the inherent dilemmas of that class, and play an integral part in the process of change. When *organic intellectuals* emerge from everyday life into that role, their specific purpose is raising the critical consciousness of the people; they remain central to the creation of a just society.

> The organic intellectual of the working class is a builder, an organiser, a permanent persuader so that he [sic] is able to engage in all aspects of the struggle.... These attributes, developed before the revolution, will serve after the revolution as the tasks of the organic intellectual continue in all these areas, from the organisation of socialist production to the building of a new culture ... the creation of a new intellectual begins in the heart of the old society. (Showstack Sassoon, 1987a: 149–50)

This reminds me of Cathy McCormack, an inspirational community activist from Easterhouse, Glasgow, who is a true *organic intellectual*, in every sense of the concept. She learnt about popular education in Nicaragua after becoming political in a housing campaign in Easterhouse in the 1980s.

> It was only through my experience in Nicaragua that I started to understand the truth. Now I was getting to the roots of my own poverty. That's when I really became involved in the international struggle for justice.... I wanted the people in both communities to learn and benefit from each other's experience. So I established the Greater Easterhouse Nicaragua Solidarity Link Group. (McCormack with Pallister, 2009: 116)

She brought popular education to Easterhouse from her encounter with Freire in action in Nicaragua.

> Whether you live in a village in Central America or in a Glasgow scheme, the people's experience is still the same and they want their voices heard. When I started on this journey, I was politically ignorant but I was able to make sense of things and start making connections. I was experiencing an education no university could have given me, but it was a shattering education because I was realising how badly human beings could treat each other'(McCormack with Pallister, 2009: 104).

After an intensive Training for Transformation programme in Ireland, she set up, with others, the Popular Democracy Education Resource Centre (PODER) in Easterhouse, which led to her involvement in the Scottish Popular Education Forum, aiming to bring popular educators together from all over Scotland to constitute a movement for change. I had the great pleasure of meeting Cathy in Edinburgh in 1999, when she came to talk about her experience at the International Association for Community Development (IACD) Conference in Edinburgh. Her book, *The Wee Yellow Butterfly* (2009), is a vital resource for community development workers who want to understand the work of organic intellectuals.

> "I never thought in my wildest imagination when I took my first step toward my community's fight for social, economic and environmental justice that I would end up in the ozone layer or the international struggle for justice, but that's what happened when we started to make links between sick houses, sick children and sick planet." (Cathy McCormack speaking to The Women's International Group at Royston Wardieburn Community Centre, 10 November 2013)

In 1994, Cathy found herself at the United Nations (UN) on a panel with an ambassador, academics and UN advisors. She said: 'It was the first time in my life I felt overdosed with being empowered and I didn't like it. It was one thing challenging our own government's health policies, but the world's? But as it turned out, I was one of the real experts on poverty' (McCormack, nd).

Organic intellectuals become leaders in the process of change, but they are not an elite. Gramsci distinguished the role by its function rather than its status. In this sense, he moves beyond a revolutionary leadership model to one where these key roles function within an overall unity in non-hierarchical relationships inspired by critical consciousness. This unity can be seen in the type of socialism discussed by Fromm (1962), by which people become the conscious subjects of history, experiencing themselves as powerful, not powerless, and by such intellectual emancipation are able to free themselves from the chains of *false consciousness*:

Through a constant process of theoretical preparation and political education, members of the rank and file could develop their political capacities and eventually become leaders. In this way the necessary division between leader and led was no longer arbitrary and formal, but merely functional. (Showstack Sassoon, 1987a: 85)

According to Gramsci, *common sense* is a collection of myths and superstitions that is resilient to spontaneous critical thought. The *traditional intellectual* unlocks popular critical consciousness by offering a coherent understanding of oppressive forces in history and society. In contrast to this initial function, the *organic intellectual* integrates this critical consciousness into everyday culture. Everyday thought and action are questioned, transformed and, in turn, collectively transform society. The organic intellectual movement grows both qualitatively and quantitatively, for every person is innately an intellectual, and by this process *false consciousness* transforms into *critical consciousness*.

Philosophy of praxis

Gramsci's insight into the complex nature of *hegemony* changed the very essence of the concept by recognising that people are not only controlled by coercion, but also consent to their own oppression when the dominant narrative is so powerful that they are persuaded that their subordination is a consequence of their own inadequacy. Stories told with conviction and repeated often enough become internalised as a truth. Again, consider this point in relation to Imogen Tyler's important research into the use of stigma in dominant ideology as a means of mass control (see Tyler in Chapter 2). As a powerful form of control, dominant attitudes and values permeate people's lives through civil institutions – the media, the family, schools and all other social groups that we experience. The result is *cultural invasion* (Freire, 1972): our minds become colonised with how we *are told to* think, feel and act. We are robbed of the confidence to be critical because the interests of power and privilege invade our minds, influencing our perceptions of the world and our place in it.

Gramsci's emphasis was on praxis in the process of change. The term he frequently used in his notebooks, *philosophy of praxis*, is the concept of a unity of theory and practice. 'For Gramsci the philosophy of praxis is both the theory of the contradictions in society and at the same time people's practical awareness of those contradictions' (Forgacs, 1988: 429). bell hooks (1993: 151) talks about making a commitment to work from a 'lived understanding' of people's lives rather than accepting as authentic the distortion of a 'bourgeois lens'. She cites Freire's words from *Pedagogy in Process*: 'authentic help means that all who are involved help each other mutually, growing together in the common effort to understand the reality which they seek to transform. Only through such praxis – in which those who help and those who are being helped help each other simultaneously

– can the act of helping become free from the distortion in which the helper dominates the helped'.

If we work with a greater understanding of power embedded in the structures of society, in civil society, and in everyday encounters, we begin to see much more clearly that action for change needs to target each of these levels in order to make a difference. How then do we begin to operationalise these ideas in practice?

Locating and dislocating oppression

An analysis of power and the structures of discrimination is needed in order to develop practical strategies for change. This analysis needs to incorporate not only race, class and gender, but it needs to embrace intersectionality as the whole complexity of interlinking, overlapping patterns of discrimination that exist as a hugely successful white supremacist, patriarchal, neoliberal class project (Tyler, 2013; 2015; Eddo-Lodge, 2018).

Discrimination as formalised oppression

An understanding of Gramsci's concept of *hegemony* is essential to this analysis. Maintaining power by persuading people that dominant attitudes are *common sense* works in a much more subtle way than a dominant group overtly coercing others into subordination. Power is located within a multidimensional system of oppressions in which we are all simultaneously oppressors and oppressed. It is essential that we see this as a complex whole that interlinks and reinforces at every level.

Ideology – the ideas that are formed around values and beliefs in society and inform the way society is organised – reinforces and justifies the divisions and power imbalances between groups in order to maintain the *status quo*. These ideas are difficult to change because they have been sold as *common sense* – a term that Gramsci defined as fragmented, disjointed, contradictory thinking that justifies reality for the mass of the people (Hall, 1996c). In these ways, the ideas of the most powerful in society sustain their own interests. This can be seen in relation to 'normality'. Take *the family*, which has fundamentally changed in role and structure over recent decades. A 'normal' family, despite an understanding of difference and changing structures, is still perceived in a white, Western, heterosexual, fully able, middle-class way as a man and a woman living together with their two perfectly formed children. Anything different is 'Other', deviant and undesirable, and therefore undermining of the moral base of society. This thinking, in turn, justifies policy decisions that target groups that do not conform to this norm – and, ironically, this constitutes the majority of people in society. But, due to the power of dominant thinking, it is perceived as a statistical norm rather than an ideological norm (Thompson, 2016), with the result that the *deviant* label is perceived as *common sense*.

Ideology not only defines what is *normal*, but also what is *natural*. Discriminatory ideas become embedded in the structures of society and accepted as *common sense*, so are not questioned (Thompson, 2016). The way in which biological or medical determinism is used to justify *normal* stereotypical roles in society (women as natural carers; black people as less intelligent; old people as feeble; disabled people as dependent) presents a false logic, what Thompson (2016) terms the *logic of discrimination*. These are powerful ideas, appealing to a *common sense* of what is normal and natural, which, in serving the interests of the *status quo*, not only subordinate, but diminish life chances by creating poverty, poor health and reduced opportunities. This terrain of ideological struggle is where prejudice, discrimination and oppression interact to weave power relationships into everyday lives. By locating the sites of prejudice and discrimination, we are also locating the most powerful points of intervention and transformation.

The first step in locating power and control is to understand the ways in which the legitimising of power is achieved. By this, I mean that prejudiced social attitudes reflect social divisions in society and help to reinforce them. *Prejudice* is an irrational thinking that primarily operates at a personal level, but reflects structural discrimination. It is often based on *stereotypes*, and works in a way that limits people's potential (as in the case of disabled or older people being treated as dependent, poor people and immigrants treated as scroungers, and so on), and at worst can be life-threatening (as in domestic violence and racist attacks). *Discrimination* defines the way in which *prejudice* is structured in society by powerful and privileged dominant groups exploiting and subordinating groups who are less powerful, and therefore less able to act in their own interests. *Oppression* refers to the subordination, marginalisation and exclusion from society of these groups, thereby denying them social justice, citizenship and full democratic rights to participate in society.

Empowerment is a term that can be applied simplistically. As Barr states (1995: 121–2), 'we need to be clear about the framework of reference within which we use the term because different agencies, and within them different actors, appear to have different expectations of empowerment and there is often a credibility gap between aspirations of communities and actual achievements'. This is explored further in the discussion of Thompson's PCS model below. In radical community development, empowerment is a consequence of critical consciousness, the ability to make connections by seeing power and control in action and the confidence to act collectively to bring about change.

Thompson's PCS model

An excellent model, which is widely used in community development practice, is Thompson's (2016) PCS model (Figure 6.1). Three concentric rings indicate the three levels of interaction that we have considered in our exploration of Gramsci: the *personal, cultural* and *structural*. The model is particularly helpful because it symbolises the ways in which these different levels mutually reinforce

Figure 6.1: The PCS model

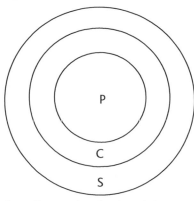

Source: Thompson (2016) with permission.

each other. Too often, analysis stops at the P-level – that of individual, personal prejudice. Challenging sexist comments, or even tackling the behaviour of racist groups in community, will never be enough to redress the problems of inequality in society. It will not even be enough to stem the tide of discrimination that constantly reinforces attitudes by permeating our thoughts and actions in the most subtle of ways.

Thompson, in a simple but effective way, embeds the P-level (the personal or psychological – a level of thoughts, feelings, attitudes, action and prejudice) at the centre of his model. Empowerment at this level involves: believing in people in order to foster self-belief; trusting in people in order to develop confidence and self-esteem; creating the opportunity for people to explore their stories, their histories, their experience in dialogue; deepening a sense of identity and personal autonomy. This is set within the C-level (that of the cultural, shared ways of seeing, thinking and doing – a level of community, commonalities, consensus and conformity). Empowerment at this level is influenced by Foucault's (1980) insights into power as discourse, as threaded through everyday conversations to convey meaning, assumptions and behaviour through the dynamics between language and social relationships. It is vital to know how this works if we are going to challenge and change the way that these assumptions reproduce the dominant power relations – related to class, race, patriarchy and white supremacy – that become so embedded in our cultural attitudes that they construct our reality, defining what is normal and acceptable and so come to frame our identities (Thompson, 2007). At the C-level, working in culture circles/community groups, people engage in dialogue that explores common experiences and builds a sense of connectedness and belonging. This, in turn, is set within the S-level (the structural level where social divisions are sewn into the fabric of society and oppression and discrimination become institutionalised – the socio-political power base) (Thompson, 2016). Structurally embedded in society is a hierarchy of power relations based on race, class and gender as central dimensions of power, but within this we also have to understand a complexity of other oppressions that intersect to greater or lesser degrees – age, disability, sexuality, religion, language, body, status, education … Critical consciousness is the form of empowerment that is needed for action at a structural level. Through a process of problematising, people begin to identify the complex nature of power that has created poverty and privilege, a living contradiction in a democracy, and has become embedded in the structures of society to be legitimised as *common sense*.

Each level indicated on the PCS model interacts with the others in ways that mutually reinforce prejudice and discrimination. This understanding is important. It indicates why it is impossible to counter oppression by targeting one level at the exclusion of the others. This dynamic is so powerful that it negates any action that fails to address the whole as a mutually reinforcing unity. In this way, individual prejudice can only be understood within the cultural context, which in turn needs to be made sense of in relation to the structural context. These levels can never be seen in isolation from one another, simply because they form an interactive dynamic that constantly maintains social divisions to serve the power relations in society. The PCS model offers an analysis that helps us to see the need for action to extend beyond community to address change at all levels, in order to bring about transformative social change.

Thompson's four types of power

In addition to the PCS levels of power, Thompson (2007) offers an analysis of four types of power: (1) power to; (2) power over; (3) power with; and (4) power within. The relevance of these to community workers is that they give us an insight into the nature of power on which to build theory in action, making interventions on all levels within all dimensions in order to work effectively with the concept of empowerment.

1. *'Power to'* can be understood as personal power to achieve our potential in life, and so is important for community development in understanding that self-esteem and self-belief are fundamental to the process of change. It links to Doyal and Gough's emphasis on personal autonomy as the foundation of collective action (see p 103). It helps us to understand how domination leads to a 'culture of silence' by diminishing self-esteem and pathologising poverty, that is, convincing people that their social status is due to their own failings. In this sense, 'power to' is vital to releasing the energy for change.
2. *'Power over'*, on the other hand, is related to relations of dominance and subordination that get acted out at structural, cultural and personal levels. These levels do not operate exclusively: they interact and reinforce, and that is why change has to take place at all levels before empowerment and equality will be cultural norms that replace disempowerment and inequality. The dominant ideas that are embedded in structural relations feed interpersonal attitudes and vice versa.
3. *'Power with'* is particularly important to the process of change. It implies not only solidarity among groups of people who identify with each other, but also alliances across difference in mutual commitment to change for the greater good for everyone. 'Power with' is central to collective action as a collective power that brings about more equality than any disconnected projects can achieve. It links local community projects to movements for change to bring about a better world for everyone.

4. *'Power within'* is a personal resilience that connects the individual to the collective. It is an inner dimension that is the basis of self-worth, dignity and self-respect, the very foundation of integrity, of mutual respect and equality, a dislocating of 'better than' or 'worse than' in order to create a world that is fair, just and equal. It embraces the confidence to act and take risks.

Power is reproduced on all these levels and in all these ways to legitimise knowledge that maintains domination and subordination. In the very language we use, dominant knowledge that reinforces power differentials is implicit in every encounter, in every spoken or written word, even in body language, which is speechless. However, these sites also provide the key to interventions that open the imagination to create counternarratives that challenge and replace dominant narratives. Foucault (1980) directs our attention to the way that power produces knowledge in discourses themselves, and the beginning of the process of empowerment for the community worker is to shift power from object to subject, from the known to the knower, from the pathologiser to the pathologised, as the basis for transformation.

Radical community development calls for anti-discriminatory practice to be set within the social, cultural and political context. The first step to this is an openness to exploring attitudes, values and beliefs in ways that are both critical and self-critical. Out of this comes the courage to experience challenge and a willingness to understand different ways of engaging with the world. We need to become 'border-crossers', that is, we have to let go of the cultural, theoretical and ideological parameters that enclose us and offer us the security of 'home', the familiar and the known. 'To move away from "home" is to question in historical, semiotic and structural terms how the boundaries and meanings of "home" are constructed in self-evident ways often outside of criticism' (Giroux, 1993: 179). Becoming 'homeless' in this sense is to shift to a space where life can be seen more critically, and possibilities for change can be explored. This is why creating contexts for critical debate in democratic public spaces is a vital concept for the community worker; by decontextualising the taken-for-grantedness of everyday life we see things from an altered perspective. From here we can focus on the individual in relation to the cultural and political context. And this is exactly what the PCS model, in all its simplicity, helps to locate: it is a structure that represents the embeddedness of discrimination at every level of society.

Making even more critical connections

The strength of the PCS model is that it takes community workers beyond a simplistic notion that we can change the world by challenging oppressive behaviour on a personal or even community level. It emphasises the importance of collective action beyond the boundaries of community, emphasising yet again that decontextualised from its political context nothing capable of radical change is ever going to come from community development. The limitations of this model are that it does not offer critical connections with the complex interweavings and intertwinings of oppressions in a multidimensional structure needed to move Gramscian/Freirean thinking from dichotomy into complexity. In relation to classroom teaching, Magda Lewis captures this complexity as follows:

> Pedagogical moments arise in specific context: the social location of the teacher and students; the geographic and historical location of the institutions in which they come together; the political climate within which they work; the personalities and personal profiles of the individuals in the classroom; the readings selected for the course; and the academic backgrounds of the students all come together in ways that create the specifics of the moment. (Lewis, 2000: 104)

Gramsci's contribution to action can be seen in the way that he refocuses our attention from the state to civil society and the way in which it serves the interests of the state. Community, in this analysis, is pivotal in the process of liberation – not only a site for critical education, but also a site for critical action. Gramsci's use of military terminology is unfortunate, but this should not detract from the conceptual insight it offers. He warned against a *war of manoeuvre*, a targeting of the state apparatus, in the first instance at least. Instead, he saw revolution as a process of consciousness rooted in popular adult education in the context of civil society. Gramsci's *war of position* involves linking all manner of social organisations in alliance, and, importantly, identifies a space for the role of social movements in this process (Mayo, 1999). Community work has always paid attention to networking and alliances, but we now need more complex levels of action. In globalised times, the dynamic between the local and the global challenges reflection and action that is preoccupied with neighbourhood as the definitive site of community work. The Occupy Movement, in this sense, can be seen as a movement of loose connections triggered into global action by social media, which then creates communities of solidarity as tent cities (see pp 130-1).

Gramscian and Freirean thought remain as relevant as ever if we re-vision the insights they offer within an analysis of diversity and biodiversity. 'Gramsci's specters are whispering to us, reminding us that the struggle ahead is a politics of passionate remembrance, of re-visiting anti-fascist struggles of the past, of recognizing the lessons embedded in history's dreams and nightmares, of moving forward into the new millennium with renewed hope and an optimism of the will' (McLaren et al, 1998: 30).

So, finally, let's move on to explore some practical possibilities for working in these ways in community.

Practical feminist approaches to dislocating oppression

Hustedde and King (2002) cite Dillard's feminist spirituality approach to individual and collective inner journeys to the soul, which help to dislocate prejudice that is held deep inside us. This is an inner rather than outer spirituality, one in which the concrete realities of our lives remain the focus of our attention: 'when individuals and communities go within they meet the violence and terror within themselves that they project on to others. We hate others because we can't face the enemy within; so we project that enemy onto people of other races and classes or other institutions and communities' (Hustedde and King, 2002: 341). The tools that they offer community development for undertaking this approach are based on story as a route to engaging community in self-inquiry and self- knowledge. 'the telling of a story slows the mind down and lets the story sink underneath the skin to reveal something of the spirit' (2002: 342). They also emphasise the importance of rituals to community as 'part of the search for who we are and the search for meaning as a community ... community rituals can provide stability and continuity and can promote a sense of solidarity and cohesion' (2002: 343). The process takes communities forward as the creators of their own futures.

They identify the following rituals as practice tools:

1. *Rituals of transition* create order out of the chaos of change. The Native American tradition of acknowledging seven generations of community takes the past–present–future dimension from solid historic connections through to marking change and planning directions for the future. This could be a valuable approach where family, community and tradition have gone through massive transitions. Another example they use is the Samoan Circle (developed by Lorenz Aggens in Chicago in 1970) where everyone is allowed to speak in turn in a safe, democratic listening environment, not led or chaired. This has been found to be effective if there are controversial issues to be tackled by a large group of people, as everyone has a stake in the success of the meeting. Conflict is more likely to be resolved because people are giving others their full attention.

2. *Rituals of healing* are based on empathy, compassion, forgiveness and justice. Community healing rituals can be used for reconciliation and dialogue. The authors give an example of the way that a unity candle was used in a public meeting in a community torn apart by land disputes and coal mining. The meeting opened with community leaders and coal mine operators symbolically lighting candles to indicate their willingness to talk, and then lighting one unity candle together to symbolise their desire to find a common resolution to their differences. This set the tone for cooperation as a value for healing divisions. Other examples include the Vietnam War Memorial in Washington and the AIDS quilt.

3. *Rituals of celebration* build on common solidarity and cohesion by expressing gratitude, joy and a sense of belonging. They focus on abundance rather than poverty, on strengths rather than weaknesses. Festivals celebrate the roots of a community, generating a sense of pride, confidence and belonging. They can also bring people from all walks of life together to learn and to negotiate differences.

Gramsci's pivotal relevance today

The main aim of this chapter is to revisit Gramsci, a Marxist thinker, in today's neoliberal context of extreme inequality. Paul Mason explains that Marx's interpretation of the prime purpose of human beings is to set themselves free, but the fundamental problem is that we embody our sense of self in objects or ideas. This is how Marx saw alienation: the fact that we allow external things to assert power over us, religions or superstitions, consumer goods, or mindlessly sticking to routines and disciplines we have created. 'The real goal of human history is individual freedom and self-realisation' (Mason, 2018): communism is not the goal of human history, it is simply a transient point that frees us from hierarchical organisation. Mason (2018: 29) asserts that it is Marx's faith in the individual that makes him a key thinker for the age of automation. The increasing development of robotics in the workplace, rather than being feared as a route to unemployment, could be a point at which we are freed from the demands of the market to pursue self-realisation in the name of a common good and a life worthy of human aspiration! (To develop this idea further, see Andrew Sayer on p 47.)

Gramsci's concept of *hegemony* is powerful in its simplicity, helping us to understand the power of ideas and the ways in which our minds are colonised unquestioningly by dominant attitudes using the power of persuasion and the control of coercion. This goes a long way to helping us understand the way in which stigma is such an effective and integral component of the neoliberal project (Tyler, 2013; 2015), and why George Eaton (2018) calls Gramsci the Marxist thinker for our times

Moving these ideas on, in the next chapter I want to engage with critiques that move us further towards the concept of *intersectionality* as a means of countering the neoliberal power we find ourselves up against today. We need sharper thinking and sharper action. This is because intersectionality transcends simple binary opposites, such as rich/poor, to embrace the interweaving, overlapping power relations of social injustice, cognitive injustice and environmental injustice, helping us to get to grips with their interlinking complexity for the urgency of our times. If these oppressions are all integral to the neoliberal project, our challenge is to stop being piecemeal and fragmented and grasp a counter-analysis fit for purpose, and this begins in critique.

HEGEMONY IS ACHIEVED WHEN WE SPEAK IN THE LANGUAGE OF THE DOMINANT CLASS AND SEE THROUGH THEIR EYES

IDEAS CREATE CHANGE

HEGEMONY

COERCION ⟷ CONSENT

STATE USES FORCE TO MAINTAIN DOMINANCE — ARMY, POLICE, PRISONS, LAW, COURTS

STATE USES IDEAS AND VALUES TO PERSUADE SUBORDINATE CLASSES TO CONSENT TO ITS DOMINANCE

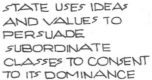

7

Critiques of Freire
and Gramsci

Critique and dissent are vital processes in deepening democracy. This chapter takes thinking from the class-based dichotomous analysis of Freire and Gramsci into critiques that are crucial for developing the relevance of their thinking for current times into our emerging understanding of intersectionality. I demonstrate the ways that making sense of the world through a dichotomous analysis reduces life experience to an either/or, 'this' or 'that', binary simplicity, which is only capable of defining something in relation to its 'Other' (for example, male/female, black/white, young/old). This denies the overlapping, intersecting reality of oppressions.

It was the predominant emphasis on a class analysis that subsumed women's experience within the working-class struggle. In turn, the same dichotomous thought blinkered white women to see women's experience only from a male/female analysis, overlooking the centrality of racism as an interlinking oppression (see Reni Eddo-Lodge in Chapter 2). Today, we are much more aware of the complex nature of oppressions, so, this is a good point at which to explore current challenges for community development theory and action:

> Freire's original work emphasized class while ignoring gender ... [he] did conceive his pedagogy in singular 'class terms' growing out of his experiences among peasants and workers in impoverished Brazil. Therefore, as feminist educators have proposed, his foundational work from forty years ago needs correction for a theme like gender, among others. Freire himself acknowledged this missing dimension; he also urged educators to avoid copying him and to develop pedagogy suitable for their local situation. (Shor, 2000: 6)

I begin my inquiry by relating it to my own community development practice. The period from the 1970s to the early 1990s was an inspiring time for community workers, which emerged from the optimism of the 1960s. 'Freirean and feminist pedagogies emerged at about the same time ... just after the activist 1960s, when dissent and participation were ideas whose time had come ... that legendary age of civil rights actions, student protests, anti-war campaigns ...' (Shor, 2000: 2). This was the birthing ground for new social movements and the time when Freire made a massive impact on emancipatory practice – including liberation theology, radical community development and human rights activism. Second-wave feminism, and other new social movements, emerged from grassroots dialogue and changed our understanding of the world – anti-racist, black women, green, lesbian and gay, disability, 'grey power' – and we began to stretch our minds from the limitations of either/or dichotomous thought, framed by Enlightenment's search for a single truth, into the complexities of difference and diversity.

Freirean pedagogy has been the biggest single influence on radical community development theory and practice in the UK from the early 1970s. Emphasising *dialogue* as a critical encounter between people, and the centrality of *praxis* in that process, Freire located theory in everyday experience. More than this, he helped community workers to understand that the practice of social justice is rooted in its ideology of equality. In this way, democratic values create a frame for the way we see the world, analyse experience of the world and challenge the world. Beginning with every encounter, we learnt that true reflection leads to action: that personal consciousness is the basis of collective action for change, but that 'action is human only when it is not merely an occupation but also a preoccupation, that is, when it is not dichotomized from reflection' (Freire, 1996: 35). This period saw community development redefine itself as a radical emancipatory praxis based on critical consciousness.

There was an immediate feminist backlash against Freirean pedagogy, initially because of his use of dominant male language in *Pedagogy of the Oppressed* (Freire, 1970). Since then the feminist critique has developed a wider analytic perspective, which offers insight into the limitations of Freire and the benefits of a feminist re-visioning of his work. Freirean pedagogy and feminist pedagogy have had a rocky ride in relation to one another, but they have much in common. Beneath the surface of commonalities lies a tangled web of what Shor terms 'conflict and convergence' (2000: 3), and it is that web that I want to explore here.

Freire and feminism

> The desire for transformation and the critique of inequality are …
> common ground shared by Freire-based critical pedagogy and feminist
> pedagogy, two dissident schools of thought with a close and troubled
> relationship in recent years. (Shor, 2000: 2)

I have been profoundly influenced and inspired, in theory and practice, by Paulo Freire, and I witness the ways in which he continues to have that same impact on practitioners in community development today. I want to begin this critique by exploring why a Brazilian man should continue to attract feminist attention.

Feminist pedagogy, like Freirean pedagogy, is founded on grassroots education for critical consciousness as a tool for understanding the nature of structural oppression. Crucial to this understanding is an awareness that emancipatory potential lies in collective action for change for a just and sustainable world. Feminist and Freirean pedagogies converge in their fundamental assumption that dominant ways of knowing need challenging, and that all people have a basic human right to be valued and active in their world. Freire, in offering a praxis of liberation that involves an understanding of the nature of oppression, the process of *conscientisation*, and the importance of culture and history in the struggle for transformative change, complements feminism. Feminist pedagogy diverges from Freire, however, in its challenge to patriarchy as a fundamental oppressive structure that echoes through women's lives everywhere, complexified by difference.

Feminism has had a powerful influence on community development. The ways in which women at grassroots level have demonstrated that *the personal is political* have been transformative for both theory and practice. Prior to this, women's experience, in the home and community, was seen as 'soft' and apolitical. These altered perspectives led to an analysis of the way in which the public/private divide has oppressed women for generations by creating the myth that politics stops at the parameters of our communities, and certainly at the thresholds of our homes. Let us apply this thinking to a practical issue. This way of seeing things was so deeply entrenched in the public psyche that such injustices as the police refusing to intervene in incidents of domestic violence led to women being denied the protection that was their human right. The women's refuge movement, pioneered by Erin Pizzey in the 1970s, shunted domestic violence into public awareness. Yet, domestic violence remains a worldwide violation of human rights, transcending all aspects of cultural diversity. In 1990, in my practice in Hattersley, Janice came to see me. "My ex-husband came to the house and started knocking me around. I managed to get him out and lock the door, but I was terrified for my life, so I called the police. They took me seriously until I gave them my Hattersley address: 'If you live there you must be an old slag, and you're getting no more than you deserve!' and they put the phone down on me." These are the types of experience that feminists challenge as hidden-from-view by a class analysis.

In these ways, we begin to understand why, despite Freire's compatibility with second-wave feminism's emphasis on the personal as political, he received harsh criticism from feminists. His pedagogy is based on a universal analysis (oppressor/oppressed) that denies the complexity of different experiences of oppression. The sexist language of his early work was also seized on as evidencing an unconsciously gendered approach to his pedagogy. His response was that *Pedagogy of the Oppressed* needs to be set in its historical and cultural context. It cannot be read as if it were written yesterday and retrospectively criticised, with the benefit of hindsight, using conceptual tools that were not available at the time it was written (Freire and Macedo, 1993). The influences of postmodernism and an increased understanding of *difference* challenged the assumptions of metanarratives that are based on a universal, collective perspective as reducing the nature of lived experience to a naively simplistic unity. A theory of liberation that glosses over divisions in society, attempting to universalise experience shaped by gender, race, ethnicity, age, sexuality, disability … entrenches those divisions still further.

bell hooks poses an interesting contradiction. She states that Freire offered her a structure within which she could define her own experience of racism on a global level, when 'the radical struggle of Black women to theorize our subjectivity' was not welcomed by early, white, bourgeois feminist thinkers (hooks, 1993:

151). hooks refers to Freire's 'blind spot' to questions of gender, and his failure to acknowledge the specific gendered nature of oppression. Nevertheless, she honours the way that his pedagogy gave her the conceptual tools with which to analyse her own oppression as a black American woman, helping her to see herself as a subject in resistance. These themes are developed in Chapter 8.

Freire emphasises that we all have a right and a duty to participate in the transformation of society because the struggle belongs to us all, wherever its specific location. He emphasises that his pedagogy is not universal, that it emerged from his own experience, and needs to be adapted for other contexts. Engaging in different cultural contexts, in a climate of political change, calls for critical questioning as the basis of an ongoing analysis. Freire was clear that giving answers, rather than asking questions, is 'the castration of curiosity' (Freire and Faundez, 1992: 35). hooks challenges feminist thinkers who separate feminist pedagogy from Freirean pedagogy: 'For me these two experiences converge.... I have taken threads of Paulo's work and woven it into that version of feminist pedagogy I believe my work as a writer and teacher embodies' (hooks, 1993: 150).

Feminist pedagogy, like Freirean pedagogy, places everyday stories at the heart of the process of critical consciousness. The notion that the deeply personal is profoundly political leads to a critical understanding of the nature of structural oppression, and the way that we are shaped in all our difference by structures of power that permeate our lives. By exploring the political nature of everyday encounters, we move towards the critical consciousness necessary to demystify the dominant hegemony and to change oppressive structures.

In much the same way as feminists challenged the universality of Freire's theory, black feminists challenged white feminist analysis on grounds of difference. In other words, white feminists stood accused of defining 'woman' from a generic male/female perspective, which overlooked racism as a major structural oppression. This is typical of the limited binary thinking that epitomises Western ideological thought. Stereotypes, or controlling images, mystify the nature of social relations and confound the ways in which race, class and gender intersect with each other. These images are 'key in maintaining interlocking systems of race, class and gender oppression' (Hill Collins, 1990: 68).

Western consciousness, in its 'despiritualisation of the universe' (Richards, 1980, cited by Hill Collins, 1990: 70), required the separation of the 'knowing self' from the 'known object' in preparation for a materialised world based on profit and exploitation. Inevitably, in a subject/object analysis, those who are seen as 'Other' are subordinated to 'object' because their reality is named by those who have the power to locate themselves as 'subject'. This power relationship dehumanises people as malleable objects rather than subjects in control of their own lives (Freire, 1972). In our unravelling of the nature of oppressions, it is easy to see how readily we fall into the trap of this dichotomy at successive stages of our understanding. Criticising the universality of Freire, second-wave feminism failed itself by overlooking the different experience of black women. We need to *problematise* power, not only powerlessness, in the struggle for liberation.

By tracing the limitations of dichotomous thought, based on oppositional difference, we come to realise it achieves a hierarchy of fragmentation: an incompleteness held together by relationships of superiority/inferiority. Within this concept, 'as the "Others" of society who can never really belong, strangers threaten the moral and social order. But they are simultaneously essential for its survival because those individuals who stand at the margins of society clarify its boundaries' (Hill Collins, 1990: 68). Hill Collins suggested that African-American women stand at the convergence of a series of the inferior halves of these dichotomies and that this is central to the understanding of their subordination (Hill Collins, 1990).

Angela Davis vividly captured the dangers of dichotomous thought in relation to the way that class can fragment black women's activism:

> Black women scholars and professionals cannot afford to ignore the straits of our sisters who are acquainted with the immediacy of oppression in a way many of us are not. The process of empowerment cannot be simplistically defined in accordance with our own particular class interests. We must learn to lift as we climb. (Davis, 1989: 9)

In these ways, feminism, as a political movement, powerfully placed patriarchy as an oppressive force alongside that of class. However, because its analysis was dichotomous, it fell into the trap of seeing 'woman' as a unitary category in relation to its 'Other', 'man', as if all women had the same experience in relation to ethnicity, class and culture. This is not a simple oversight. It represents a struggle of consciousness that, in focusing on this essentialist analysis of patriarchy, fails to offer an adequate explanation of the complex oppressions that construct female identities, including historical and cultural dimensions of gender relations. The endemic racism of white feminism not only failed to recognise the anti–racist struggle as central to feminism, but also overlooked the way it pathologised black people in relation to sexuality and family relations (Anthias and Yuval-Davis, 1992).

So, while Freire was criticised for not dealing with the specific nature of the subordination of women within a class analysis, white feminists stood accused of failing to engage with racism within a feminist analysis. The assumption of a universal sisterhood rendered black women invisible. This ethnocentric approach overlooked cultural and historic relations, and in its preoccupation with the male/female dichotomy became oblivious of the hegemonic white, female, often middle–class focus (Anthias and Yuval-Davis, 1992). Critique is essential to unpacking the complex interactions of race, class and gender and other aspects of difference, otherwise we move from one form of fragmented consciousness to another. We are now challenged to take feminism, with its commitment to flourishing people in a flourishing world, into intersectionality, with a particular focus on white privilege and its enduring capacity to resist change.

Reflecting on the process of my own consciousness, I am aware that I owe my altered perceptions of social reality to Freire. His pedagogy equipped me with the conceptual tools necessary for my own struggle, and in turn this gave me the confidence to grapple with understandings that were outside my own specific experience. In this respect, bell hooks (1993: 148) says that while Freire adopted a 'phallocentric paradigm of liberation – wherein freedom and the experience of patriarchal manhood are always linked as though they are one and the same', his profound conceptual insights cannot be rejected. Without his help in deepening my own understanding of *praxis* in the process of change, it is likely that I would have remained ignorant of just how necessary it is that 'our lives must be a living example of our politics' (hooks, 1993: 148).

> Words seem not [to] be good enough to evoke all that I have learned from Paulo. Our meeting had that quality of sweetness that lingers, that lasts for a lifetime, even if you never speak to the person again, see their face, you can always return in your heart to that moment when you were together and be renewed – that is a profound solidarity. (hooks, 1993: 154)

Despite the range of criticism that Freire generates among feminists, we continue to be moved by his visionary humanity, humans as subjects making our own history. The essence of feminist critiques of Freire is that he did not understand the complex nature of patriarchal, white privilege or the complexities of overlapping, intersecting oppressions (Weiler, 2001).

Freire and class

Lockhart (1999: 92) claims that there is no evidence that Freirean pedagogy is capable of transformative social change, that he was 'always more important in terms of educational method than "revolutionary futurity"'. This is a position hotly contested by Paula Allman (1999), who attributes the dilution of Freire's potential to the way he is often reduced to a technique by pedagogues; we cannot be partially Freirean, she warns (see Chapter 4).

Allman (1999, 2001, 2009, 2010) and McLaren (2000) both challenge the potential of a critical pedagogy that is based on reformism, within rather than against the existing structures of society, and they emphasise that Freirean concepts disjointed from the whole pedagogy simply give the illusion of addressing capitalist social relations, 'a limited praxis ... that simply reproduces the given social relations' (Allman, 2009: 419). However:

> ... reform, and struggling for it, is crucial both because we must attempt to make life more palatable for those suffering the harshest consequences of capitalism and because we must try to forestall environmental collapse. But it is also important as well as essential

> because it is through and within the struggles for reform – the shop floor, the community, the environment or any other site where the ramifications of capitalism are experienced – that critical revolutionary praxis develops. (Allman, 2001: 139)

McLaren warns of setting class relations against cultural insights, and advocates a re-reading of Marx with the insights of identity politics if we are to attain any coherent theoretical challenge to globalisation. Knowledge, he says, is transformed through an epistemological critique, which not only examines the content of knowledge, but also the way in which we produce and reproduce that knowledge. He calls for greater collective links between critical educators and students, community activists and the people, to come together in a dialogical relationship in the process of collective action for social change, in praxis.

Paula Allman (2001, 2010) poses some crucial questions for our time. How does capitalism seduce us into accepting massive contradictions of suffering and excess as natural and inevitable? How has it managed to win widespread consent at the same time as creating a culture of constant discontent? Her thesis is that a Marxist analysis provides the most complete interpretation of the nature of capitalism, and that the greatest barriers to our understanding remain a misinterpretation of Marx's work. Praxis, for her, embraces all thought and action, not merely the application of theory to practice. Uncritical praxis has the potential for reproducing the conditions for capital to flourish; critical praxis has the infinite possibility to transform our engagement with the world. By exposing the ways in which global capitalism has been internalised and integrated into everyday subjective awareness, we thus begin a process that becomes ever critical and self-critical.

Both McLaren's and Allman's arguments are based on the premise that we remain uncritical as long as our practice relocates us within the same social relations of power. Praxis only assumes its critical potential when we become aware that ideological statements are partial truths that, in turn, partially distort the truth they are based on, thus reducing our understanding at the same time as convincing us that the version of reality they portray is the real truth. Capitalism, Allman stresses, cannot be reformed; the only way forward is a new worldview founded on justice, both within humanity and between humanity and the natural world. The fundamental role of critical education in this process is in *problematising* reality, constantly probing into how we know and feel. While acknowledging the contribution of the 'new antagonists' – environmentalists, feminists, human rights organisations and other new social movements – she claims that these can do no more than shake capitalism. Her criticism is that some of our finest minds remain trapped within the parameters of capitalism and liberal democracy.

According to Allman, critical pedagogy that has transformative potential needs to be informed by Marx's theory of consciousness, in which principled ethics of compassion and social justice reach out in a form of social interdependence based on a re-reading of class relations. She envisages collective action for change in the form of an international alliance. This strategy is based on an analysis of the way that capitalism cleaves social divisions based on racism, homophobia, environmental destruction, gender disparity and so forth, and so recognises that capitalism is the common enemy, that oppression has a common core. From grassroots organisations, she sees this alliance gradually growing into a global movement (Allman, 2001, 2010). Think about Allman's point in relation to the EU and the demise of the nation state (discussed by Dasgupta, 2018, and examined earlier, in Chapter 1 on pp 35–6).

Paula Allman, until her death in 2011, worked tirelessly for social transformation, and her insight into capitalism as the common core of all oppressions takes us into the context we struggle to analyse today. We have failed to develop a critical praxis capable of halting neoliberalism in its tracks and its devastation and degradation continue. This is precisely why I refer you to my selected intellectual activists – Mendoza, Sayer, Dorling, Wilkinson and Pickett, Tyler, Monbiot, Klein, Eddo-Lodge, Raworth, Lowrey, Hall and Tandon, and Bregman – to add to the eclectic body of community development theory by collectively: (a) offering incisive critiques of advanced neoliberalism and the ascendance of the New Right within which practice must be contextualised; thereby (b) shocking us out of the 'coma' we have created for ourselves (Bregman, 2016) and triggering our imaginations to see that a new social order is possible at this point of crisis; (c) based on the overt naming of different values as the basis for counternarratives in the process of change.

Freire was always very clear that his pedagogy needed to be adapted to, not superimposed on, different political and cultural contexts. Any pedagogy can only be as effective as the integrity and vigilance of its practitioners. While we need to be critical in re-visioning Freire in relation to our rapidly changing world and our equally rapidly changing understanding, maybe we also need to get better at practising Freire. Arguably, we are all inextricably trapped in our experience of the world, struggling for an uncluttered, unambiguous clarity. While the criticisms levelled at Freirean thought should be taken seriously, they also give it increased strength. As we push beyond the parameters of the dichotomous thinking that formed Freire's worldview, we are beginning to grapple at the edges of complexity, and develop his pedagogy in accordance with these new awarenesses.

> It is precisely his refusal to spell out in a 'bag of tricks' fashion alternative solutions that enables his work to be re-invented in the contexts in which his readers find themselves, thereby enjoining a contextually specific translation across geographic, geopolitical, and cultural borders. It also grants to Freire's corpus of works a universal character, as they are able to retain their heuristic potency (much like the works of Marx) such that they can be conscripted by educators to criticize and to counterpoint pedagogical practices worldwide. In fact, Freire urged his readers to reinvent him in the context of their local struggles. (McLaren, 2000: 164)

Gramsci and Foucault and the microaggressions of everyday life

Gramsci's significance is profound in the search for an understanding of the subtle nature of power reaching from the state not only into civil society but directly into people's minds. Foucault – even though he is associated with post-structuralism and postmodernism – adds to rather than detracts from Gramsci's analysis by suggesting that power is everywhere, not only on a mega-level of state and at the local level of civil society but permeating the micro-relationships of everyday life. As with Gramsci, he sees knowledge and power as inseparable, and this adds to community development's emphasis on critical consciousness as a liberating process, placing critical education at the heart of change and connecting with knowledge democracy as a crucial component of liberation. Foucault, like Gramsci, is preoccupied with how people become the conscious subjects of history by intellectual emancipation, and by this I mean that by questioning our lived experience we expose the contradictions we live by, and by seeing the world through a different lens, we claim back our power as subjects in the world. Once again, it reminds us that the key to unlocking grassroots action for change lies in freeing the mind from the chains of *false consciousness* that persuade us to be passive objects in the world to become 'self-determining agents that resist and challenge power structures' (Danaher et al, 2000: 150). Foucault has been embraced into the evolving body of literature that searches for an analysis of power for critical praxis to help us to understand the ways in which a social hierarchy is constructed through power/knowledge relations and reinforced in everyday encounters. Some have the privilege to assert a truth as a statement of power; others accept its truth and transmit it. This is a cumulative process, reinforcing power structures at street level (Giroux, 2009). 'For Foucault, power comes from everywhere, from above and from below; it is "always already there" and is inextricably implicated in micro-relations of domination and resistance' (McLaren, 2009: 72). This calls on us to identify the ways in which power embedded in classed, racialised and gendered relations becomes reinforced in the practices and discourses of everyday life as microaggressions.

> Power must be analyzed as something which circulates, or rather as something which only functions in the form of a chain. It is never localized here or there…. Power is employed and exercised through a net-like organization. (Foucault, 1980: 98)

In these ways, power is 'an active process constantly at work on our bodies, our relationships, our sexuality, as well as on the ways we construct knowledge and meaning in the world' (Darder et al, 2009: 7). Power is embodied in the self, as well as embedded in society, not only out there in structures of domination, but also in sites of resistance interacting within the relationships of those who claim to be on the same side. Importantly, Foucault identifies the dangers of a society that 'neither questions itself nor can imagine any alternative to itself … [feeding]

… the growing ineptitude, if not irrelevance, of (in)organic and traditional intellectuals whose cynicism often translates into complicity with the forms of power they condemn' (Giroux, 2009: 177).

Thinking of power in this way, rather than only a polarity between the state and civil society, we are more able to see how dominant ideology reaches into the processes of life permeating people's relationships in every interaction, influencing attitudes, identities and perceptions (Foucault, 1980). For instance, when my younger son Duncan's black British friend Owen came to stay with us after our move from culturally diverse Manchester to predominantly white Lancaster, I asked him how he found it. "The gaze lingers for just a little bit too long," he said. It lingers, of course, just long enough to make a statement of 'Other' as part of the myriad microaggressions that are part of daily life. Power relations, according to Foucault, are acted out in all our practices – educational, scientific, religious, legal – that embed dominant discourse in their processes.

'Critical educators argue that *praxis* (informed actions) must be guided by *phronesis* (the disposition to act truly and rightly). This means, in critical terms, that actions and knowledge must be directed at eliminating pain, oppression, and inequality, and at promoting justice and freedom' (McLaren, 2009: 74). As McLaren points out, *empowerment* means not only setting the learning context for participants to understand the world around them, but also to find the courage to speak truth to power, as Quakers would say. This is what Freire meant by denunciation. We need to be able to understand power in order to denounce it, and by denouncing it we create an interruption in *what is*, a space in which to build new possibilities for *what could be*. In these ways, much as Gramsci redefined *hegemony* to include power as ideological persuasion, not simply coercion, so Foucault argues that we must direct our attention from a concentration on the role of the state and the institutions of civil society to include the micro-levels of social interaction.

> Hegemonic or global forms of power rely in the first instance on those 'infinitesimal' practices, composed of their own particular techniques and tactics, which exist in those institutions on the fringes or at the micro-level of society. (Foucault, 1980: 99)

These analyses give us a better idea of what form power takes in different contexts and at different levels, and how community development needs to engage with each appropriately.

Kothari (2001), Craig et al (2008) and Darder et al (2009) warn of the dangers to any liberatory practice of simplifying the nature of power. Kothari says that while we fail to see knowledge as an accumulation of norms, rituals and practices that are embedded in power relations, we fall back on simplistic dichotomies of power, and change nothing. Gary Craig (2008) warns that an inability to analyse power at policy and personal levels has led to an inability to understand racism or multicultural societies, so that issues of social justice, culture and identity constantly get swept under the carpet. Darder et al (2009) note that there was a point at which postmodernism threatened to fragment understanding of major structures of power by reducing critical theory to a disconnected whole while 'advanced capitalism whipped wildly around the globe, [consolidating] the neoliberal effort to perpetuate structures of economic domination and exploitation' (Darder et al, 2009, pp 16-17). As I address in other parts of this book, within a multiplicity of power relations that get acted out on all levels, race, class and gender remain crucial overarching sources of oppression and exploitation. But, without getting to grips with intersectionality, and the way that power intersects all oppressions, we not only reduce the social justice intention of our practice, but, much worse, we also unwittingly reinforce the *status quo*.

Gramsci and feminism

Capitalism and patriarchy are interrelated systems of oppression, and the view that feminism is less important than class or even divisive of class has been a contentious issue. Here, I will explore the invisibility of male power to Gramsci in an investigation of the contradictions between his intellectual and personal/emotional understanding of power relations. Paradoxically, yet unsurprisingly, Gramsci owed his personal sustenance during his prison years, and the survival of his contribution to thought in the form of his *Prison Notebooks*, to his sister-in-law, Tatiana Schucht, yet any political analysis of her 11 years of commitment to him was overlooked by Gramsci. Holub (1992: 195) reminds us that we should not 'assiduously polish the tainted mirrors of theoretical heroes'. By the same token, it is equally important not to dismiss significant contributions to the development of our own thought, as women, out of hand. We need to engage with this paradox. As with Freire, Gramsci's thinking was historically and culturally specific, and it is therefore hardly surprising that it fell foul of the public/private divide. His thinking did not benefit from the coherent feminist awareness that has developed over the last few decades. The deep affection and admiration he felt for his mother, his sister Teresina, his wife Giulia and his sister-in-law Tatiana are well documented and undisputed (Kenway, 2001). Paradoxically, Gramsci accepted as 'natural' the roles of the women in his personal life without recognising their political implications.

However, there is a glimpse that he was aware at some deeper level of the complex subordination of women. In 1916, Gramsci's first public address was on the emancipation of women 'taking as his cue Ibsen's play "A Doll's House"' (Hoare and Smith, in Introduction to Gramsci, 1971: xxxi). In his discussion of Americanism and Fordism he not only acknowledges women's exploitation in the public domain, but also recognises women's vital function in the reproduction of the workforce, thereby identifying sexuality as a locus of oppression. However, 'although Gramsci supported women's rights and saw sexuality as a basic aspect of emancipation, women's issues were not central to his thought' (Kenway, 2001: 56). Holub, too, points to an inherent contradiction in his thinking from a feminist perspective: 'Gramsci insists on the centrality of sexuality, a woman's rights over her body, when it comes to the emancipation not only of women, but of society as a whole', but this is contradicted by the way his analysis is limited to 'the need to discipline women's sexuality for economic and political purposes' (Holub, 1992: 197–8).

By gaining insight into the subtle ways in which power transcends the divide from public to private through the institutions of civil society – religion, education, the family and other forms of daily life – Gramsci offers understanding of the ways in which domination permeates the most intimate aspects of our being, transcending the public/private divide. This is the basis for Gramsci's acknowledged contribution to feminist thought through his concept of hegemony, which has provided a tool of analysis for understanding the sites of gendered oppression in society. Feminists have found the concept of hegemony to be a powerful conceptual tool. For instance, Arnot in the early 1980s argued that male hegemony consists of a multiplicity of moments that have persuaded women to accept a male-dominated culture and their subordination within it. The result is a constructed reality that is qualitatively different from that of men (Kenway, 2001). In understanding the nature of consent, we come to see that hegemony is always in process, in continuous struggle, and we begin to see that feminist consciousness has grown through questioning the nature of consent in relation to women's lives.

Holub's (1992: 197) interpretation of Gramscian feminism is that Gramsci saw economic independence as only part of the story; true emancipation involves freedom of choice in relation to sexual relationships. What he referred to as a 'new ethic' is the transformative moment gained from a war of position that frees women in a truly liberatory way. Gramsci's feminist consciousness therefore connects women's sexual rights not only with women's liberation, but with the total transformation of society. Gramsci in this sense gives us a model of the way in which the *personal* is fundamentally *political*. Disappointingly, though, he loses credibility by calling for a sexual discipline that serves the economy:

> So the promising concessions Gramsci makes to the liberation of feminine sexuality are severely curtailed by his deterministic view of progress, his belief in the liberatory potential of industrialisation and above all his uncritical deployment, indeed, his 'forgetting', of one of his own powerful analytical tools in the demystification of power: the ubiquitous operations of hegemony, of certain ways of seeing and validating relations in multiple sites of political and social relations, in the public, but above all in the private sphere, in political, but above all in civil society, in the social, in the cultural, in the micro-spaces of everyday life. (Holub, 1992: 198)

Here is a story from practice, from the micro-spaces of life where community development works to protect women who are abused by the dominant hegemony. A young community worker, Delaram Ali, talks about her participatory practice in reducing high-risk behaviours among female sex workers in Iran in 2013.

Performance was the key we were looking for

My story dates back to five years ago, when we were trying to carry out some activities to prevent high-risk sexual behaviours among a group of women with a background of drug abuse and sex work (in which some were still involved), in one of the high-risk southern neighbourhoods of Tehran.

We started by weekly gatherings in 'Khane Khorshid',[1] a Drop-in Centre (DIC) in the neighbourhood, to discuss what high-risk sexual behaviour means, how it is experienced by sexual workers and how it could be prevented or reduced. Using participatory methods, our meetings began with seven or eight participants, including me as the facilitator trying to encourage greater involvement from the attendees, as well as encouraging more people to join the group. These group discussions continued for about nine months and attracted up to 18 participants.

In the process ideas emerged, became polished and resulted in new forms of practice. One of these, which aimed at reducing high-risk behaviours among sex workers in the community, was to launch a peer outreach initiative in the neighbourhood. It took about two months for the group to agree an exact outline of the scope and limits of the project. In the meantime, we noted that World AIDS Day (1 December) was near. Thus the group, as its first activity, decided on holding an event for this occasion in the Drop-in Centre in order to both introduce participants to the ways of preventing high-risk behaviours and to get them interested in joining the project and expanding the group.

So we continued planning the event, until finally it was decided to choose a presenter from amongst ourselves, to hold a competition to enhance the knowledge of the participants about high-risk sexual behaviours, to perform a short play, and finally to sing and dance together.

Four members of the group volunteered to write and perform the play. Their choice was a musical, and it took them ten days to write and practise the lyrical dialogues. The play was about a sex worker waiting for customers on the street who finally chooses one of the passers-by and gets in his car. The man insists on offering more money for sex without a condom, but the woman persistently argues against such an offer. Eventually, having reached no agreement, she gets out of the car and leaves the man behind.

On World AIDS Day, our performers, all women, did each other's make-up to take on male and female roles with much excitement, while they also feared that they might forget their lines. But, on the whole, although they did forget some lines (and were helped by other members' whispering!) their performance was great and very well received. The audience really enjoyed the show and for a long time everybody in the centre talked about it and repeated the slogans. The show was effective in recruiting new volunteers for the group and, before long, these newcomers performed another play. The original play was also performed in other Drop-in Centres to the warm reception of the audiences.

After a year working together, this performance helped us recognise different abilities in ourselves: how we could write, be satirical, and act in a play. It showed us how, by translating our experiences into a play and sharing it with others, we could intrigue and encourage them to get involved.

Later on, together we also launched the peer outreach initiative and did much more in our two years of activity. Yet we knew well that performance was the prime key in helping us tell our stories in new ways, it opened the doors to new people and created an unforgettable experience.

[1] Khane Khorshid (House of Sun) is a well-known Drop-in Centre in Tehran, established in 2007 by Leila Arshad, a social worker and women's rights activist, providing services for abused women. The scope of the service has since expanded to include street children/workers.

(Source: Delaram Ali's story translated into English from Persian by Manizheh Najm Araghi. See also Maaref-vand (2016), *Evidence-based Intervention in Social Works*, which we hope to be available in English.)

~~~~~~

So, while Gramsci helps us to understand that without consent the whole nature of domination is weakened, it has taken Foucault to illuminate the ways in which power permeates these nooks and crannies of everyday existence. This understanding of power extending from state to civil society to the micro-spaces of life helps us frame our analyses for action.

Patti Lather in her work in the mid-1980s drew on Gramsci's notion of the *war of position* and the role of the *intellectuals* in relation to feminist political action. She chooses to substitute 'counter-hegemony' for 'struggle', inasmuch as it puts the emphasis on ideological alternatives, fitting in well with what I have said about shifting our focus from critique to counternarratives for a new social order based on values of cooperation and connection. Lather takes Gramsci's belief in everyone's innate capacity to be philosophers and considers this in relation to the way that women have documented experience-based knowledge and acted to become prominent in all social institutions, claiming that this constitutes a *war of position*: 'many small revolutions ... many small changes in relationships, behaviors, attitudes and experiences' (Lather, cited in Kenway, 2001: 59). She places particular emphasis on the role of the intellectuals in the tide of developing critical consciousness, but raises a note of warning about the need to stay critical, vigilant and self-questioning. Jane Kenway (2001) calls for a renewed Gramscian perspective from which we could engage with the big issues of our times, but Peter Mayo points out that 'one has to go beyond Gramsci to avoid Eurocentrism and beyond both Gramsci and Freire to avoid patriarchal bias' (Mayo, 1999: 146). However, together Gramsci and Freire present a profundity of thought that offers us the basis for a critical approach to community development. 'And where they relate most clearly is in Freire's consideration of the political nature of education and in Gramsci's consideration of the educational nature of politics' (Allman, 1988: 92). Our responsibility is to wrestle with these ideas with the privilege of our new understandings.

We must hold this vision in a past–present–future dynamic, 'moving between present and past with a view to contributing towards a transformed future' (Mayo, 1999: 147). Throughout their radical past, Freire and Gramsci have inspired community development and popular education. The critiques explored in this chapter, linked to the body of thought summarised in Chapter 2, provides a foundation of knowledge for a new possibility for radical community development praxis. (For a fuller discussion of Gramsci and feminism, see Ledwith, 2010.)

Social justice, environmental justice and sustainability

> Unless development leads to greater equality, environmentally sound outcomes, and improved opportunities for human growth it cannot meet the goals of sustainable development. (Gamble and Weil, 1997: 220)

The eco-pedagogy movement grew out of discussions at the Earth Summit in Rio de Janeiro in 1992, extending Freire's 'love for all life' from diversity to biodiversity. Since Freire's death, the race into a headlong environmental disaster has magnified to the point that, 'just as there is now a socio-ecological crisis of serious proportions, there is also a crisis in environmental education over what must be done about it' (Kahn, 2009: 526). Kahn calls for a radical eco-pedagogy, a plan for action that reconstructs and re-dreams our educational institutions to play a part in social and ecological change, getting our feet in the door: 'let's storm the entrance and let love live! It is one thing to do in these desperate times … it could mean the difference between today's rage and tomorrow's hope' (Khan, 2009: 538). The knowledge democracy movement is trying to get its foot in the door of our educational institutions to revolutionise what we understand as knowledge, but radical eco-pedagogy must be integrated into the emergence of knowledges …

From an environmental justice perspective, Freire and the Freirean movement stand accused of neglecting both globalisation and the environmental crisis (Bowers and Apffel-Marglin, 2004). The argument is that Freire's emphasis on critical consciousness in relation to class liberation, most particularly through literacy, is founded on Western assumptions that prioritise humanity, freedom and empowerment through dialogue over subordinated indigenous belief systems that are founded on biodiversity, with claims that critical pedagogy 'fractures knowledge and supports the further alienation of human beings from nature' (Darder et al, 2009: 17). These critiques have sharpened our understanding of the inextricable relationship between social justice and environmental justice. Community development has embraced this understanding and now overtly claims to be predicated on principles of social and environmental justice. The Paulo Freire Institute for Ecopedagogy is committed to 'the construction of a planetary citizenship, so that all, with no exception or exclusion, may have healthy conditions, in a planet able to offer life because its own life is being preserved' (Darder et al, 2009: 18). In this way, ecopedagogy embraces all forms of life on earth in diversity and biodiversity as a love for all life. Paulo Freire was working on ecopedagogy when he died, and some of these ideas are included in his posthumous *Pedagogy of Indignation* (2005).

Other examples of Freire's ongoing influence on early action for social and environmental justice and the connectedness between community, empowerment and sustainability include Blewitt's (2008) work under the banner of 'The Converging World', a charity which links people to address education, poverty and environment developed by local, community-led sustainability groups in a process of action and reflection towards a movement for change. This all started off in 2004 with the Coffeehouse Challenges, which gained inspiration from the coffee shops of 18th-century London which were the context for critical dialogue on big issues as the basis of action.

 ## Coffeehouse Challenges

A series of meetings held in a Bristol branch of Starbucks – ironically – led to a series of coffeehouse conversations in the nearby village of Chew Magna looking at how residents wanted their community to develop and how they could move towards a zero-waste society. One person who was a common denominator in both processes gathered support in the village, and each time they met numbers grew:

> The first response was surprising – something had tapped deeply into the consciousness of the local population and had released energy. Not only were people concerned, even anxious, but it was apparent that they were keen to make something happen. When, one evening, more than forty people turned up, it was too late to stop the momentum and soon four groups formed to take action. (Roderick with Jones, 2008: 18–19)

Freire has been accused of failing to understand the ecological crisis the world faces because he emphasises poverty in relation to capitalism and its economic domination in the process of globalisation. Ecological thought emphasises that diverse indigenous cultures live in harmony with their natural environments. Cultural diversity thus becomes essential for biological diversity, and histories based on local economic development offer alternatives for the future that reflect values other than consumer lifestyles: a harmonious co-existence between social justice and environmental justice.

Gamble and Weil were early commentators on the necessity of understanding the interconnection between community development and environmental justice because:

> the concept of sustainable development now functions as a unifying concept in several ways. It connects local and global perspectives; it provides a focus on protection of both the physical environment and human populations; it imposes a long-term view of the consequences of present-day activities; it can serve the goals of gender equity; and it provides a way effectively to integrate social and economic development. (Gamble and Weil, 1997: 211)

They cite Estes' seven fundamental concepts as a frame for analysis and action:

a. the unity of humanity and life on earth
b. the minimisation of violence
c. the maintenance of environmental quality
d. the satisfaction of minimum world welfare standards
e. the primacy of human dignity
f. the retention of diversity and pluralism
g. universal participation.

Riordan, in her essay on adapting to climate change in Africa, warns that the absence of a gender analysis 'can obscure the gap between having a stake in environmental protection and the capacity to act on it. Some essential differences in the way in which men and women typically organise environmental action (usually formal among men, informal among women) can be missed ... [leading] to a failure to identify the constraints that women face and need to overcome for their effective involvement in the formal institutions of local resource management' (Riordan, 2008: 47). Research constantly reaches similar conclusions:

• women in poverty are most at risk from dangers associated with climate change
• women are largely ignored in climate research, policy and development
• women are key actors in developing local coping strategies for climate change
• women are critical agents of change in communities
• women's skills and leadership are crucial for survival and recovery of all
• women's empowerment is needed for sound management of environmental resources

- women possess initiative, creativity and capacity to find grassroots solutions for climate change.

Lack of a gender analysis not only places a disproportionate burden on poor women the world over in relation to action on climate change, but it also limits the effectiveness of initiatives. (Riordan, 2008: 49)

Ecofeminism's embrace of the environment and sustainability arises from a critical connection between the 'death of nature' and the rise of patriarchy, and can be explored through the work of such people as Charlene Spretnak, Carolyn Merchant, Arundhati Roy and Vandana Shiva. The central argument from ecofeminism is that 'a historical, symbolic and political relationship exists between the denigration of nature and the female in Western cultures' (Spretnak, 1993: 181). Ecofeminism is rooted in principles of 'harmony, co-operation and interconnection' that challenge the perceived male principles of competition, 'discrimination, extremism and conflict' (Young, A., 1990: 33). This competitive worldview elevates men over both women and the natural world in a system of ranked order importance, deifying a male God, and downplaying the femininity of God, illustrating how organised religion plays a key hegemonic role in legitimising the common sense of subordination (McIntosh, 2001). Women continue to be active in organising and theorising an alternative worldview based on harmony and cooperation, non-violence and dignity, a view that embraces both public and private, local and global, humanity and the natural world in equal measure. It reflects women's concerns for preserving life on earth over time and space. Our Western worldview, founded on a complex system of domination and subordination, creates physical and spiritual alienation. This calls for a new way of seeing the world:

> We need, I believe, a way of knowing which helps us to heal this split, this separation, this alienation. We need a way of knowing which integrates truth with love, beauty and wholeness, a way of knowing which acknowledges the essential physical qualities of knowing. We need a new story about our place in the scheme of things. (Reason, 1994a: 14)

In relation to the interface of social justice and environmental justice, Crescy Cannan made an immense impact on community development thought when she stated that the environmental crisis is a crisis for us all, but it disproportionately affects both the poor and the South and so 'intensifies forms of inequality and threatens collective goods – thus it is a human crisis as well as a threat to the entire planet' (2000: 365). Her argument is linked to the impact of globalisation and the way that massive increases in economic growth have simultaneously been accompanied by massive poverty gaps, both between nations and within nations. Neoliberalism, with its emphasis on individual greed, has given rise to levels of consumption are not only creating global ecological degradation but unsustainable social inequalities, crises of diversity and biodiversity. Sustainability and social justice are intertwined in this crisis.

We must celebrate the role of the media in raising public consciousness about the reality of environmental degradation. TV programmes such as David Attenborough's *Blue Planet* series, together with Liz Bonnin's *Drowning in Plastic* and Stacey Dooley's investigative journalism into '*Are your Clothes Wrecking the Planet?*' (all available at bbc.co.uk) have done much to shock public consciousness as to how our daily consumption and waste are killing the planet and how we have a responsibility to change our behaviours. I forced myself to watch all three in one week – try it!

An alternative ideology, based on the principle of a common good rather than individual greed, raises questions about a drive for profit that holds no accountability for human or environmental wellbeing. Sandra Sewell, of Tamborine Mountain, Queensland, tells this story of Freirean eco-pedagogy.

Community action against environmental injustice: towards a mountain ecopedagogy

> Dialogue, as the encounter among [people] to 'name' the world, is a fundamental precondition for their true humanization. (Freire, 1970: 133)

When I moved to Tamborine Mountain in south east Queensland in 2001, it was for the cool temperate rainforest and with the hope that I might be able, with others, to care for some small part of it. I had become increasingly concerned about loss of environmental habitat and biodiversity, the probable dire consequences of global warming for all species, including the human, and the lack of political will in Australia to acknowledge and prepare for climate change.

With Paulo Freire, I have faith in people's intelligence and, given the means, their capacity to dialogue and to call out the toxic social and political realities that poison their lives. But, as Paulo Freire knew, keeping people in the dark can be to the benefit of vested interests, which is why 'the revolutionary process is eminently educational in character' (Freire, 1970: 133). After a lifetime of educating for conscientisation, he began working on an eco-pedagogy which, after his death, others took forward to the Earth Summit in Rio in 1992, and embedded in the Earth Charter in 2001 (Kahn, 2008).

Climate change

In Australia, despite warnings that climate change may well bring a two degree rise in temperatures, with destructive consequences (Flannery, 2006), state and federal governments have been, in the main, of little practical help and sometimes blatantly obstructive. Debates about climate change have been the direct or indirect cause of five changes of Australian prime ministers in the past six years. Conflating emissions reductions with higher electricity costs, leaders of both major parties have struggled to disentangle themselves from the conservative flanks within their own parties and the powerful lobbyists and media without (Flannery, 2018). While surveys indicate that most Australians support actions to ameliorate climate change and develop renewables (The Climate Institute, 2010), vested interests such as the coal industry lean heavily on politicians and spend considerable sums of money funding conservative think tanks and contrarian scientists to unsettle the science of climate change and skew debates.

Tamborine Mountain

Tamborine Mountain is a semi-rural town of over 7,000 people, 80 km south west of Brisbane and 50 km west of the Gold Coast. Country of the Wangerriburra people, the Mountain has grown from its early logging and small farm base to a tourist destination attracting more than a million visitors a year. Among the attractions are seven national parks of cool temperate rainforest. A changing climate will affect all Mountain species in particular ways (Low, 2011: 144–5). The estimates and predictions are that plant and animal species which can move to higher ground and to cooler temperatures on the Mountain will have a better chance of survival than those which for a complex of reasons – specific food and habitat requirements; lack of widespread seed dispersal capacity - will not be able to do so. Those currently at the limit of their ranges on mountain tops may not do well, unless they can move laterally. The human species on Tamborine Mountain will also be at risk, not only from rising temperatures but also from water shortages (there is no reticulated water or sewerage on the Mountain), bush fires and, not least, pressure on land for development to house people fleeing the city heat. Unfortunately, the Mountain, as elsewhere, has its own chorus of strident climate change denialists, and the local papers have published their letters and articles, believing (mistakenly, in my view) that everyone has a right to their opinion and version of the truth.

'Belonging to Country' and climate change

In 2007, following an Indigenous seminar in Brisbane on climate change, led by women elders (Black Card Training, The Australian BlackCard, 2018), I asked whether they would be willing to bring the seminar to Tamborine Mountain. There was at that time little Aboriginal presence on the Mountain and little informed public discussion about climate change. In the course of making the seminar arrangements, the focus changed to 'Belonging to Country', a basic starting point for any Indigenous discussion of climate change. We registered 20 participants for the 2008 seminar, and it was enthusiastically received. We have since offered the seminar every two years, and it is always over-subscribed.

In these seminars, the participants' expectations and the elders' gifts have always been in learning about Aboriginal care for country. Central to that have been opportunities for dialogue and relationships. For myself, they have also been opportunities to get to know a group of local women who not only value Indigenous wisdom, but also share my aim to change local conversations about the environment and climate change. It is with this small and changing group of women I have since worked on what we could describe as mountain 'eco-pedagogy' projects.

Women environmentalists on Tamborine Mountain

It is not I think therefore I am, but I am located therefore I am. (Mary Graham, 1999)

My place, my location, is Tamborine Mountain, and its environmental history features some outstanding women – women like the naturalist and photographer Hilda Geissmann, the poet and environmental activist Judith Wright, and the collector and propagator Joy Guyatt (Sewell, 2014b). In 2012, I sought the help of women friends to present a display of photos, videos and texts of these women's lives and work, followed in 2014 by a display of a photovoice project I had undertaken with seven of them, photographs and captioned images of their connections to the Mountain environment (Sewell, 2014a). The Tamborine Mountain library hosted these displays in their foyer and on their out-facing windows.

Because of the number of participants at the Indigenous seminars, we have asked local churches to host us and, for a small donation, they have generously done so. There is a community centre on the Mountain but it has no paid worker and mainly functions as a venue hire, with spaces either too big or too small for what we have wanted to do. Libraries have become hubs of community activities, and our library has proved to be an excellent venue, the staff excellent hosts.

Libraries and community development

As in other localities, the Mountain's library, with more than 7,000 members (at August 2018, personal communication) and a range of activities for all ages, is a significant resource. In fact, libraries have changed vastly, many now resembling neighbourhood centres. Librarians look both inwards and outwards: they see themselves as a 'third space', neither private nor public/ commercial. While embracing technology, they have not forsaken their buildings, collections or, perhaps most importantly, the relationships between staff and clients.

In 'Beyond the Walls', the proceedings of the 2015 public libraries in Australia and New Zealand conference (Bundy, 2015), the term 'community development' (CD) crops up often, both in terms of a 'community-led' approach and in terms of principles, strategies and directions. What is meant by and defined as CD may be fluid, but the outreach to, for example, people with disabilities and homeless people, the partnerships library staff seek with other local service providers, the innovative staff positions they create, and their inclusiveness has much in common with traditional CD. It is true that most of these changes and innovations are non-controversial, and local libraries or local councils who fund them may feel wary of taking on partisan political activities. When a few of us began talking about a series of climate change seminars on the Mountain, we were mindful of these constraints.

Climate change seminars

In 2017 we became aware of the National Climate Change Adaptation Research Facility (NCCARF) whose administrative hub (now defunded) was located in nearby Griffith University on the Gold Coast. We visited, and NCCARF staff directed us to numbers of useful resources on Australian and overseas climate change adaptation research. When we said we were planning a series of seminars on the likely consequences of climate change for the Mountain, they put us in touch with possible speakers from Queensland universities and the CSIRO (Commonwealth Science and Industrial Research Organisation).

There were risks, and we were cautioned that we would be preaching to the converted, that the local climate denialists would attend and be disruptive, and that the presentations would be too academic. We went ahead anyway, inviting our local councillors to open the series and offering each local environment group a week's display space to showcase their work. The format was 20 minutes presentation and 40 minutes discussion.

For the first series, we chose the theme 'Refugia' (Reside et al, 2013), and asked speakers to share what their research was telling them about probable survival rates of montane flora and fauna. The aim was both to learn more about species' responses to warming temperatures and to appreciate what was already being done on the Mountain, such as creating wildlife corridors, undertaking regular species counts, and restoring and preserving specific habitats. The speakers were hands-on young women researchers who vividly communicated the emerging science in words and pictures. The ensuing discussions were long and lively, no denialists showed up, and the talks were well received. Emboldened, we organised a second series of seminars a few months later on climate change itself, inviting a botanist, a planner, a restoration researcher, and a project officer from an expert group of 'concerned scientists'. We liaised with a local bookshop and the library staff themselves to provide a book and information display for what were, again, well-attended and well-received presentations and dialogues. Again, no denialists showed up, the information was readily accessible, and those who consider themselves already 'converted' said they felt strengthened in their commitment to keep on keeping on.

Where to from here?

Across Australia, temperatures are rising and we are witnessing some of the most extreme droughts, storms and floods on record. Most animals and plants are temperature-sensitive, either because of their metabolism (for example, temperature triggers reproduction) or because their food sources and habitats are. We are talking about frogs, insects, reptiles, birds and mammals, as well as the trees and plants in our gardens and in Mountain parks and rainforests. We are also talking human beings, especially the most vulnerable.

We can't know to what extent our eco-pedagogy efforts have changed people's understandings and conversations, or prompted them to take action. We do know that it is difficult to leverage structural changes or national policies from local level, and that it isn't always straightforward to shape action out of dialogue. Some participants have said that they feel both more confident and competent to 'speak truth to power' about all kinds of issues, including racism and environmental care. While the politics of climate change remain stuck in Canberra, householders, businesses, and some councils in Australian states and territories are investing in renewables: on the Mountain, there are fewer contrarian letters to local papers, and other groups, such as school parents' and citizens' assocations, are now taking up environmental care. Change is slow, but the dialogues continue, and the work goes on.

In his notes towards eco-pedagogy, Paulo Freire wrote:

> It is urgent that we assume the duty of fighting for fundamental ethical principles, like respect for the life of human beings, the life of other animals, the life of birds, the life of rivers and forests ... it seems to me a lamentable contradiction to engage in progressive, revolutionary discourse and have a practice which ... does violence to the mountains, the cities, to our cultural and historical memories. (Freire, 2005)

After Sandra's detailed and carefully connected story of community development in Australia, I will move on to capture a different story of government-supported environmental abuse that has outraged residents in Lancashire, not far from where I live in North West England.

 ## 'Frack Off': Extreme Energy Action Network

Fracking (hydraulic fracturing) drills vertically two to three kilometres into the ground and sends out horizontal drills for over a mile to inject a mixture of water, sand and chemicals at high pressure to fracture the rock that lies under communities in order to release methane gas. Each well uses five million gallons of clean water, and in return the water comes back out contaminated, as well as leaking toxic chemicals into ground water, poisoning wildlife. Local residents have an increased risk of breathing problems and skin conditions. Fracking employs very few people, is non-renewable, short-term, destroys the environment and depresses house prices, but is profit-driven, owned by private companies who will sell the fracked gas on the European market. The Frack Off network (www.frack-off.org.uk) identifies the fracking sites and offers information.

The story of Preston New Road, near Blackpool

Many countries have banned fracking, including Ireland, Wales and Scotland, but when local residents voted against fracking at Preston New Road in Lancashire, backed by the local government, the UK government committed an anti-democratic act by overriding participatory democracy to allow fracking to take place. Since that time, activists have joined local people to demonstrate on the access route to the site. I have witnessed the bravery of local people in standing up for their rights, and have witnessed aggressive policing by large battalions of police to intimidate and frighten ordinary people, many women and some elderly and disabled, from exercising their right to protest against what they feel is wrong. And the earthquakes just keep coming, with tremors felt for miles around. Other local groups have been formed, such as Lancaster Fights Fracking – which says that individually the task is enormous but together we can do it! (Facebook: Lancaster Fights Fracking)

~~~~~~~~~~~~~~~~~~~~~~~~

The anti-fracking activists from Preston New Road make connections from local to global and have a presence at demonstrations that connect neoliberal politics with the destruction of humanity and the planet. They joined the Extinction Rebellion action in London on 17 November 2018 to swell collective power under the banner of 'What kind of world do we want to leave our grandchildren?'. Protests are recognised to be more successful if they are not a one-off action, but sustained over time. To illustrate this point, let's take a look at sustained action from the individual to the collective.

Collective action: from individual to social movement

My focus here is on the ways in which social action can be sustained and extended into global movements for change.

Fridays for Future

Greta Thunberg, aged just 15, started her 'School Strike for Climate' alone, outside the Swedish Parliament, in August 2018. Inspired by Rosa Parks, she realised that one person can make a huge difference – 'I can't vote so this is one of the ways I can make my voice heard!' (www.bbc.co.uk). This turned into 'Fridays for Future', striking from school every Friday to maintain momentum. Attention was magnified when she spoke at the UN Climate Talks in Poland in December 2018. Her school strikes have motivated young people around the world: in a global day of school strikes on 15 March 2019, tens of thousands joined in with her Fridays for Future demonstrations, and she continues to prompt people of all ages into action against climate change.

Extinction Rebellion

Extinction Rebellion's mission is:

> To spark and sustain a spirit of creative rebellion, which will enable much needed changes in our political, economic and social landscape. We endeavour to mobilise and train organisers to skilfully open up space, so that communities can develop the tools they need to address Britain's deeply rooted problems. We work to transform our society into one that is compassionate, inclusive, sustainable, equitable and connected. (www.rebellion.earth)

Extinction Rebellion aims to use creative, peaceful action to demonstrate that the impossible is possible, to trigger a national conversation about our ecological crisis and the way in which it is a consequence of the political, economic and social landscape that we have created under neoliberalism. Their message is that action is urgent, and their process is to connect people from community to movement for change though 'Rising from the Wreckage', a citizens' assembly, linking communities to the state to demand change. Extinction Rebellion now has local groups for people wanting to take non-violent action to raise awareness of the looming climate catastrophe as well as providing an umbrella movement for change for the many emerging climate action groups, such as the Frack Off: Extreme Energy Action Network featured above.

In November 2018, five London bridges were occupied by thousands of Extinction Rebellion climate change protesters. On 15 March 2019, the youth of the world – including my granddaughter, Grace – following Greta Thunberg's lead in Sweden, came out on strike under the banner 'Youth Action for Climate'. They stated clearly: 'We will no longer accept this injustice. We demand justice for all past, current and future victims of the climate crisis, and so we are rising up. Thousands of us have taken to the streets in the past weeks all around the world. Now we will make our voices heard. On 15 March, we will protest on every continent' (Carrington, 2019).

Then, eight days in April 2019 saw a wide range of acts of non-violent civil disobedience from Extinction Rebellion in different venues in London, bringing parts of the City to a standstill. For example, three activists super-glued themselves onto a Docklands Light Railway train at Canary Wharf, disrupting rail services. Others glued themselves to the garden fence at the home of Jeremy Corbyn, the Labour Party leader. A gathering of young activists flew a banner asking 'Are we the last generation?' from a traffic island outside Heathrow airport. Greta Thunberg spoke to the gathered crowds with passion, shaming governments for complacency 'despite all the beautiful words and promises' and Massive Attack played. Scores of protesters occupied the Natural History Museum and staged a 'die in' underneath the blue whale skeleton to raise awareness of the threat of mass extinction of species. Extinction Rebellion claimed it to be the largest civil disobedience event in recent history, with over a thousand arrests by police, while still more people joined in support. Eventually, protesters were persuaded to move to Marble Arch, having been given official permission to gather in a main camp. Everything remained peaceful and there seemed to be general agreement that there was an air of dignity that prevailed (Perraudin, 2019).

On 6 May, the UN's Intergovernmental Science–Policy Platform on Biodiversity and Ecosystem Services (IPBES) report appeared. It named consistent failure to address the bourgeoning loss of biodiversity, and shamed the lack of progress made to halt the damage being done by humanity in relation to extinctions and habitats, let alone restoring the environment to safe ecological margins. 'Nature's dangerous decline "unprecedented"; species extinction rates "accelerating"' hit the headlines. The message is that there is overwhelming evidence from a diversity of knowledge bases to say that the health of ecosystems is increasingly deteriorating, killing the foundations of our economies, livelihoods, food supplies, health and overall quality of life on a worldwide scale. Action needs to be immediate, there is no time to be complacent, and it needs to be at all levels, from local to global. In this way, through transformative action, we could restore our ecosystem but it calls for fundamental systemic change across technological, economic and social factors – which means changing our values, expectations and lifestyles – this is not only a question of greenhouse gases and climate change, but an ecological crisis, the result of our lifestyles causing the destruction of nature. It is now our job not only to protect what is left, but to restore what has been lost (www.rebellion.earth). Public consciousness of the urgency of this ecological crisis has deepened due to Extinction Rebellion's bravery in the face of arrests and sustained action to alter the face of public consciousness and responsibility. Lorna Greenwood, from Extinction Rebellion, said:

> The natural world is collapsing because of how we live and we will go with it unless we act now. We must accept that we can't go on as we are. Not only are we destroying nature but we're worsening our own health and making it harder for us to feed ourselves. It's time to rethink how we grow food, travel and look after the countryside. It may mean hard choices but the rewards are enormous. Within our lifetime we could see nature restored and our children's future secured. The alternative is not an option. We have no choice but to rebel until our world is healed.' (www.rebellion.earth)

Community development practice and sustainability

Community action can be strengthened in partnership with a diversity of campaigning bodies to gain the support of those experienced in non-violent action and strategic tactics, to great effect. This action, in turn, inspires other communities.

The problems that we face today around health, poverty, inequality, education and the environment have become perceived as inevitable rather than as a consequence of neoliberal capitalism. Community development practice needs to develop strategies that challenge this consciousness and balance the needs of business against the needs of local communities.

One of the ways in which this understanding can be incorporated into our practice is by joining forces with the New Economics Foundation (www.neweconomics.org) which embraces many of the ideas I have focused on and operationalises them. They have a six-point plan for a new economy:

- A purposeful economy
- Urgent green transition
- More worker power
- Homes for all
- Decent quality of life
- A digital revolution

In a call for 'truly radical thinking for truly radical times' they develop these ideas as the beginning of a conversation. Join in their conversation to explore how you can develop a practice capable of change to counter these social and environmental crises by improving lives for the many. They incorporate many of the ideas in this book and take them into action. 'Sustainable solutions to local environmental problems require wider issues to be addressed' (Burningham and Thrush, 2001: 44). In these ways, we tease out the links between environmental and social justice, and local to global action.

Critiques of Freire and Gramsci from coherently argued perspectives provide us with the basis for extending community development theory into more adequate analyses of *diversity* in relation to social justice and *biodiversity* in relation to environmental justice. Within this, it is important to take into account critiques of capitalism as a system incapable of reform and the call for a new social order, one that is based on an ideology of cooperation rather than competition. *Praxis* is the bedrock of this process: theory in action, building a body of knowledge based on experience. The collective struggle for social justice and environmental justice is the basis for alliances between community activists and environmental activists in global times. In fact, many community workers are seeing this as a natural extension of their traditional work. The local/global dynamic is vital here: local people experience the impact of environmental degradation most immediately, and action is more relevant when it begins in people's communities as part of the process of critical consciousness and grassroots action. From local participation, this reaches out beyond community to engage with movements for change that take on global issues of diversity and biodiversity in crisis.

> We're all interconnected, interdependent. Lose the planet and we lose our habitat and means of survival. (Higgins, 2010: 24)

And one way of moving into such an alternative worldview is to build a pedagogy of intersectionality fundamentally rooted in an ideology of cooperation, where a desire for peace and non-violence forms the basis of the drive to open up new possibilities. This is the subject of the next chapter.

BIODIVERSITY

PAULO FREIRE
ECO-PEDAGOGY

THE NOTION SEEMS DEPLORABLE TO ME OF ENGAGING IN PROGRESSIVE, REVOLUTIONARY DISCOURSE WHILE EMBRACING A PRACTICE THAT NEGATES LIFE - THAT POLLUTES THE AIR, THE WATERS, THE FIELDS AND DEVASTATES FORESTS, DESTROYS THE TREES AND THREATENS THE ANIMALS

VANDANA SHIVA
ECO-FEMINISM

THE PRIMARY THREAT TO NATURE AND PEOPLE TODAY COMES FROM CENTRALISING AND MONOPOLISING POWER AND CONTROL. NOT UNTIL DIVERSITY IS MADE THE LOGIC OF PRODUCTION WILL THERE BE A CHANCE FOR SUSTAINABILITY, JUSTICE AND PEACE

8

Taking Freire into intersectionality

The basis of community development's transformative potential lies in its analysis of power in relation to changing political times. The challenge remains to more fully engage with white privilege and the way that it reinforces racism as a political ideology that acts in the interests of white people at the expense of non-white people. Stripping back the layers of consciousness leads to the insight that not only does racism result in *disempowerment* for black people, but at the same time it *empowers* those who are white. This calls for a complex intersectional analysis that embraces the tangled web of overlapping, intertwining injustices that work together as a whole to reinforce oppressions. Intersectionality explains the way that *all* injustices are interconnected to operate in the interests of white, patriarchal, supremacist privilege as part of the neoliberal project.

The insight into the workings of power offered by Gramsci and Freire gave community development a foundation for the process of radical social transformation. Power became more fully understood as a mutually reinforcing process operating from the bottom up as well as the top down. Critical consciousness, as an intervention at the heart of change, detects power in the stories of everyday life in community. This served us well until the mid-1980s, when postmodernism led us from metanarratives towards mini-narratives, emphasising multiple identities rather than political identities, obscuring the need for collective action (Kenway, 2001: 60). Retrieving our position from this analytic fragmentation, bell hooks reminded us that Freire had 'offered her insight into the nature of her own oppression as a Black American woman, helping her to see herself as a subject in resistance, thus locating a contradiction between White women and a third-world man' (hooks, 1993: 150). In these ways, Freire has spoken with integrity to people from a non-white, non-European, developing world perspective.

Neoliberalism's marketisation of life on earth operates on a multiplicity of hegemonies, reproducing a multiplicity of oppressions. Gary Craig et al (2011) reiterate the need for a strong theoretical base for community development if we are to preserve our distinctive identity, claiming that our poverty of literature has weakened our capacity to develop sufficiently strong race and gender analyses to sit alongside class as the three pervading structures of oppression that subsume but do not exclude others. Problematising power shifts us from a preoccupation with powerlessness to *powerfulness* in the struggle for liberation, with anti-racism and anti-sexism at its heart (Fine et al, 1997). This is an important point to reflect on, and in this respect I want to re-engage with Peggy McIntosh's seminal essay 'White privilege: unpacking the invisible knapsack' (2004). More than ever our reflections on everyday experience, the stories we tell, hold the answer to the change we want to live. The dangers of overlooking whiteness mean that multicultural reforms are routinely 'sucked back into the system' and the 'multicultural paradigm is mired in liberal ideology that offers no radical change in the current order' (Ladson-Billings and Tate, 2006: 579). Times are urgent for radical change and I propose that the cutting edge lies at the interface of whiteness, feminism and class.

White privilege

In Western culture the same structures that silence and subordinate women intersect with race, class, ability, culture, religion, status ... to marginalise and oppress in the name of white patriarchal supremacy to weave a net of overlaying oppressions. Just some opportunities are allowed to sift through in the name of tokenism, giving the illusion of change without changing anything.

As community development practitioners we are also action researchers engaged in theorising everyday lives in dynamic with changing political times. In our theorising, we have failed to understand whiteness as a key source of power, and in overlooking it, we leave it invisible. Critical whiteness, a move to explore the tenacity of white privilege in the face of civil rights, emerged from the USA in the late 1980s (hooks, 1989; Fine et al, 1997; Frankenberg, 1993), but has still not been embraced into the theoretical base of community development. Frankenberg (1993) argues that white communities are racialised by the very act of accumulating 'unearned privileges', and unless we learn to name whiteness, it won't get questioned.

> While the elite journeys to its imaginary destination somewhere near the top of the world, the dispossessed are spiraling downwards into crime and chaos. This climate of frustration and national disillusionment is the perfect breeding ground, history tells us, for fascism. (Roy, 2003)

The fascism that Arundhati Roy talks about is evidenced today as a force of racist common sense that feeds into the fascist minds of the Far Right under the banner 'make Britain great again', with no thoughts that connect with slavery or colonialism or gender or class. Similarly, Michelle Fine (2018: 15) reflects on the process of creeping dehumanisation of the neoliberal project, referring to the 'mass incarceration seeping aggressively into the darkest neighborhoods of New York State', that of actively channelling black lives from schools to prisons. Windrush – the state deporting its own citizens, the Grenfell Tower inferno – the state cremating its own citizens, or formal education doing the work of the state by transferring bodies of colour from school to prison, the racist process of dehumanisation is the same.

Whiteness, I suggest, is an overriding political ideology that needs to be understood in relation to all injustices. An assumed privilege that affects all exploitation, it is an invisible superiority in which the colour of skin becomes symbolic of an intellectual ideal that gets acted out as moral superiority. Feminism is a movement that covers every inequality and injustice, including environmental injustice, and it offers the key to anti-racist thinking and to class politics. No wonder Eddo-Lodge (2018: 167–8) asks, 'Can you be a feminist and be wilfully ignorant on racism?' As white women, we need to take our courage in our hands and be prepared to question seriously the assumed privilege our whiteness brings. One white woman who did just that was Peggy McIntosh. She changed the face of white privilege by naming its everyday, unconscious nature as an assumed power.

Peggy McIntosh's invisible knapsack

The cultural reproduction of whiteness as privileged and superior plays a central role in the embeddedness of race and racism.

> I think whites are carefully taught not to recognize white privilege, as males are taught not to recognize male privilege. So I have begun in an untutored way to ask what it is like to have white privilege. I have come to see white privilege as an invisible package of unearned assets that I can count on cashing in each day, but about which I was 'meant' to remain oblivious. (McIntosh, 1989, available at http://nationalseedproject.org/white-privilege-unpacking-the-invisible-knapsack)

McIntosh (2004), in her compelling self-definitions of moments in everyday life that contain the unconscious privilege of whiteness, exposes the insidious nature of power by changing her focus from 'powerlessness' to hold 'power' unfalteringly in her gaze. When I first came across Peggy McIntosh's work on the invisible knapsack it was like music to my ears as I went deeper into my own search, propelled by my experience with Paula. A change of emphasis from understanding racism to concentrate on the invisible systems of privilege that reinforce dominance challenges white people to examine our assumptions of 'normality'. McIntosh's metaphor of an 'invisible knapsack' containing a plethora of unearned privileges that can be unpacked and examined holds the key to dismantling the way that those privileges have remained invisible, assumed, equating normality with white culture. By assumed, I mean that the subtlety of white privilege is not understood by white people. This makes it elusive and hard to challenge, as it is so fully embedded in the practices of everyday life. Mekada Graham (2007) reminds us that by concentrating on giving voice to silenced voices we have encouraged the long silence on whiteness as a social construct: 'Whiteness carries a positive identity and without racial others it could not exist' (Graham, 2007: 61). Bhavani et al (2005: 50) outline the key areas as:

- White is seen as the majority, the norm, therefore tied to power.
- Whiteness lacks racial/ethnic features, making it invisible.
- Whiteness is naturalised so has no need to define its cultural traits, as with minority groups.
- Whiteness is confused with nationality, therefore central to power.
- White is not expressed as an ethnicity, and so avoids a label.

But Peggy McIntosh, in unpacking her knapsack, finds the embeddedness of whiteness in ordinary, everyday encounters of power, a web-like reinforcement at ground level, just as Foucault identified. Instead of looking out there at the structures that reinforce these attitudes and values, we find the beginning of the process right here, under our noses, in everyday life. McIntosh, in self-reflection, discovered and named 46 daily privileges that she took for granted as normal and available to anyone. She tried to eliminate class, religion, ethnicity or geographical location from the experience in an attempt to isolate and understand the elusive nature of these 'unearned assets' and these are some of her insightful reflections:

- I can, if I wish, arrange to be in the company of people of my race most of the time.
- I can be pretty sure that my neighbours will be neutral or pleasant to me.
- I can go shopping alone most of the time, pretty well assured that I will not be followed or harassed.
- I can turn on the television or open the front page of the paper and see people of my race widely and positively represented.
- Whether I use cheques, credit cards or cash I can count on my skin colour not to work against the appearance of financial reliability.
- I can remain oblivious of the language and customs of persons of colour who constitute the world's majority without any penalty for such oblivion.
- I can go home from most meetings of organisations I belong to feeling somewhat tied in, rather than isolated, out-of-place, outnumbered, unheard, held at a distance or feared.

These statements trigger a myriad of experiences in my mind. As a woman, I find I am able to relate some of these experiences to patriarchy. But most of all, I find the story of my shared moments with Paula Asgill coming to life, and I honour the insight into whiteness that she continues to bring me in reflection on our shared moments, all these years after her death.

Paula and Margaret: the interface of black and white

In Lancaster, a predominantly white community, whenever I saw Paula from a distance, I noticed her proud and beautiful stature slumped, and her eyes cast down at the pavement. One day, at work, she greeted me with a big smile, and told me the story of Duncan, my 17-year-old younger son:

> I was walking up from town, deep in my own thoughts, feeling that I don't belong here as I did in Manchester. "Yo Paula!", echoed across the street. I looked up and there was Duncan driving his pizza delivery van, waving out of the window with a big grin on his face, so pleased to see me. It made me feel recognised, part of the place.

I laughed when I heard this, knowing that Duncan would indeed be so happy to see Paula out and about. We moved to Lancaster from Manchester at the same time as Paula, and Duncan had grown up in a multicultural community with many close black friends in his life.

In the years that we were both friends and colleagues, Paula and I used to travel to the USA on work trips. I walked through passport control and customs confidently assuming that I would not be searched. Gradually, I came to realise that inevitably Paula was the one chosen from the line of white visitors to the country to have her bag checked; these were not random acts. I used to walk over and demand to know whether there was a problem, but was always told it was 'routine'. Paula had learnt to accept it as part of her life. Despite our mutual research into the problematic relations of alliances between black and white women, we only partially addressed the very painful ways in which this got acted out in our friendship – and there were many! When we were on work trips to the USA, she was often furious that I had more privileges and was less challenged. But, when she took me into one of the most volatile black areas of Chicago, she was at home, she belonged and I received the gaze as outsider. I was scared! Stripped of the privilege of my dominant whiteness, I was dislocated from my assumed comfort and acutely aware of the danger of being different, of being a white woman in a black community, of being a minority. Over the years until she died, my deep friendship with Paula bounced through these challenging and painful encounters that educated me into racism as a lived experience.

When Paula was taken ill, and rushed to hospital, I followed the ambulance nose to tail in my little VW Polo, anxious not to lose her in the power and bureaucracy of the system. By the time I parked and got to the ward, she was already in bed, her beautiful features framed by the starched, white, linen pillowcase. The doctor interviewing her looked up at me, asking, "And who are you?" To my amusement, in her illness, her head rose slowly from the pillow, looked him directly in the eye, daring him to challenge her, and announced with some force, "'She is my *sister*!" I knew in that moment that she was acknowledging my authenticity as a sister in resistance.

The long friendship and working relationship I had the privilege to share with Paula was immensely problematic but continues to educate me in the ways of white privilege, how tenacious and elusive it is as an assumed power to those who have it – even those of us who claim to be anti-racist practitioners – and how it needs to be much more systematically analysed and understood.

Racism becomes reproduced in the everyday discriminatory practices acted out at a micro level (Bhavani et al, 2005). White people are implicated in the reproduction of inequality and need to be accountable for the role that we play in legitimising the structures that privilege whiteness. But saying it is not enough: we need to understand the subtleties which reveal whiteness as both invisible and hegemonic at one and the same time. Only in these ways will we be able to construct counternarratives of liberation that truly embrace the concept 'lift as we climb' (Davis, 1989: 9) across difference and diversity, and Reni Eddo-Lodge, one of my identified intellectual activists for this book, takes no prisoners on this score. She speaks frankly and uncompromisingly to white people: even the title of her book, *Why I'm No Longer Talking to White People about Race*, sets out her stall!

Reni Enno-Lodge is outstanding in her capacity to speak to white people who simply do not want to listen (see Chapter 2)!

Reni Eddo-Lodge

> Feminism needs to demand a world in which racist history is acknowledged and accounted for, in which reparations are distributed, in which race is completely deconstructed. (Eddo-Lodge, 2018:182)

Eddo-Lodge's provocative book title launches a challenge to white women to engage in the issue of white power. White people are simply not comfortable talking about racism in relation to white power. 'You can see their eyes shut down and harden. It's like treacle is poured into their ears, blocking up their ear canals. It's like they can no longer hear us' (Eddo-Lodge, 2018: ix). We become defensive, bewildered and offended. She challenges this emotional disconnect: that we don't listen, we don't know what it means to embrace a person of colour as a true equal, with thoughts and feelings that are as valid as our own. White denial, she says, is the ubiquitous politics of race that operates on its inherent invisibility (2018: x). This, of course, means that people of colour not only have to work at analysing structural racism, but have to tiptoe warily around the sensitivities of white people in the process. It is simply not good enough! If we won't accept that the problem exists, we are not alerted to recognising the thousands of racist microaggressions that are a lived reality on a daily basis for a person of colour. Even worse is when we say we don't even notice people of colour as any different from ourselves, so claim that we enter conversations as equals. White people's entitlement is always having permission to speak and never having to listen. If we want to eliminate oppression, white people have to be humble, to listen, to be open to challenge, brave enough to reflect on it and to change!

Eddo-Lodge's emphasis is that 'Colour-blindness does not get to the root of racism' (2018: 83). So, if you are white, listen to what she has to say:

> White privilege is instrumental to racism … whiteness as a political ideology … favours whiteness at the expense of those who aren't … like yin and yang. Racism's legacy does not exist without purpose. It brings with it not just a disempowerment for those affected by it, but an empowerment for those who are not. That is white privilege. Racism bolsters white people's life chances. It affords an unearned power; it is designed to maintain a quiet dominance. Why don't white people think they have a racial identity? (Eddo-Lodge, 2018:116)

REFLECTION and DIALOGUE: Britain's inheritance from slavery

Read Eddo-Lodge's story of Britain's unacknowledged common inheritance from the profits of slavery, and discuss your thoughts in your dialogue group.

 **A story of slave history and inheritance**

The Albert Dock opened four decades after Britain's final slave ship, the *Kitty Amelia*, set sail from the city, but it was the closest I could get to staring out at the sea and imagining Britain's complicity in the slave trade. Standing on the edge of the dock, I felt despair. Walking past the city's oldest buildings, I felt sick. Everywhere I looked, I could see slavery's legacy. … But slavery wasn't just happening in Liverpool. Bristol, too, had a slave port, as well as Lancaster, Exeter, Plymouth, Bridport, Chester, Lancashire's Poulton-le-Fylde and, of course, London … The Society for Effecting the Abolition of the Slave Trade, founded in London in 1787, mostly by Quakers, campaigned for 47 years before it was successful in abolishing slavery in the British Empire in 1833. But the recipients of the compensation for the dissolution of a significant money-making industry were not those who had been enslaved. Instead it was the 46,000 British slave-owning citizens who received cheques for their financial losses. Such one-sided compensation seemed to be the logical conclusion for a country that had traded in human flesh.

Source: Eddo-Lodge (2018: 5-6).

For many years, aware that my adopted home town Lancaster was complicit in 'this trade in human flesh', having made the pilgrimage to the grave of a slave in a lonely, windswept corner of a field on Sunderland Point, the northern bank of the Lune estuary passed by slave boats on their way into the Port of Lancaster, I have asked myself about the inheritance of those still living who continue to benefit from this dark shameful legacy. How can we continue to revere status and privilege and envy its trappings? We need to question its origins. For these reasons, the laws of inheritance must be seen as not only perpetuating inequality, but doing so on the proceeds of unacceptable exploitation (see Andrew Sayer's argument on common inheritance discussed in Chapter 2). Perpetuating these benefits is to perpetuate the suffering of those who paid the price in past generations. The story goes on.

Feminism as anti-racist praxis

> Feminism needs to demand a world in which racist history is acknowledged and accounted for, in which reparations are distributed, in which race is completely deconstructed… these demands are utopian and unrealistic. But I think feminism *has* to be absolutely utopian and unrealistic, far removed from any semblance of the world we're living in now. (Eddo-Lodge, 2018: 182)

Feminism is a praxis; it is both a theory and a movement for change concerned with understanding how power interests create injustice for their own gain, and acting to create a better world for everyone and everything.

> Feminism, at its best, is a movement that works to liberate all people who have been economically, socially and culturally marginalised by an ideological system that has been designed for them to fail. That means disabled people, black people, trans people, women and non-binary people, LGB people and working class people. (Eddo-Lodge, 2018: 181)

Contrary to popular belief, feminism does not fight its own corner, but believes that every suffering affects the whole. This is why a counternarrative that addresses every inequality and injustice, including environmental injustice, is at the heart of women's action. But, to be effective, this calls for a complex analysis based on intersectionality and the tangled web of overlapping, intertwining injustices that work together to reinforce oppressions. Fighting our own corner can be unhelpful if it results in divide-and-rule, defending ourselves against other oppressed groups rather than standing back and taking a long look at the way that white, patriarchal, supremacist power is playing all of us off for its own gains. We need to see through this clever tactic once and for all. It is keeping all marginalised groups poor, at the same time as it creates a global super-rich, a sector that is amassing excessive global wealth. We need a key to understanding how inequalities are mutually interconnected, rather than segmented.

Let's start with the knowledge that feminist thought offers the key to anti-racist thinking and to class politics. Let's explore why Eddo-Lodge (2018: 167–8) asks 'Can you be a feminist and be ignorant on racism?'. White feminists have, for too long, lacked the courage to engage with racism as a priority, instead falling into a trap of defending whiteness and its entitlement. Yet, if feminism can get to grips with analysing patriarchy, why have we been so resistant to questioning white privilege. Her argument is that our political structures are dominated by the authority of men, often middle-aged white men reinforcing their own power, with the occasional middle-aged white woman as a token gesture to diversity. Nowhere is there a concerted challenge to this white consensus.

Feminism is a movement that offers the key to anti-racist thinking and to class politics. Well, can you be a feminist and be wilfully ignorant on racism? To answer this question, white women need to be prepared to question their own racial identity. If we begin to engage with complex questions on race and gender, perhaps we will be more readily prepared to engage with the thorny questions of race, class and gender intersections, asking why it should be that a middle-class job, say that of university professor, inevitably calls for a working-class candidate to turn their back on their class and culture of origin. This is surely tokenism?

> Our strategy should be not only to confront empire, but to lay siege
> to it. To deprive it of oxygen. To shame it. To mock it. Without art,
> our music, our literature, our stubbornness, our joy, our brilliance, our
> sheer relentlessness – and our ability to tell our own stories. Stories that
> are different from the ones we're brainwashed to believe. (Roy, 2003)

Tackling white privilege would take us a long way in pursuit of a world informed by values of diversity and biodiversity. George Monbiot (discussed in Chapter 2) dispels the myth of individualism, providing evidence that the human condition thrives on belonging, on connection, kindness and compassion, and this provides the key to healing our alienated world. To get beyond tokenism we must change our focus to the real source of the problem, and deconstruct neoliberalism as a universal, imperialist, white supremacist capitalist patriarchy, with its legacy of slavery, colonialism and dominance, that is playing us all off against each other.

Engaging with white privilege

There are pioneers in institutions who are engaging with white privilege, like Diane Warner, a black teacher educator who talks about ways in which whiteness is reproduced. Her research into understanding the very essence of the black experience in teacher education exposes how the culture of the black trainee teacher is marginalised both in the learning context and in schools. This is research which needs to be heard. Diane captures the resistance of white superiority to questioning its own privilege, at the same time as demonstrating the capacity of a skilled black educator to work across difference in supporting student teachers to reflect on the ways in which white privilege reproduces itself. It is a warning that if we leave the system unquestioned, it reproduces the same inequalities, increasing dominance of the already powerful and reinforcing marginality of difference based on race, ethnicity, class and gender. She is nurturing 'seeds of resistance', as a black woman in a dominant white context. However, considering Frantz Fanon published *Black Skin, White Masks* in French in 1952 (Fanon, 2008) based on black experience of Western domination, it is high time, as white people, that we seize the baton and take responsibility for exploring the injustice of white privilege more systematically if we are seriously committed to a just world.

Bhopal (2018), in her analysis of the intersections of race and class in the struggle to name white superiority, engages with the complexity of neoliberalism's racist connections that elevate whiteness and encourage racist attitudes to black and minority ethnic groups. This connects with Imogen Tyler's (2013; 2015) research on stigma. Bhopal talks about the way that threats of terrorism or fears of our borders being breached by migrants and refugees key into deep feelings of poorly understood dimensions of Britishness that often reinforce racist stereotypes. The othering of black and non-white identities then becomes 'another threatening element in a climate dominated by fear, terror and risk' (2018: 10). She engages with the current climate of Brexit, the way that in the aftermath shock of the referendum 'people's social lives had changed and the perception of what British identity might constitute changed quickly and irrevocably', evoking for pro-Europeans 'not just disbelief at the decision, but also feelings of great abjection and despair for their futures' as a significant rise in hate crime was witnessed across the country. Those who voted to leave the EU were mostly from the lowest social class, with lower levels of education and from a white background:

> The vote to leave was a clear indication of the predominance of whiteness. It was a reaction to mass immigration in which many white (working class) people felt they were being disadvantaged; immigrants were taking their jobs and were a strain on education and the National Health Service. And for once, they could have a voice in which they could use their vote as a legitimate platform to voice their racist views. Brexit was an 'us versus them' vote in which white privilege was used at its most powerful – to separate out those who were *allowed* to belong and those who were *not,* and racism was used as a vehicle to promote this. (Bhopal, 2018: 12–13).

The Far Right identified this niche of fear and hopelessness, and played the racist card, fuelled by Nigel Farage's infamous 'Breaking Point' poster.

Bhopal (2018) highlights the peculiarly British whiteness experience, that of an imagined threat of black and non–white identities as a '"danger" to the British way of life' (Bhopal, 2018: 10). This notion of what constitutes Britishness as whiteness is culturally embedded and needs to be understood in order to get under the surface of neoliberalism's role in the rise of the Far Right, and the part that racism is playing in constructing Brexit Britain and the Trump regime in the USA.

Problematising neoliberal capitalism

Capitalism has been conflated with democracy. This is problematic for social justice, as it obscures the way that capitalism is predicated on exploitation of all that it subordinates, including the natural world. For example, under capitalism race is exacerbated by the relations between race and property ownership, perpetuating privilege and creating unequal relations. A critical paradigm disconnects democracy from capitalism, and identifies alternative economic systems that are based on justice and sustainability. If we fail to problematise capitalism and only focus on deepening democracy, we leave the structural inequalities of capitalism intact (Ladson–Billings and Tate, 2006: 573). The tenacity of inequality remains a conundrum simply because we miss the dialectical relationship between capitalism and democracy.

As an example, Michael Apple raises the issue of cultural capital's exploitation of the market. For example, education is increasingly marketed as a commodity. Universities have been transformed into business enterprises which charge for the benefits of a degree at the same time as marketing their products according to demand: 'markets are marketed, are made legitimate, by a depoliticizing strategy. They are said to be natural and neutral, and governed by effort and merit' (Apple, 2006: 471). By unquestioningly accepting these assumptions as common sense, we miss the way that the most privileged get the biggest slice, that it is a system designed for those with all the confidence, ease, wealth and natural assumptions of power that are so much less accessible to those who are 'Other'.

Linked to this analysis are the critical connections that ensure that education fails children who are from subordinated groups, while maintaining its neutral stance as awarding merit. Children living in overcrowded homes – or homes without books, or homes in which languages other than English are spoken – cared for children, children from families that are minority ethnic or have an unemployed parent or a single parent or a disabled parent and so on are failed by the education system. Yet, *false generosity* or tokenism creates the illusion that the system is fair and just, so, every so often, a child from one of these backgrounds proves the exception.

We can no longer afford to deal with discrimination as a fragmented experience. It must be seen as a sustained and central theme of the neoliberal project to subordinate a multiplicity of identities in the name of making the rich richer at the expense of the poor. The longer we fail to engage with the intersectionality of discrimination, we get even more of the same.

Eddo-Lodge talks about being constantly looked at as an alien in your country of birth, a sustained racism carried forward in the microaggressions of everyday life. But the Windrush scandal, unfolding in the spring of 2018, exposed the complicity of the Conservative Brexit Government under the leadership of Theresa May in a shameful, dehumanising stage of the neoliberal project – to keep aliens out. White and black citizens alike have been appalled by the denial of British citizenship to what has become known as 'the Windrush generation', so named after the ship that brought the first Caribbean migrants by invitation of the government to help rebuild post-war Britain. The truth has unveiled the suffering of generations of families who have legal rights to citizenship being denied passports, losing jobs, being stranded in Caribbean countries and refused re-entry to Britain, being refused health care, social care and benefits, because the government had destroyed their legal documentation, so denying them evidence of residence. The world has been horrified that an anti-immigrant government intent on building walls around the country could arrogantly assume that public opinion would let them get away with retrospectively applying this hatred to generations of settled migrants here by invitation.

Problematising gender

Racism, sexism and heterosexism work in overlapping but different ways. As Audre Lorde expressed as long ago as 1980: 'As a forty-nine-year-old Black lesbian feminist socialist mother of two, including one boy, and a member of an inter-racial couple, I usually find myself a part of some group defined as other, deviant, inferior, or just plain wrong' (Lorde, 1980).

Much as whiteness is assumed, so is patriarchy. The everyday encounters between men and women reinforce gendered differences. A patriarchal hierarchy of privilege remains resilient among the myriad of hegemonies that reach from street to structures. It calls for a radical questioning into the ways that patriarchy and racism are overt oppressions, but the key to unlocking that power lies in understanding the way that they become embodied in male and white identities and played out in subtly powerful ways. Patricia Williams (1991: 216) says that 'blacks in a white society are conditioned from infancy to see in themselves only what others, who despise them, see'. The freedom struggles that we place on black women are powerfully expressed in this story told by Diane Watt, previously of Manchester Metropolitan University, about her friend (and my friend) Paula.

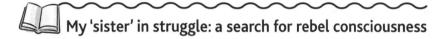

My 'sister' in struggle: a search for rebel consciousness

My friend Paula who was also my 'sister' in struggle was born in Jamaica, the third largest of the Caribbean islands after Cuba. It is an island where the sounds of Bob Marley's 'No Woman Nuh Cry' and the rhythms of Africa are ever present, a place of oral tradition, where stories such as 'Nanny of the Maroons' abound. In her fight against the British, and drawing upon the powers of her Ashanti heritage, Nanny is said to have bounced bullets off her bottom.

At the age of seven, Paula left Jamaica to join her mother and stepfather in England. Although Paula was not among the thousands of children left behind with the promise that within five years their parents would return 'home' financially secure, she nevertheless found separation from her mother extremely traumatic, an effect of migration which is rarely spoken about. Paula had enjoyed sharing her mother with other members of her extended family, and these family members, in turn, mothered her after her mother left. She was surrounded, in her own words, by a battalion of little 'mothers' who all played a role in passing on the oral tradition with their parables and storytelling.

Paula arrived in England at a time when language was seen as one of the key factors influencing the decision by many local education authorities to send an unprecedented number of black children from the Caribbean to special educational needs schools. This was an issue of growing concern among black parents throughout the country, and in preparing her for her first day at school, she recalled her mother telling her that "They'll say things to you and you won't understand, but all you have to do is to say 'pardon' and they'll say it again."

Looking back, Paula felt that her mother's advice was quite radical in the sense that it was not intended to silence her. Initially, she found speaking and understanding English within the British context challenging. Paula's transition from the primary school girl who arrived at Manchester Airport in the middle of winter, wearing a little yellow and brown crinoline dress, to that of community activist was very much influenced by her mother's experience.

This involvement gave her a greater understanding of the position of black women of her mother's generation within the labour market, most of whom, irrespective of their skills, found themselves doing unskilled work. Prior to coming to England, her own mother was a successful, self-employed seamstress, and she found packing crisps soul destroying. This was not unlike the experience of the Jamaican feminist writer Una Marson who, despite her educational achievements and professional credentials, was unable to find employment as an office worker in England during the 1930s. Marson has since been described as the first black British woman to speak out against racism and sexism, as she did at the 12th Annual Congress of the International Alliance of Women for Suffrage and Equal Citizenship which was held in Turkey in 1935. In Manchester, there were also the 'coloured' passengers on the number 53 bus, which local whites renamed the 'African Queen' in reference to the large number of black immigrants who travelled daily to what was then one of Europe's largest industrial estates.

These are some of the experiences of the black community that inspired Paula's involvement with community-based activism aimed particularly at championing the rights of black women. This at times meant her active participation in anti-deportation campaigns, as in the case of the West African woman whose marriage had broken down and who, together with her six children, faced deportation. Campaigns of this nature also provided Paula with the opportunity to engage in conscious struggles against race- and gender-related forms of social and political injustice. It was through her involvement with the Manchester Black Women's Co-op, in particular its Saturday Supplementary School activities, that Paula met the late Olive Morris, one of the founder members of the Organisation for Women of Africa and African Descent (OWAAD). In terms of political activism, she described Olive as a trooper and a young woman of wisdom who both mothered and sistered her. Throughout their friendship, Olive taught her that she didn't have to conform to all the shit to be a fighter and survive. Olive was both inspirational and fundamental to Paula's development as a young black woman in search of that state of rebel consciousness.

~~~~~~

Kathleen Weiler calls for counter-hegemonic opposition: 'the creation of a self-conscious analysis of a situation and the development of collective practices and organization that can oppose the hegemony of the existing order and begin to build the base for a new understanding and transformation of society' (2009: 235). In order to resist the sexism of black British culture and the racism of white British culture we need to understand that:

> ... resistance and ... 'reading' of the ideological messages of schools
> will differ in specific school settings. And of course girls of different
> class and race subjectivities will be met with varying expectations on
> the part of white and black, male and female teachers, depending on
> these teachers' own views of what is gender appropriate. By adding
> the categories of race and class to that of gender, we can begin to

reveal the diversity and complexity of girls' and women's experiences in schools. (Weiler, 2009: 226)

According to Gramsci, any theory of change must be grounded in the struggles of everyday life. 'The task of counter-hegemonic groups is the development of counter-institutions, ideologies, and cultures that provide an ethical alternative to the dominant hegemony, a lived experience of how the world can be different' (Patti Lather, 1984: 55, cited in Weiler, 2009: 226). In these ways, we can build counternarratives based on a critical understanding of existing society as the basis for an alternative value system based on justice and sustainability.

Feminism's emphasis on *difference* has given profound insight into the complexity of lived experience, which places us all within a matrix of oppressions, variously positioned as both victims and perpetrators. Similarly, feminism's emphasis on non-hierarchical structures of peace and non-violence has developed altered views on both human rights and environmental justice. The challenge is now to develop an integrated praxis that informs a pedagogy for our times.

Towards intersectionality

Perhaps bell hooks captures the argument that feminism misses the point if it seeks to make women equal with men when not all men are equal. Eddo-Lodge (2018) identifies hooks' work as a platform for more inclusive feminist theory that allows for the long-standing idea of sisterhood within a consideration of gender's relation to race and class, acknowledging that much as white women need to do their part in the struggle for change, so do men. This is a bid for a more inclusive feminism, one that focuses on a common good based on acceptance of and kindness towards others. It calls for another gap to be bridged: the anti-intellectualism that is foisted on the poor creates a divide that brings privilege.

The education system places controls on whose knowledge matters that ultimately decide whose lives matter, and the condition for acceptance into this system of privilege is to live by the cultural values that it embodies, creating a further separation between poor and rich. Our struggle for knowledge democracy needs to embrace the diversity of subordinated knowledges if we are to bridge this separation, and those of us who write and talk about social inequalities need to write in ways that speak to everyone. In demystifying the myths of neoliberal dominant ideology, we simply need to question the finger of blame that has served neoliberal *common sense* so well. Every time that finger points to an immigrant, a poor person, a black person, a Muslim, a woman, a homeless person … we need to question, to challenge and to expose the agenda of the rich that it serves. More than that, we have to expose the way that during 'austerity' measures, while the rest of us have been forced to pay for the risks of greedy bankers, the rich have got richer than ever.

Feminist approaches attempt to place women's ways of knowing at the centre of knowledge generation, not to exclude men, but because 'by looking at human experience from the point of view of women, we can understand male experience and the whole of cultural history with greater depth' (Callaway, 1981: 460). This constitutes a critical repositioning that embraces a multiplicity of ways of knowing the world, challenging gender and cultural dominance. Within this frame, 'the act of looking back, of seeing with fresh eyes, of entering an old text from a new critical direction' (Adrienne Rich, cited in Callaway, 1981: 457) allows us to 're-vision' Freire and Gramsci, using the analytic tools they offered us to expand our feminist consciousness in the first place. Looking back with our new awarenesses offers new ways of exposing the contradictions embedded in the taken-for-grantedness of daily life, and, in turn, 'the imaginative power of sighting possibilities and thus helping to bring about what is not (or not *yet*) visible, a new ordering of human relations' (Callaway, 1981: 457).

Towards an intersectional critical pedagogy: a loci of oppressions

Radical community development needs to step up to play its role in a praxis for our times. This calls for extending our ideas, our analyses and our theories, adding to the body of knowledge capable of taking community development forward. I see Freirean pedagogy and anti-racist, feminist pedagogy as a powerful combination, informed by analyses of class, patriarchy and racism as overarching structures of oppression that intertwine with each other. These forces are woven into the fabric of life through different contexts at different levels in a complex system of domination and subordination. This is absorbed in the public psyche as common sense, and thus legitimate. A Freirean-feminist-anti-racist pedagogy is also profoundly concerned with other aspects of difference and diversity, seeking a worldview that is equal, harmonious and respectful of all life on earth. Exploring the ideas of Allman, McLaren and Hill from a class perspective and Spretnak and Shiva from an ecofeminist perspective, this worldview is not possible within a system of capitalism that is built on domination and exploitation for profit. In other words, capitalism is inherently incapable of reform because its success depends on exploitation and profit, and, within this, class, race and gender are prime forces of exploitation that serve its interests.

The 14 intellectual activists I introduced in Chapter 2 and incorporated into the body of this book take forward the challenges of critiquing neoliberalism, imagining counternarratives and offering ideas that turn the current state of society on its head. We cannot do this within an ideology of profit that absolves itself of any accountability for human and environmental wellbeing in the interests of the excesses of the few. We need to unlock our imaginations to find a new way of seeing the world that is based on the common good of the many. It simply does not have to be like this: there are many alternatives. Radical community development calls for analyses of power that take thinking and action from a local to a wider collective potential for change.

To illustrate the idea of a multiplicity of oppressions intersecting to privilege the powerful, I offer a loci of oppressions matrix (Figure 8.1): a three-dimensional model that moves through (i) **difference** (race, class, gender and so on) on one axis, through (ii) **context** (family, workplace, streets, schools and so on) on another, and between (iii) **levels** (local, national, global and so on) on a third, to illuminate intersectionality between a complex set of interrelationships that interweave between axes, but also intertwine on any one axis. The elements are not fixed; they are interchangeable on each face; the model is designed to probe critical thinking, stimulating questions rather than offering definitive answers. It calls for three-dimensional thought, as opposed to the simplistic linear rationality of Western consciousness. Students have said it helps to imagine this as a Rubik's cube, each section capable of changing and being re-examined in relation to the whole. It is only by struggling to locate these complex intersections that we begin to understand the root causes of oppression, and in doing so locate potential sites of resistance. So, for example, the model not only helps us to explore the interrelatedness of race and gender on one face, but to locate this within an environmental context, and on a community level. Then, if the level is shifted from local to, say, global, different but related issues emerge.

Figure 8.1: Loci of oppressions matrix

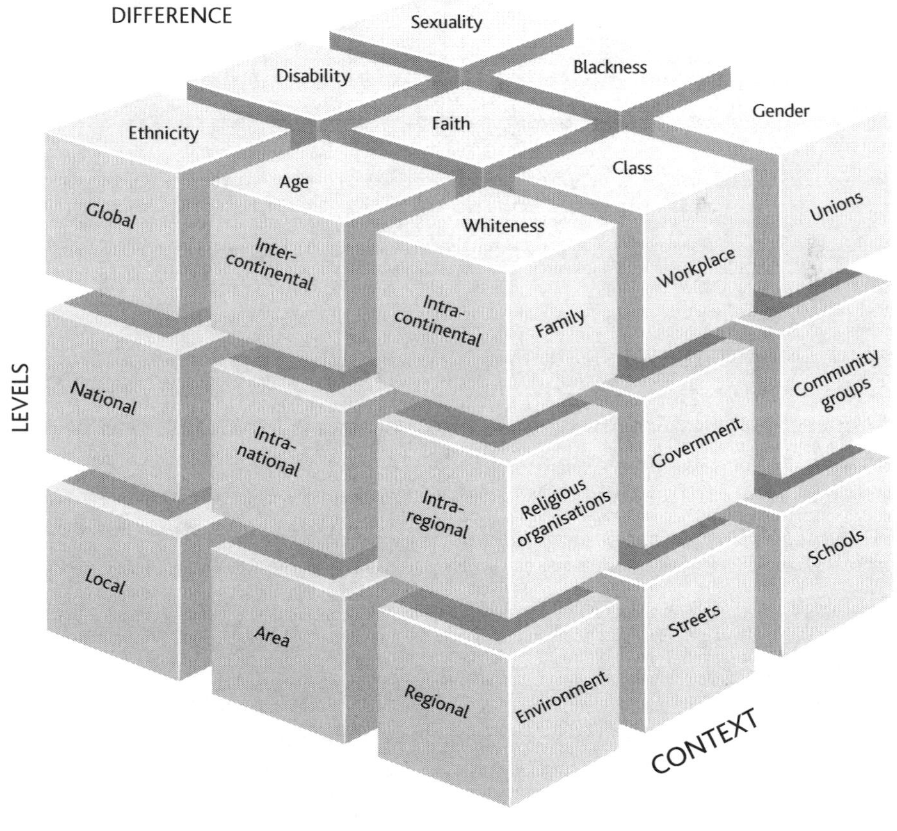

The purpose of the model is to stretch our thinking in a multidimensional way by locating the intersections of different dimensions of oppressions, and, in doing so, pose questions that deepen our analysis and make our practice more critical. The critical potential of this model is that it teaches us to question in the most complex of ways. Beginning in an aspect of everyday reality, using problem-posing as part of this multidimensional model, could open us to new understandings and new forms of action. The dialogue is kept critical, based on Hope and Timmel's (1994, Book 1, p 58) six stages of questioning:

1. description (What is happening?)
2. first analysis (Why is it happening?)
3. real life (Where is it happening?)
4. related problems (What else is happening? What other related symptoms?)
5. root causes (political power – ideology and policies?)
6. action (How can we act locally, nationally, globally to bring about change?)

Working with people in a community group, *problematise* a local issue by using a photograph as a *codification*, capturing the essence of this issue from the reality of their lives. The 'description' stage is merely asking what the photograph depicts. What is in the photo? What do you see? Who is in the photo? What do you think they are doing? What are they feeling? This moves into 'first analysis', which questions why this thing is happening, a shift of focus from observing the photograph to thinking about it. As confidence grows, and the group gets more involved, ask 'Does this happen in "real life"?' If you have chosen a generative theme, one that is relevant to the everyday lives of the people, and captured it well, it will generate a passionate response: 'It happens to me!' 'It happens every day in our community!' 'This is the way it is here!' In this way, the outward focus on the codification, in this case a photograph, shifts inward to the group and critical dialogue is generated by the relevance the issue has to the reality of its members. Curiosity and mutual inquiry will often stimulate the group to identify 'related problems'. In this way the group moves beyond the concrete situation, making connections across difference, time and space. Your role is to probe in a *problematising* way. If you challenge the group to take its analysis to a deeper level, the inquiry will go beyond the symptoms to the root causes of the problem, which truly pushes towards *critical consciousness*. New ways of knowing are explored. Social relations are transformed as people experience each other differently. There is a move towards critical thought for transformative action.

Try experimenting with some of your own experiences to see if this model extends your analysis. Consider how, on one axis, difference is compounded by, say, whiteness, gender and age to give us profoundly different experiences of being a 'woman'. If we then consider how this is further compounded by context – say, the public world of work as opposed to the private world of family – further patterns of difference emerge. Finally, if we follow this through to make global links with local experiences, we can begin to see realities that are constructed by the interaction of these forces. By struggling to analyse these complex intersections, we get nearer to connecting with the root causes of oppression, and in doing so locate potential sites of resistance. Because the elements are not fixed, the model becomes adaptable to multiple possibilities.

If you begin to see more complex connections through the matrix, consider using it as a structure for teaching to question with your community groups. Reflect on the nature of your own power, status and authority as an educator in relation to the difference represented in your groups. This may operate in half–hidden, subtle ways. How do you see the interaction of power and difference within the group? What evidence is there of different ways of knowing within the group, for example emotionality and rationality? Is your way of knowing different from that of the group? In a mutual relationship as co–educators/co–learners in an evolving process, explore the gendered, racialised nature of accepted knowledge, and discover ways in which dominant views of the world and the nature of truth may not be the same for men and women, or for different cultures. This takes us nearer to the cutting edge of a pedagogy of difference.

The matrix offers a focus for investigation of the many possible interlinked sites of oppression and deepens an awareness of the ways in which these are structurally reinforced at different levels. As the group grows in confidence and awareness, they own the process in a mutual and reciprocal way. *Critical consciousness* is an outward–flowing energy. Personal empowerment involves a sense of self in the world that gives rise to personal autonomy. This process becomes collective as critical consciousness leads to critical autonomy. Links are made with other groups in the community and alliances are formed with groups outside the community, generating a collective energy for change that has the potential to connect through levels from local to global. A coherent and strategic model of intersectionality offers community development a radical possibility.

But the beginning of the process starts with critical reflection on experience: Peggy McIntosh (2004) has demonstrated that everyday experiences hold the key to power and powerlessness. In dialogue, in a process of connected knowing (Belenky et al, 1986), we pay full attention to others by suspending our own truth, and develop new insights that are the basis of counternarratives of liberation, new stories about new possibilities. Reni Eddo-Lodge places white privilege at our feet as a persistent remnant of colonialism, slavery, racism and patriarchy that must be engaged with by both white women and men if we are to progress. A Freirean, feminist, anti–racist pedagogy based on intersectionality uses a starting point of lived experience. Beginning in dialogues of trust, it operates from a kind heart in non–hierarchical, reciprocal relations. It is a revolutionary approach because it embodies values that are the antithesis of those embedded in the dominant ideology of neoliberalism: cooperation replaces competition. As Paula Allman (2009) says, dialogue involves the struggle to transform relations, therefore sows the seeds of a radical praxis which experiences different ways of relating, leading to a different way of seeing the world, which forms the basis of re-visioning a new world and acting together to change the course of history. And Reni Eddo-Lodge says: 'Feminism will have won when we have ended poverty' (2018: 181), and that is poverty for all. 'The mess we are in is a deliberate one. If it was created by people, it can be dismantled by people, and it can be rebuilt in a way that serves all, rather than a selfish, hoarding few' (Eddo-Lodge, 2018: 181–2).

Freirean pedagogy and feminist pedagogy

My proposal is that Freirean pedagogy and feminist, anti-racist pedagogy are powerful and complementary in their potential for critical practice in global times. In support of this claim, I will explore the development of feminist pedagogy and consider the similarity of process and goals. The political activism of the women's movement of the 1960s and 1970s developed out of a challenge to a dominant way of seeing the world based on patriarchy and pragmatism, which denies the validity of *experience* and *feeling*. Women rose to claim the *personal as political*. There was a groundswell of grassroots activism in which women came together in leaderless groups to explore consciousness from our own experience, making feminist theory in action. We translated this into collective action for change based on a vision of peace and justice. An outstanding example of the collective potential of this movement is the way in which, in August 1981, a group of women who had never been involved in political action before marched from Cardiff to Greenham Common to protest against the siting of cruise missiles in Britain. This marked the beginning of the Greenham Women's Peace Movement, which gave focus to 'an ideology that countered patriarchy and offered women an alternative worldview' (Dominelli, 2019: 119). A praxis began to evolve with emphasis on lived experience as the basis of theoretical understanding.

At this time, Sylvia Walby (1992, 1994) critiqued the limitations of poststructuralism and postmodernism as 'a neglect of the social context of power relations' (1992: 16). Her argument was that postmodernism fragmented concepts of race, class and gender. Whereas Marxism subsumed all forms of discrimination under class, postmodernists swung with the pendulum to disintegrate these concepts altogether. She illustrated the dangers of this in relation to black women who raise three important aspects of analysis: (1) racist structures within the labour market; (2) ethnic experience and racism; and (3) locating the intersection of ethnicity and gender, both culturally and historically. Disintegration overlooks these patterns of race, class and gender oppressions and their local/global dimensions. She cited Swasti Mitter's call for a 'common bond on women in the new globalized economy' (Walby, 1994: 234) within a recognition of difference, as unfolding insights enabled us to work with *conscientisation* from a wider perspective as analyses of power moved the dynamic of praxis further towards achieving a shared vision of freedom.

In these ways, Freire and anti-racist feminism enrich each other in the struggle for transformative social change. Together, they provide a pedagogy with which to denounce social injustices in all their complexity, 'for to be utopian is not to be merely idealistic or impractical but rather to engage in denunciation and annunciation', the 'act of analyzing a dehumanizing reality, denounce it while announcing its transformation' (Freire, 1985: 57). For Freire, *utopia* is a fundamental necessity in the process of becoming fully human, 'in favor of dreaming, of utopia, of democracy is the discourse of those who refuse to settle and do not allow the taste for being human, which fatalism deteriorates, to die within themselves' (Freire, 2007b: 26).

The most compelling analysis of Freire from a feminist perspective continues, for me, to come from Kathleen Weiler. She profoundly influenced my thinking with her challenge to engage with 'Freire and a feminist pedagogy of difference' (Weiler, 1995: 23). Her point is that collective action will not emerge naturally from contradictory histories and experiences. We need to engage with the contradictions of privilege, oppression and power by acknowledging our own histories and selves in process from an 'acute consciousness of difference' in order to move more critically towards our 'goals of social justice and empowerment' (Weiler, 1995: 35). She calls for a feminist pedagogy that enriches and re-visions Freirean goals but is framed more specifically in the context of feminist struggle. In this sense, the concept of *denunciation* suggests that we need to develop better strategies to help us name and analyse our insight into a multiplicity of oppressions, and *annunciation* suggests the need for new forms of action across difference that unite us in mutual struggle.

Weiler offers three key areas of analysis with which to extend Freirean pedagogy into feminist pedagogy: the role and authority of the teacher; experience and feelings as sources of knowledge; and the question of difference.

The role and authority of the teacher

While Freire emphasises the horizontal, reciprocal role of the educator as a co-teacher/co-learner, he fails to address issues of power according to ethnicity, gender and status. Weiler suggests that *authority* can be problematic. The vision of a mutual, reciprocal, non-hierarchical way of working can be driven by hope rather than reality if issues of power, hierarchy and culture are overlooked. Women in community are not a homogeneous group; they are diverse. They are also situated within a competitive and individualistic culture. As feminist community workers, we are vested with the role, authority and status that render us different. If we are working towards consciousness and collective action for change with groups within which issues of power are ignored, we are not likely to be successful. However, it is possible for the anti-racist, feminist educator, through the process of *conscientisation*, to name difference and reach a shared critical understanding of the forces that have shaped that difference and, in doing so, reach a collective unity for change. For example, anti-racist, feminist thought, by engaging with male privilege as a corollary of white privilege, is able to extend beyond linear rationality to gain insight into the nature of contradictory oppressions. Let me illustrate this with a reflection from Peggy McIntosh (cited in Weeks, 2009: 7): 'As a white person, I realized I had been taught about racism as something that puts others at a disadvantage, but had been taught not to see one of its corollary aspects, white privilege, which puts me at an advantage. I think whites are taught not to recognise white privilege, as males are taught not to recognise male privilege.' In becoming open to understanding our privileged identities as well as our oppressed identities we develop the confidence and autonomy to work collectively for the common good.

Experience and feeling as sources of knowledge

We need to identify a feminist knowledge of the world as the basis for social change. Freire placed great emphasis on the questioning of experience to come to an understanding of power in order to transform the world: in knowing it, we can recreate it. In the same way, feminist knowledge of the world is the foundation for action. Belenky et al (1997) have made an immense contribution through their research into *Women's Ways of Knowing*. They emphasise the quest for self and voice, which plays a key role in the process of transformation for women. The self, in an inner and outer process, is transformed: 'weaving together the strands of rational and emotive thought and of integrating objective and subjective knowing [lead to a] new way of thinking' (Belenky et al, 1997: 134-5). Traditionally, *feeling* has been seen as the domain of women, as of the private domain and not a reliable basis for rational action. Women are denied the value of their being in the world by a positivist, patriarchal system that places emphasis on science, on rationality, on pragmatism rather than emotion, experience or feeling. In feminist analysis, universal truths about human behaviour are challenged and increasingly *feeling* has contributed to feminist pedagogy as a balance between the inner self and the outer world, between the public and private, the personal and political. Audre Lorde captures the essence of feelings as a guide to analysis and action, keeping us in touch with our humanity:

> As we begin to recognise our deepest feelings, we begin to give up, of necessity, being satisfied with suffering and self-negation, and with the numbness which so often seems like their only alternative in society. Our acts against oppression become integral with self, motivated and empowered from within. (Lorde, 1984: 58)

There are strong links here with Freirean emphasis on humanisation as a way of being in the world. In identifying the ways in which our experience of power relationships is structured, the act of knowing, of critical insight, generates energy and motivation for action. Out of a state of dehumanisation, we are freed to humanise ourselves, creating alternative worldviews based on justice, fairness and equality.

The question of difference

The assumption made by white feminists of a universal sisterhood rendered black women invisible. Black feminists and postmodern feminists challenged the unitary and universal category *woman* as fundamentally racist on the one hand, and socially constructed and shaped on the other. Feminist pedagogy has focused on narratives of lived experience as a participatory strategy with groups of women to identify the social and historical forces that have shaped these narratives. For instance, Weiler (1994: 31) cites Sistren, a 'collaborative theatre group made up of working-class Jamaican women who create and write plays based upon a collaborative exploration of their own experiences'. The collective sharing of experience is the key to the knowledge of our socially and politically given identities. It is the process by which we discover our power as subjects in active, creative process in our world, rather than as objects that are fixed, defined and static. The Combahee River Collective argue that 'the most radical politics come directly out of our own identity, as opposed to working to end someone else's oppression' (Weiler, 1994: 32).

In 2001, in a further critical re-reading of Freire, Weiler flags up the dangers of discourse that rests on social and cultural definitions of men's and women's natures as some *given truth*. Difference between men and women is useful in thinking about feminist knowing, but must not be seen as innate. Failing to acknowledge the social and historical construction of the idea of women's natures would be to subscribe to Western patriarchy's *male rationality* versus *female nurturance* dichotomy. Weiler advocates the need to write from a discourse of *feminist rationality*. By this, she means that women have the capacity to think in rational and abstract ways: women's knowledge is not solely defined by emotion.

Gloria Anzaldúa's conception of the *new mestiza* as a postcolonial feminist emphasises that set patterns of women's behaviour are invasions of the self, and that any critique of patriarchy must include Western conceptions of: (i) linear rationality, (ii) white privilege and (iii) assumptions of universal truths (1987). Anti-racist feminist educators have 'stressed that critical and feminist pedagogies, whilst claiming an opposition to oppression, are in danger of taking a kind of imperial and totalizing stance of knowing and "speaking for" those who are to be educated into truth' (Weiler, 2001: 72). Weiler raises *social identity* and *authority* in speaking for silenced others. Are we acting out privilege by taking on an unquestioned authority in speaking? Reflecting, she asks, 'How then do I, a white woman from the US, approach the work of a Brazilian man who spoke for the subjugated and oppressed?' (Weiler, 2001: 73).

Sylvia Walby: patriarchal sites of oppression

At this point, I want to return to the ideas of Sylvia Walby (1992; 1994) and examine their specific use in relation to a Freirean-feminist-anti-racist pedagogy. Clearly Walby put emphasis on the centrality of patriarchy as a prime oppressive force. This has helped us gain insights into the way that unitary concepts can hide more than they reveal. Walby's argument is that patriarchy, as a blanket theory, denies the complex ways in which women's experience varies across difference. Her solution is to identify six structures of analysis within which to analyse patriarchy: (i) paid work, (ii) housework, (iii) sexuality, (iv) culture, (v) violence, and (vi) the state. She suggests that the interrelationships between these elements create different forms of patriarchy.

Walby contested if we fail to theorise new patterns of gender, ethnicity and class oppressions, our practice will be uncritical. For example, while the feminisation of poverty continues to be a concern within the UK, on a global level consumer-driven profit under capitalism is dependent on the exploitation of women and children in the developing (and industrialising) world who are becoming the prime producers and suppliers of some of the cheapest goods for Western markets. Walby concluded that the concept of 'patriarchy' is a vital component of gender inequality, and we ignore it at our peril. Patriarchy as a concept and theory is essential to 'capture the depth, pervasiveness and interconnectedness of different aspects of women's subordination, and can be developed in this way to take account of the different forms of gender inequality over time, class and ethnic group' (Walby, 1992: 2).

Freire vehemently believed that empowerment is a collective experience, that true freedom is to work to transform all society (Freire, in Shor and Freire, 1987). *Pedagogy of the Oppressed* continues to offer critical pedagogues around the world hope, passion and theoretical justification for their work. How, then, is it possible to address the problems it presents to feminist, anti-racist pedagogy? The major problem lies not so much in its sexist language, which was addressed in Freire's later work, but in its failure to fully engage with difference and diversity, overlooking the 'possibility of simultaneous contradictory positions of oppression and dominance' (Weiler, 1995: 27). However, Freire was emphatic that his work should always be open to critique and that it be re-visioned based on the experience of others and changing political contexts:

> Many things that today still appear to me as valid (not only in actual or future practice but also in any theoretical interpretation that I might derive from it) could be outgrown tomorrow, not just by me, but by others as well. The crux here, I believe, is that I must be constantly open to criticism and sustain my curiosity, always ready for revision based on the results of my future experience and that of others. And in turn, those who put my experience into practice must strive to recreate it and also rethink my thinking. In doing so, they should bear in mind that no educational practice takes place in a vacuum, only in a real context – historical, economic, political, and not necessarily identical to any other context. (Freire, 1985: 11)

Now, in current times of crisis and change, having failed to halt the neoliberal project, we have reached unsustainable extremes of inequality and neoliberal capitalism continues to drive us headlong on a trajectory of disaster for humanity and the planet. We must try to think harder: instead of fragmenting oppressions or concentrating solely on disempowerment, we need to focus on power, critique the way it works, expose its consequences. We need to attach the symptoms to the root source of oppressions! At the same time as we develop these insights, we need to name the world we want in a counternarrative of possibility. As Reni Eddo-Lodge (2018: 182-3) says, we need to name our own utopia:

> We have to hope for and envision something before agitating for it, rather than blithely giving up, citing reality, and accepting the way things are. After all, utopian ideals are as ideological as the political foundations of the world we're currently living in.

INTERSECTIONALITY
ONE OVERARCHING SYSTEM OF DOMINATION

INTERSECTIONALITY IS ABOUT SEEING OPPRESSIONS AS AN INTERLINKING, OVERLAPPING, MUTUALLY-REINFORCING SYSTEM OF DISCRIMINATION. IT OFFERS DEEPER KNOWLEDGE FOR SOCIAL JUSTICE PRACTICE TO COUNTER NEOLIBERAL POWER

PATRICIA HILL COLLINS

BLACK FEMINIST THOUGHT DEMONSTRATES BLACK WOMEN'S EMERGING POWER AS AGENTS OF KNOWLEDGE. BY EMBRACING A PARADIGM OF RACE, CLASS AND GENDER AS INTERLOCKING SYSTEMS, BLACK FEMINIST THOUGHT RECONCEPTUALISES THE SOCIAL RELATIONS OF DOMINATION AND RESISTANCE (1991)

9

Reclaiming the radical agenda

Figure 9.1:

Seven steps to a radical agenda

1. • Voicing values
2. • Making critical connections
3. • Critiquing and dissenting
4. • Imagining alternatives
5. • Creating counternarratives
6. • Connecting and acting
7. • Cooperating for a common good

Community development is predicated on principles of social justice and environmental justice: a sustainable world in balance, an ecosystem in which everyone and everything flourishes, a democracy based on participation and collective wellbeing. Its vision is of a peaceful, just and sustainable future. Its practice is critical pedagogy, rooted in a 'profound love for the world and for people [and] because love is an act of courage, not of fear, love is commitment to others' (Freire, 2018: 89). The process of liberation begins in dialogue, a trusting, critical encounter which enables people to speak their word and name their world. And Freire was clear that the purpose is freedom, 'the conquest of the world for the liberation of humankind' (2018: 89).

What happened to radical community development?

Radical community development emerged at a historic juncture: social and political change in the late 1960s and early 1970s came together with the revolutionary ideas of Freire and Gramsci becoming available in English for the first time (see Chapter 3). This combination was the basis of a unity of praxis. The Community Development Programme (CDP) challenged the pathology-based assumptions of the government's 'cycle of deprivation' theory by developing a critical approach to practice based on a structural analysis of poverty. As Lena Dominelli says, 'CDP's activities challenged the social pathology theory of poverty for being unable to explain structurally induced poverty' (2019: 187). This was not a message that the state wanted to hear, that is, that the gap between rich and poor is not due to personal pathologies, but is a direct consequence of the exploitation of profit generation and accumulation under capitalism.

After the emergence of radical, transformative community development in the early 1970s, there was a period of sustained action against injustice, challenging class, patriarchal, racist and heterosexist traditions which erode human rights and undermine democracy. This involved campaigns to end violence against women and children, to end poverty, to end the corporate degradation of the environment, against homophobia, racism and sexism, against the deportation of asylum seekers, and much more. At the same time as acting on bigger issues, practice focused on the development of cooperative local economies and healthy convivial communities. New social movements gathered momentum from grassroots practice to change the face of society. Class–based grand narratives were critiqued as inadequate analyses of discrimination and a process of deconstructing binary opposites began. Prior to this, discrimination had been subsumed under a class analysis of oppressor/oppressed, and many of the critiques of Freire and Gramsci were levelled from this perspective, that is, that a simplistic binary analysis conceals more than it reveals. However, postmodernism became increasingly contradictory for community development by dismantling binary opposites at the same time as it fragmented any sense of the collective.

During this period, community development lost its way from the radical agenda of the 1970s and 1980s as, through the 1990s, neoliberalism insidiously crept through every aspect of our being, and community workers, trapped in the headlights, became depoliticised. Shifting boundaries between the state, the market and civil society blurred the way for practitioners, who forgot about their radical agenda, to be persuaded to perform policy delivery on behalf of the government. In doing so, they unwittingly played a part in dismantling the welfare state (Craig et al, 2011). We became drawn into a culture of bureaucracy and managerialism, chasing our own funding and jumping to the tune of performance indicators. As the hijacking and dilution of our radical concepts were imported into policy, we failed to see that there were contradictions between what we said we do and what we were doing in practice. This opened the way for community development to be misappropriated in the interests of top–down agendas.

Pitchford with Henderson (2008) argue that the plethora of competing policy agendas that renamed community development as community *involvement* or *engagement* or *participation* muddied understanding of community development as a distinctive political process for progressive social change. The consequence is that we became distracted, lost our way and had little sense of direction or overarching purpose. 'The case can and should be made for how community development can deepen democracy' (Pitchford with Henderson, 2008: 94–5). Without effective and relevant theoretical analyses we are vulnerable to this sort of manipulation. It is vital that we develop theoretical analyses of power that are incisive and properly adequate to inform action against poverty, racism, patriarchy and all their intersections that feed into the neoliberal class project, including environmental degradation. In order to bridge the persistent gaps in community development praxis, gaps that not only reduce our potential to contribute to radical, transformative change, but leave us in grave danger of reinforcing the neoliberal structures of discrimination that we claim to be against, I offer you a seven-stage structure for reclaiming the radical agenda.

Seven steps to a radical agenda

(1) Voicing values

How many times do you explain your community development role as being founded on principles of social justice and environmental justice and grounded in values of dignity, respect, reciprocity, mutuality, trust and cooperation – values that lead to diversity and biodiversity in balance, and to human and environmental flourishing? In Chapter 2, I introduced George Monbiot's emphasis on the centrality of values to the process of change: 'Values are the bedrock of effective politics. They represent the importance we place on fundamental ways of being, offering a guide to what we consider to be good and worthwhile (2017: 7). He suggests that they can often be captured in single words, and these profound concepts capture values that connect to the way we think and behave. I demonstrated in Chapter 1 that the values that led to the welfare state were based on a common good that was at variance with the values of neoliberalism that were introduced by Margaret Thatcher. Cooperation was traded in for competition, as the dominant ideology persuaded us to believe that the market was effectively in control of society rather than the other way round, that it was necessary for the rich to become richer in order for the rest of us to benefit, that there was no such thing as society, only individuals and their families, and that there was no alternative to this neoliberal ideology, which as a whole package represented the real truth!

The tragedy is that we had reached a point in history, from 1968 to 1978, when society was at its most equal and, as Danny Dorling (2018b) pointed out (see p 51), we could have chosen to go down a different route, making different decisions based on values that reflect human and environmental flourishing. But we didn't, and it's taken us headlong into world crises, caught like rabbits in the headlights, unable to think of any alternative. As Rutger Bregman (2016) says, we seem to be in a coma, lacking the ability to understand what is happening, let alone the imagination to see a new world order to replace it.

When people are asked what they care about, community, friendship, compassion, kindness and equality come top of the list (Common Cause Foundation, 2016). George Monbiot (2017) emphasises that despite our natural capacity to feel compassion and our need to feel connected in reciprocal relationships, we have made the opposite choice by going down the route of neoliberalism with its emphasis on individualism and competition. The results of the *UK National Values Survey: Increasing Happiness by Understanding What People Value* identify a critical connection (see p 59): whereas there is a strong correlation between people's personal values and their desires for a culture rooted in those values, their perceptions of current British society are at variance with the kinder world in which they want to live. Monbiot (2017: 12) emphasises: 'A politics that has failed to articulate its values and principles leaves nothing to which people can attach themselves but policies.'

(2) Making critical connections

> To escape from this trap, we first need to perceive it. We need to name the power that has exacerbated our isolation and our collective loss of identity. This power is neoliberalism, the story it tells and the political programmes that arise from it' (Monbiot, 2017: 182–3).

Monbiot calls for a politics of belonging, and to secure this we need to change the lens through which we see the world. We need to find the criticality to name this neoliberal politics of disconnection and exploitation, and identify the contradictions we live by. Andrew Sayer (2016: 366) leads us in this direction with his provocation: 'We can't afford the rich!' He continues: 'They are living beyond our means and those of the planet, and their interests are at odds with those of the 99% and the environment.'

Provocations are good way to stimulate critical questioning.

> 'And the rich continue to get richer, even in the worst crisis for 80 years – they can still laugh all the way to their banks and tax havens as the little people bail out the banks that have failed.'
>
> Sayer (2016: 1)

This statement names contradictions and, if presented to a group of people, it would excite dialogue and debate. If you look at the section on Dorling (pp 50-2), you will find he has made similar comments in connection with the film *Eat the Rich*. By these means, we expose the way that the dominant ideology uses stigma to stir up a politics of hatred in order to justify the extreme inequalities created by neoliberal capitalism, so well explained by Imogen Tyler in her research (see pp 56-8). Wilkinson and Pickett (2018), in their latest book *The Inner Level*, offer incisive analysis into the way that inequality invades our minds, increasing anxiety levels, affecting the way we think and feel and relate to each other, causing ill health and social problems. They illustrate how more equal societies benefit everyone, including the rich. Use these insights as resources to encourage critical questioning.

(3) Critiquing and dissenting

Creating the context for critical questioning is vital in the process of radical community development praxis. It happens in those spaces we create for dialogue and our practice, as popular educators, sets the scene for questioning through Freirean problematising (see p 116).

Take a living contradiction from everyday life that is relevant to the people in your community, one that you hear repeated in conversations. Capture it in a relevant form for your community – as a provocation, photograph, song, drama, poetry or cartoon – in order to engage your group's attention. All you have to do is to ask what's going on! You don't give any answers, you simply ask questions that go deeper into the issue at stake. Eventually, the group will ask its own questions and come up with some ideas to take it further. Use Mendoza's critique of austerity (see p 42).

Critique is at the heart of deepening democracy. Through a process of critical consciousness, in dialogue with local people, community development questions the dominant story and exposes its contradictions. And, once we begin to question, we see things differently, and when we see things differently, we do things differently. These are all vital stages in the process of change.

(4) Imagining alternatives

We believed it when Margaret Thatcher repeatedly told us there is no alternative to this system that has so badly failed us. We doubted ourselves and lacked the imagination to come up with an alternative, Monbiot suggests that this failure has resulted in the evaporation of hope and descent into despair and disillusion.

Now we need to excite people's imaginations to see that an alternative world is infinitely possible. People create politics, but to create the politics that we want, we have to come up with an alternative, otherwise we will continue to get what we deserve! Revisit Dorling's ideas to free imaginations by projecting ourselves 100 years into the future: imagine a different future how we might control the rich, create greater diversity and opportunity, live in harmony with Europe, elect our politicians, police ourselves, deal with terrorists, welcome immigrants, create full employment 'without current obsession with the market'. Imagine a single well-funded education system for all, based on the right for all children to have the best education possible: what would it look like? (see p 52).

Re-read Annie Lowrey (2018) on p 72 and imagine universal basic income (UBI) as a simple, radical and elegant transformation of the dehumanising impact of the welfare scrounger stigma. 'Imagine that a check showed up in your mailbox or your bank account every month', she says: it restores human dignity and confidence, and it has been proven to work. It is a much healthier, more positive and cheaper solution than a means-tested benefit system. This idea is endorsed by Kate Raworth (2018) (see pp 65–71), who says that the evidence is there to show that people tend to work harder and seize more opportunities when they have the safety net of UBI. Bregman, too, reminds us that 'it's precisely because we're richer than ever that it is now within our means to take the next step in the history of progress: to give each and every person the security of a basic income. It's what capitalism ought to have been striving for all along' (2018: 46).

Dorling claims that inequality has harmed our imagination, leaving us stuck. We need to imagine how placing different values at the heart of the way we live and relate to each other and to the environment releases new possibilities for changing the course of history.

(5) Creating counternarratives

Up to now, we have failed to come up with a compelling counternarrative of change, offering nothing to put in the place of the dominant neoliberal narrative that has created our current crises of social inequality and environmental destruction. Let's return to Monbiot's idea of a politics of belonging. Our counternarrative should emerge from the values and principles we have named, which need to be compellingly woven through a new story that has instant appeal. And, as Bregman challengingly asserts, for the story to reach out to as many people as possible, it needs to be written in an accessible style that can be understood by a 12-year-old!

I think George Monbiot is saying much the same as this when he suggests that this story has to inspire hope and possibility for a new future 'faithful to the facts, faithful to our values, and faithful to the narrative patterns to which we respond' (2017: 6). This counternarrative needs to engage with intersectionality, identifying interconnected, overlapping oppressions that cannot be fully understood in a fragmented way. Monbiot talks about a counternarrative of belonging, which I see as a healing, a reconnection from the alienating way of life creating by neoliberalism, one that is inclusive and honouring of all. To achieve this, we are called on to pay full attention to others by suspending our own truths in a process of connected knowing (Belenky et al, 1986). In this way, we develop new insights that form the basis of counternarratives of liberation, new stories about new possibilities. Reni Eddo-Lodge places white privilege firmly on the table as the sticking point of colonialism, slavery, racism and patriarchy. White women and men must heed this challenge!

Starting in dialogues of trust and operating from a kind heart, we put new values into place that open new ways of relating to each other, and this is the basis of seeing new possibilities for a new story. It is a revolutionary approach because it embodies values that are the antithesis of those embedded in the dominant ideology of neoliberalism: cooperation replaces competition. As Bregman says, 'a crisis should be a moment of truth, the juncture at which a fundamental choice is made' (2018: 242).

(6) Connecting and acting

Changing the way we see the world changes the way we act in the world. Once we begin to see that another world is possible, we realise that our ideas need to be connected to action. For instance, if we challenge the concept of people being governed by the market, and turn this on its head to say that the market is there to serve the wellbeing of people and the planet, we do things differently. Engage with Kate Raworth's remarkable Doughnut model on p 66 and explore how we can have healthy, happy lives by replacing consumer greed with a new ideal, that of meeting human need for everyone, at the same time as dealing with diversity and equality, and supporting biodiversity and a flourishing planet. Explore the drive behind knowledge democracy: how it is concerned with the subordination of other knowledges in the pursuit of a single, dominant truth that overtly favours discrimination and subordination in order to maintain the interests of the rich and powerful (see Hall and Tandon, discussed on p 73).

(7) Cooperating for a common good

Raworth says that 'The twenty-first century task is clear: to create economies that promote human prosperity in a flourishing way of life so that we can thrive in balance within the Doughnut's safe and just space' (2018: 287). Her Doughnut model offers a simple, graphic model of how to maintain that balance for the good of all within the means of the planet. This model flies in the face of neoliberal elevation of the market over society by emphasising that 'every economy – local to global – is embedded within society and within the living world' (2018: 287). It recognises that the household, the commons, the market and the state all provide for the needs of society, best of all when they work together. In these ways, 'by deepening our understanding of human nature we can create institutions and incentives that reinforce our social reciprocity and other-regarding values, rather than undermine them' (2018: 287). An interconnected, rather than disconnected, praxis addresses the interlinked crises of climate change, violent conflict, forced migration, widening inequalities, rising xenophobia, and endemic financial instability. With the resources, the knowledge and the technology we already have and by simply changing our focus from profit to human and environmental flourishing, we can come up with an economy that operates within a healthy web of life on earth, in perfect, respectful balance, in which the household, the commons, the market and the state work together to provide for the needs of everyone within the means of the planet. Here we have an ingenious solution from an economist who fundamentally turns neoliberalism's emphasis on profit on its head. The economy must serve the needs of people and the planet!

Connect with movements for change. Connect with the New Economics Foundation to find out how to put Raworth's ideas into action. Engage with the intellectual challenges of intersectionality and learn to listen from the heart to other experiences. Actively explore the concept of knowledge democracy and be open to other knowledges that challenge the role of schools and universities as purveyors of a dominant truth. Have the courage to get together in groups of white people to take the burden of white privilege off black people. Engage with Sayer's ideas on common inheritance which expose any notion that we have an entitlement to any more than our fair share as nonsense. Reparation for the wrongs of the past could be righted if we take seriously Sayer's analysis of our common inheritance in relation to redistribution of resources, fair taxation, collective responsibility, the right to human dignity and right to a fair and relevant education that offers all children the chance to flourish. It is a future predicated on diversity and biodiversity, and exciting ideas on how to make it a reality.

But Naomi Klein (2018) warns of the dangers when a story is ruptured and we do not understand the crisis we find ourselves in. By this, she means that we have been living with the dangerous stories told by neoliberalism for a long time – no such thing as society, greed is good, profit is more important than people, white men are best, the poor are wasters, the natural world is ours for the taking, as are the commons, that there is no alternative – and much more. By elevating subordinated knowledges in a drive for inclusion, as discussed by Hall and Tandon in Chapter 2, we discover other truths informed by other values, other ways of seeing the world and other ways of being in the world that put less value on money and more value on caring for each other and the planet.

> For Paulo, throughout his life and work, the essential questions ... remained: What kind of world do we live in? Why is it like that? What kind of world do we want? How do we get there from here?'
> (Ira Shor, 2018: 188)

This is our task: to critique the world we live in and spell out the world we want, only then does it become very straightforward to make it a reality!

Kickstarting a new narrative with provocations

The essence of Paulo Freire's approach to social and environmental justice lies in his belief in people. He believed that everyone has a right to human dignity and respect; that everyone is capable of the thought and action needed to change their world into a better place. The world is diminished by dehumanising acts, and poverty is the key way that people are robbed of the right to be fully human in the world.

BOX 9.1: A counternarrative founded in Freirean dialogue

• Human beings are subjects fully able to think and act for themselves.

• Freirean values based on respect, dignity, reciprocity, mutuality, cooperation and compassion offer a lens through which to frame every encounter and interaction.

• *Dehumanising* stories are part of dominant hegemony, reviling the vulnerable in order to maintain dominance of the powerful. These stories filter into public consciousness as an unquestionable truth that becomes embedded into the structures of society.

• *Cultural invasion* refers to the colonisation of one social group by another, imposing cultural values that become dominant and seen as desirable and superior to those of the subordinated group. This concept is key to understanding knowledge democracy and the concept of *epistemicide*.

• Social change will come from below; power will not be relinquished from above.

• Dialogue is the conduit of critical consciousness: respectful, mutual, reciprocal conversation between equals develops a process of *conscientisation*, or 'the deepening of the coming of consciousness' (Freire, 1993: 109). In dialogue groups, people question the contradictions of everyday reality and become aware of the connections between their personal lives and the structures of society that create social divisions.

• Problem-posing, or *problematisation,* is used to trigger dialogue. Freire referred to *codifications,* a way of capturing an aspect of lived reality and removing it from everyday taken-for-grantedness for dialogue groups to question what is happening with new eyes. This may be a provocation, a photograph, poem, story, drama – anything that is familiar to the lives of the participants and gets them questioning. Focus on the codification lessens as the participants become more confident and begin to take their questioning deeper. They seek answers and decide how to go about increasing their understanding. The educator/facilitator/provocateur/animateur offers questions, never answers!

• Creating critical public spaces is essential for dialogue. The development of new ideas is transformative and challenges the *status quo*, which is why so much neoliberal effort has gone into preventing people meeting, talking and protesting. It threatens power. Out of this critical space a counternarrative is born. It links with those of other communities, networks, alliances, into a movement for change that works towards a world worthy of human aspiration, based on values of human dignity and respect for the Earth.

At this point, I want to focus on ideas for kickstarting a counternarrative of connection based on diversity and biodiversity. Presenting some thought-provoking ideas from all of the 14 intellectual activists I have identified as sources for deepening community development's body of knowledge, I offer you a starting point for reclaiming the radical agenda.

Provocations provide an interruption in daily taken-for-granted assumptions. Questioning the *status quo* through reflection and dialogue deepens critical consciousness. Critiquing the dominant neoliberal narrative frees the space to imagine alternatives. Starting with values, we imagine the world we want to live in, and these values provide a lens through which to see a counternarrative.

Provocations from 14 key intellectual activists

Here, I have chosen a cross-section of thought-provoking statements, selected on the basis that as they inspired my thinking to go deeper, I felt they could work well to stimulate critical dialogue. These provocations are supported by related ideas. They could be projected, or handed out as hard copies, accompanied by cartoons or photographs, or used on their own or made into cards, depending on the nature and experience of your dialogue group. These are tools that are capable of triggering the process of radical community development to deepen critical consciousness at each stage of its process. Take a glance and see what you think. Go back to Chapter 2 and read the summarised ideas of these intellectual activists to deepen your understanding of the related issues. Try putting some of the most thought-provoking ideas onto cards to extend your set of provocations.

Provocations from 14 key intellectual activists

(1) Voicing values

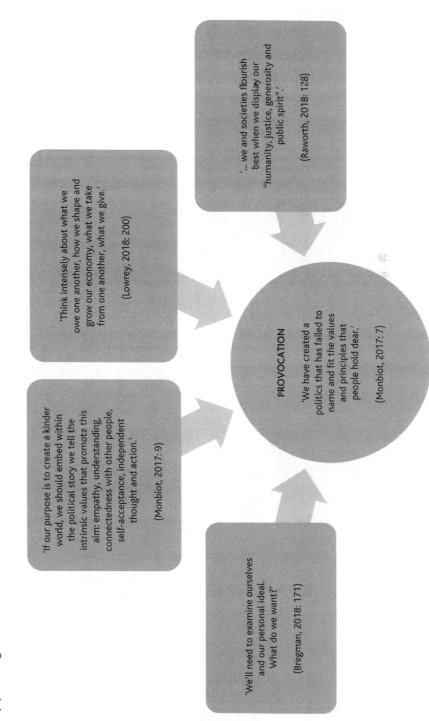

'Think intensely about what we owe one another, how we shape and grow our economy, what we take from one another, what we give.'

(Lowrey, 2018: 200)

'... we and societies flourish best when we display our "humanity, justice, generosity and public spirit".'

(Raworth, 2018: 128)

'If our purpose is to create a kinder world, we should embed within the political story we tell the intrinsic values that promote this aim: empathy, understanding, connectedness with other people, self-acceptance, independent thought and action.'

(Monbiot, 2017: 9)

PROVOCATION

'We have created a politics that has failed to name and fit the values and principles that people hold dear.'

(Monbiot, 2017: 7)

'We'll need to examine ourselves and our personal ideal. What do we want?'

(Bregman, 2018: 171)

(2) Making critical connections

'The contemporary university is often characterized as working with colonized knowledge ... The epistemologies of most peoples of the world, whether Indigenous, or excluded on the basis of race, gender or sexuality are missing.'

(Hall and Tandon, 2017: 7)

'Racism's legacy does not exist without purpose. It brings with it not just a disempowerment for those affected by it, but an empowerment for those who're not. That is white privilege.'

(Eddo Lodge, 2018: 115-16)

'Abjection describes the violent exclusionary forces of sovereign power: those forces that strip people of their human dignity and reproduce them as dehumanized waste, the disposable dregs and refuse of social life.'

(Tyler, 2015: 21)

PROVOCATION

'The rich are having a good crisis ... in fact, the rise of the rich is an integral feature of the crisis ... many of the rich have not only got richer in the build-up to the crisis but ... after it too.'

(Sayer, 2016: 179)

'We live in time of peak inequality. It pervades almost every aspect of our lives in Britain in ways that we now accept as normal ... but it isn't ... a child born in Sweden is half as likely to die in childhood as a child born today in the UK.'

(Dorling, 2018b: 31)

(3) *Critiquing and dissenting*

'The inevitable endgame of neoliberalism is corporate fascism, and the de-civilization of our world... Some would argue that capitalism is trade, or ownership of property, or profit. But capitalism is not any of these things. It is an ideological basis for *how* we do these things.'

(Mendoza, 2018: 78)

'Stigmatization operates as a form of governance which legitimizes the reproduction and entrenchment of inequalities and injustices which impact on us all.'

(Tyler, 2016 212)

'The first Occupy protest "We are the 99%" in September 2011 ... focused attention on how much the richest had helped themselves to wealth generated by austerity, creating the level of inequalities that lead to unhealthly, unhappy societies.'

(Dorling, 2018b: 23)

PROVOCATION

'Austerity is not a short-term disruption to balance the books. It is the controlled demolition of the welfare state – transferring the UK from social democracy to a corporate power.'

(Mendoza, 2016: 7)

'To get started, we first need to understand what we're saying no to – because that *No* ...is not just to an individual or even a group of individuals ... We're also saying no to the *system* that has elevated them to such heights. Then let's move to a yes – a yes that will bring about change so fundamental that today's corporate takeover will be relegated to a historical footnote.'

(Klein, 2018: 11–12)

(4) Imagining alternatives

'We're all one race, "the human race"... Discussing racism is about discussing white anxiety. It's about white anxiety. It's about asking why whiteness has this reflexive need to define itself against immigrant bogey monsters in order to feel comfortable, safe and secure.'

(Eddo-Lodge, 2018: 215)

'Nature needs respect and a sense of wonder, not plunder ... Nature provides things like soils, water, fish and plants for free, but it makes no sense to regard them as free to be used without limit, regardless of the health of the biosphere. Nature doesn't respond to the signals of the market.'

(Sayer, 2016: 347)

"Inequality actually harms the imagination ... Once we imagine what could be, then it becomes easier to know what we should be dreaming of and aspiring to.'

(Dorling, 2018: 327)

PROVOCATION

'Political failure is ... a failure of imagination.'

(Monbiot, 2017: 6)

'It's precisely because we're richer than ever that it is now within our means to take the next step in the history of progress: to give each and every person the security of a basic income. It's what capitalism ought to have been striving for all along. See it as a dividend on progress made possible by the blood, sweat and tears of past generations... talk differently, think differently, describe the problem differently.'

(Bregman, 2018: 46–7)

(5) Creating counternarratives

'[The Doughnut is] a radically new compass for guiding humanity this century. And it points towards a future that can provide for every person's needs while safeguarding the living world on which we all depend.'

(Raworth, 2018: 44-5)

'Every dollar invested in a homeless person returns triple or more savings on healthcare, police, and court costs. Just imagine what the eradication of child poverty might achieve.'

(Bregman, 2018: 259)

'Imagine that a check showed up in your mailbox or your bank account every month ... The idea is a very old one '.

(Lowrey, 2018: 4-5)

PROVOCATION

'It is time to redraw ourselves as people who thrive by connecting with each other and with this living home of ours that is not ours alone ...'

(Raworth, 2018: 127-8)

'How can we organise economic life in ways that are fair, conducive to well-being, and sustainable?'

(Sayer, 2016: 342)

(6) Connecting and acting

'The right to unionize, bargain for pay and conditions collectively, and withdraw labour through strike: this co-operative approach to holding corporate power to account brought workers rising wages, reduced hours, the concept of work–life balance, the weekend, health and safety in the workplace, and an end to the slave-like conditions working people endured through the 18th, 19th and early 20th century.'

(Mendoza, 2018: 121)

'We have to hope for and envision something before agitating for it, rather than blithely giving up, citing reality, and accepting the way things are. After all, utopian ideals are as ideological as the political foundations of the world we're currently living in.'

(Eddo-Lodge, 2018: 182–3)

'Because shock tactics rely on the public becoming disorientated by fast-moving events, they tend to backfire most spectacularly in places where there is a strong collective memory of previous instances where fear and trauma were exploited to undermine democracy. Those memories serve as ... shared reference points that allow [people] to name what's happening and fight back.'

(Klein, 2018: 191)

PROVOCATION

'*Homo sapiens*, it turns out, is the most cooperative species on the planet ... along with our propensity to trade, we are also drawn to give, share and reciprocate.'

(Raworth, 2018: 104)

'Don't let anyone tell you what's what. If we want to change the world, we need to be unrealistic, unreasonable and impossible. Remember: those who called for the abolition of slavery, for suffrage for women, and for same-sex marriage were also once branded lunatics. Until history proved them right.'

(Bregman, 2018: 263-4)

(7) Cooperating for a common good

'Doughnut economics sets out an optimistic vision of humanity's common future: a global economy that creates thriving balance.... And we know full well, as an international community, that we have the technology, know-how and financial means to end extreme poverty in all its forms should we collectively choose to make that happen.'

(Raworth, 2018: 286)

'Feminism has to be absolutely utopian and unrealistic, far removed from any semblance of the world we're living in now.'

(Eddo-Lodge, 2018: 182)

'Rather than congratulate ourselves on our wealth ... we should open our eyes to our vast debts to our common inheritance from nature and the labours and achievements of previous generations.'

(Sayer, 2016: 150)

PROVOCATION

'... societies that come together around an understanding of a shared crisis can change the world for the better.'

(Klein, 2017: 1)

'The spell of neoliberalism has been broken, crushed under the weight of lived experience and a mountain of evidence. What for decades was unsayable is now being said out loud ...: *free college tuition, double the minimum wage, 100 per cent renewable energy as quickly as technology allows, demilitarize the police, prisons are no place for young people, refugees are welcome here, war makes us all less safe.*'

(Klein, 2017: 263)

 **Another week in my life**

I witness issues of moral leadership becoming key in a resurgence of a 'politics of hatred'. Misogyny, xenophobia and racism are being woven into the longstanding dominant narrative of the 'welfare scrounger', as white, patriarchal, supremacist privilege rears its ugly head. As September 2019 draws to a close with a tumultuous week in politics in both the UK and the US, I sense a pivotal moment for the Far Right extremist rhetoric that brings with it the threat of violence and civil unrest:

> The 11 judges of the UK supreme court cancelled Boris Johnson's unlawful suspension of parliament on the very day the House Speaker, Nancy Pelosi, put aside her previous misgiving and launched an impeachment inquiry against Donald Trump ... During the 2016 EU referendum campaign, MP Jo Cox was murdered; a few weeks later Trump hinted that gun owners might deal with Hillary Clinton by taking the law into their own hands. (Freedland, 2019)

At last I detect change. There is a visible outrage drawing people to stand up and speak their truth to power as they see this normalising of the unacceptable. This week has seen a minority ethnic woman, Gina Miller, take Boris Johnson to the highest court in the land and win. Out of populist political chaos we see a new dawn on the horizon ...' on both sides of the Atlantic decency is reasserting itself' (Freedland, 2019). And young people of the world are rising, inspired by 16-year-old Greta Thunberg to demand a better future for the planet. In the few months since her lone protest in Stockholm, she has triggered a global movement for change now known as Young People for Climate. On 20 September 2019, four million young people took to the streets in countries around the world demanding action on climate change: 'We are not just some young people skipping school. We are a wave of change. Together we are unstoppable' (Greta Thunberg, in *The Guardian*, 21 September 2019).

Our crisis is a crisis of values. Claiming back values based on human worth and our place on the planet, values of diversity and biodiversity in mutual balance in an interconnected whole, is the basis of a powerful counternarrative. Get the values right and the story writes itself to provide deeper critiques of the problems we face and the imagination to create a new, flourishing world order out of the ruins of the old!

> **'Those who tell the stories run the world.'**
> Monbiot (2017: 1)

References

Adams, R. and Barr, C. (2018) 'Oxford faces anger over failure to improve diversity among students', *The Guardian*, 23 May

Alinsky, S. (1969) *Reveille for radicals*, New York: Vintage Press.

Allman, P. (1988) 'Gramsci, Freire and Illich: their contributions to education for socialism', in T. Lovett (ed) *Radical approaches to adult education*, London: Routledge, pp 85–113.

Allman, P. (1999) *Revolutionary social transformation: Democratic hopes, political possibilities, and critical education*, Westport, CT: Bergin & Garvey.

Allman, P. (2001) *Critical education against global capitalism: Karl Marx and revolutionary critical education*, Westport, CT: Bergin & Garvey.

Allman, P. (2009) 'Paulo Freire's contributions to radical adult education', in A. Darder, M.P. Baltodano and R.D. Torres (eds) *The critical pedagogy reader* (2nd edn), New York: Routledge, pp 417–30.

Allman, P. (2010) *Critical education against global capitalism: Karl Marx and revolutionary critical education*, Rotterdam: Sense.

Allman, P. and Wallis, J. (1997) 'Commentary: Paulo Freire and the future of the radical tradition', *Studies in the Education of Adults*, vol 29, pp 113-20.

ALP (Adult Learning Project) (2017) ALP Groups 2017/18. Available at: http://alpedinburgh.btck.co.uk/ALPgroups [accessed 4 December 2018].

Alston, P. (2018) 'Statement on visit to the United Kingdom by Professor Philip Alston, United Nations Special Rapporteur on extreme poverty and human rights', London, 16 November, available at www.ohchr.org

Anonymous (2018) 'Changing the Story' (P. Wilkinson, Interviewer)

Anthias, F. and Yuval-Davis, N. with Cain, H. (1992) *Racialized boundaries: Race, nation, gender, colour and class and the anti-racist struggle*, London: Routledge.

Anzaldúa, G. (1987) *Borderlands/La Frontera*, San Francisco, CA: Aunt Lute Books.

Apple, M. (2006) 'Producing inequalities: neo-liberalism, neo-conservatism, and the politics of educational reform', in H. Lauder, P. Brown, J. Dillabough and A.H. Halsey (eds) *Education, globalization and social change*, Oxford: Oxford University Press, pp 469-89.

ASH (2019) 'The truth about Grenfell Tower: A report by Architects for Social Housing', Available at architectsforsocialhousing.co.uk [accessed 12 August 2019].

Baird, V. (2010) 'The beauty of big democracy', *New Internationalist*, no 436, October, pp 15-19.

Barr, A. (1995) 'Empowering communities – beyond fashionable rhetoric? Some reflections on the Scottish experience', *Community Development Journal*, vol 30, no 2, April, pp 121-32.

Barrett, R. and Clothier, P. (2016) *The United Kingdom Values Survey: Increasing happiness by understanding what people value*, available at www.valuescentre.com

BBC (1966) *Cathy come Home*, 16 November.

Behr, R. (2016) 'How Remain failed; The inside story of a doomed campaign' in *The Guardian,* 5 July.

Belenky, M., Clinchy, B., Goldberger, N. and Tarule, J. (1997) *Women's ways of knowing: The development of self, voice and mind* (2nd edn), New York: Basic Books.

Berger, R. and Quinney, R. (eds) (2005) *Storytelling sociology: Narrative as social inquiry*, Boulder, CO: Lynne Reinner Publishers.

Beveridge Report (1942) *Social insurance and allied services*, London: HMSO.

Bhavani, R., Mirza, H.S. and Meetoo, V. (2005) *Tackling the roots of racism*, Bristol: The Policy Press.

Bhopal, K. (2018) *White privilege: The myth of a post-racial society*, Bristol: Policy Press.

Biesta, G. (2011) 'Towards the learning democracy', in *Learning democracy in school and society*, Rotterdam: SensePublishers.

BlackCard Training (2018), The Australian BlackCard Pty Ltd, Brisbane, Queensland, https://www.theblackcard.com.au

Blair, T. (1998) *The third way: New politics for the new century*, London: The Fabian Society.

Blewitt, J. (ed) (2008) *Community, empowerment and sustainable development*, Totnes: Green Books.

Boal, A. (1994) (translated by A. Jackson) *The rainbow of desire: The Boal method of theatre and therapy*, London: Routledge.

Boal, A. (2008) *Theatre of the oppressed* (new edn), London: Pluto.

Boggs, C. (1980) *Gramsci's Marxism*, London: Pluto.

Bone, J. (2015) 'False economy: Financialization, crises and socio-economic polarisation', *Sociology Compass*, https://onlinelibrary.wiley.com/doi/abs/10.1111/soc4.12300

Bowers, C.A. and Apffel-Marglin, F. (eds) (2004) *Re-thinking Freire: Globalization and the environmental crisis*, Mahwah, NJ: Lawrence . Erlbaum Associates.

Bown, L. (2011) Acknowledgments, in C. Kirkwood and Kirkwood *Living adult education: Freire in Scotland* (2nd edn), Rotterdam: SensePublishers, pp xi-xii.

Boyle, D. (ed) (2013) *What if money grew on trees? Asking the big questions about economics*, Lewes: Ivy Press.

Bregman, R. (2018) *Utopia for realists: And how we can get there*, London: Bloomsbury.

Bundy, A. (ed) (2015) *Beyond the walls: Public libraries in Australia and New Zealand engaging their communities, Adelaide, 26-27 March 2015 Conference Proceedings*, Adelaide: Auslib Press.

Burningham, L. and Thrush, D. (2001) *Rainforests are a long way from here: The environmental concerns of disadvantaged groups*, York: Joseph Rowntree Foundation.

Calder, G. (2003) 'Communitarianism and New Labour'. Available at www.whb.co.uk/socialissues

Callaway, H. (1981) 'Women's perspectives: research as re-vision', in P. Reason and J. Rowan (eds) *Human inquiry: A sourcebook of new paradigm research,* Chichester: Wiley, pp 457–71

Calouste Gulbenkian Foundation (1968) *Community work and social change: A report on training*, London: Longman.

Cameron, D. and Clegg, N. (2010) *The Coalition: Our programme for Government*, London: HMSO.

Cannan, C. (2000) 'The environmental crisis, Greens and community development', *Community Development Journal*, vol 35, no 4, October, pp 365-76.

Carrington, D. (2019) 'Youth climate strikers: "We are going to change the fate of humanity"', *The Guardian*, 1 March.

Cavanagh, C. (2007) 'Popular education, social movements and storytelling: Interview with Chris Cavanagh', in C. Borg and P. Mayo, *Public intellectuals, radical democracy and social movements: A book of interviews*, New York: Peter Lang Publishing, pp 41–8.

Commission for Social Justice (1994) *Social justice: Strategies for national renewal*, London: Verso.

Common Cause Foundation (2016) *Perceptions matter: The Common Cause UK Values Survey*, London: Common Cause Foundation, available at valuesandframes. org

Cooke, I. and Shaw, M. (eds) (1996) *Radical community work: Perspectives from practice in Scotland*, Edinburgh: Moray House.

Coote, A. (2010) 'Cameron's Big Society will leave the poor and powerless behind'. Available at: www.neweconomics.org

Craig, G. (2008) 'The limits of compromise? Social justice, "race" and multiculturalism' in G. Craig, T. Burchardt and D. Gordon (eds) *Social justice and public policy: Seeking fairness in diverse societies*, Bristol: The Policy Press, pp 231–50.

Craig, G. (undated) 'Social justice' (available from g.craig@hull.ac.uk).

Craig, G. and Mayo, M. (eds) (1995) *Community empowerment: A reader in participation and development*, London: Zed Books.

Craig, G., Burchardt, T. and Gordon, D. (eds) (2008) *Social justice and public policy: Seeking fairness in diverse societies*, Bristol: The Policy Press.

Craig, G., Derricourt, N. and Loney, M.(eds) (1982) *Community work and the state: Towards a radical approach*, London: Routledge and Kegan Paul.

Craig, G., Mayo, M., Popple, K., Shaw, M. and Taylor, M. (eds) (2011) *The community development reader*, Bristol: The Policy Press.

Crowther, J., and Martin, I. (2011). 'Preface to second edition' in C. Kirkwood and G. Kirkwood *Living adult education: Freire in Scotland* (2nd edn), Rotterdam: SensePublishers, pp xiii–xviii.

Danaher, G., Schirato, T. and Webb, J. (2000) *Understanding Foucault*, London: Sage Publications.

Darder, A. (2002) *Reinventing Paulo Freire: A pedagogy of love*, Boulder, CO: Westview.

Darder, A. (2015) 'Paulo Freire and the continuing struggle to decolonize education' in M. Peters and T. Besley (eds) *Paulo Freire: The global legacy*, New York: Peter Lang.

Darder, A. (2018) *The student guide to Freire's* Pedagogy of the Oppressed, London: Bloomsbury Academic.

Darder, A., Baltodano, M.P. and Torres, R.D. (eds) (2009) *The critical pedagogy reader* (2nd edn), London: Routledge.

Dasgupta, R. (2018) 'The demise of the nation state', *The Guardian,* 5 April. Available at www.theguardian.com [accessed 12 August 2019].

Davidson, A. (1977) *Antonio Gramsci: Towards an intellectual biography*, London: Merlin Press.

Delpit, L. (2009) 'Language diversity and learning' in A. Darder, M. Baltodano and D. Torres (eds) (2nd edn) *The critical pedagogy reader*, NY: Routledge

Department for Business Innovation and Skills (2014) *National Strategy for Access and Student Success in Higher Education* London: DBIS.

Dickerson, A. and Popli, G.K. (2015) 'Persistent poverty and children's cognitive development: evidence from the UK Millennium Cohort Study', 30 June 2015. Available at: https://doi.org/10.1111/rssa.1212 [accessed 20 May 2018].

Dominelli, L. (2019) *Women and community action* (3rd edn), Bristol: Policy Press.

Dorling, D. (2010) *Injustice: Why social inequality persists*, Bristol: The Policy Press.

Dorling, D. (2018a) *Peak inequality: Britain's ticking time bomb*, Bristol: Policy Press.

Dorling, D. (2018b) 'Peak inequality' in *New Statesman,* 6–12 July 2018, pp 30–5.

Dornan, P. (ed) (2004) *Ending child poverty by 2020: The first five years*, London: Child Poverty Action Group.

Doyal, L. and Gough, I. (1991) *A theory of human need*, London: Macmillan.

Eaton, G. (2018) 'Why Antonio Gramsci is the Marxist thinker for our times' in *New Statesman*, 5 February. Available at: www.newstatesman.com/culture/observatoins/2018/02/why-antonio-gramsci-marxist-thinker-our-times

Eddo-Lodge, R. (2018) *Why I'm no longer talking to white people about race,* London: Bloomsbury.

Entwistle, H. (1979) *Antonio Gramsci: Conservative schooling for radical politics*, London: Routledge.

Equality Challenge Unit (2019). *Equality Challenge Unit*, 30 January. Retrieved from www.ecu.ac.uk: https://www.ecu.ac.uk/

Escrigas, C., Sanchez, J.G., Hall, B. and Tandon, R. (2014) 'Editor's introduction', in GUNi (eds) *Knowledge, engagement and higher education: Contributing to social change*, Basingstoke and New York, NY: Palgrave Macmillan. Available at http://bulletin.ids.ac.uk/idsbo/issue/view/222 [accessed 18 April 2018].

Fanon, F. (2008) *Black skin, white masks* (new edn), London: Pluto.

Ferguson, I. and Lavalette, M. (2017) '1968 – the year of the barricades', *Critical and Radical Social Work,* vol 6, no 1, pp 3–6.

Fine, M. (2018) *Just research in contentious times: Widening the methodological imagination,* New York: Teachers College Press.

Fine, M., Weiss, L., Powell, L. and Mun Wong, L. (1997) *Off white: Readings on race, power and society*, New York: Routledge.

Fisher, W.F. and Ponniah, T. (2003) *Another world is possible: Popular alternatives to globalization at the World Social Forum*, London: Zed Books.

Flaherty, J., Veit-Wilson, J. and Dornan, P. (2004) *Poverty: The facts* (5th edn), London: Child Poverty Action Group.

Flannery, T. (2006) *The weather makers. The history and future impact of climate change*, Melbourne: Text Publishing.

Flannery, T. (2018) 'Energy policy captive to lobbyists and "mad ideologues", Tim Flannery says', https://www.theguardian.com/books/2018/sep/23/energy-policy-captive-to-lobbyists-and-mad-ideologues-tim-flannery-says?CMP=share_btn_link

Forgacs, D. (ed) (1988) *A Gramsci reader*, London: Lawrence & Wishart.

Foucault, M. (1980) *Power/knowledge: Selected interviews and other writings*, Brighton: Harvester Wheatsheaf.

Foundational Economy Collective (2018) *Foundational economy,* Manchester: Manchester University Press

Frankenberg, R. (1993) *White women: Race matters: The social construction of whiteness*, London: Routledge.

Fraser, W. (2018) *Seeking wisdom in adult teaching and learning: An autoethnographic inquiry*, Basingstoke: Palgrave Macmillan UK.

Freire, N. (1998) 'Paulo Freire: To touch, to look, to listen', *Convergence (A tribute to Paulo Freire)*, vol 31, pp 3–5.

Freire, N. (2007b) 'Introduction', in P. Freire *Daring to dream: Toward a pedagogy of the unfinished* (ed. D Macedo), Boulder, CO and London: Paradigm Publishers, pp vii–xix.

Freire, N., (2014) Keynote to 'Paulo Freire and Transformative Education: Changing lives and transforming communities' Conference, University of Central Lancashire, April.

Freire, N. (2015) 'Foreword: The understanding of Paulo Freire's education: Ethics, hope, and human rights' in M. Peters and T. Besley, *Paulo Freire: The global legacy,* Peter Lang: New York/Oxford.

Freire, P. (1970) *Pedagogy of the oppressed* (trs Myra Bergman Ramos), New York: Continuum/Seabury Press.

Freire, P. (1972) *Pedagogy of the oppressed*, Harmondsworth: Penguin.

Freire, P. (1985) *The politics of education: Culture, power and liberation*, London: Macmillan.

Freire, P. (1993) *Pedagogy of the city* (trs D. Macedo), New York: Continuum.

Freire, P. (1995) *Pedagogy of hope: Reliving pedagogy of the oppressed* (trs R. Barr), New York: Continuum.

Freire, P. (1996) *Pedagogy of the oppressed* (revised edn), Harmondsworth: Penguin.

Freire, P. (1998a) *Pedagogy of the heart*, New York: Continuum.

Freire, P. (1998b) *Pedagogy of freedom: Ethics, democracy and civic courage*, Oxford: Rowman & Littlefield.

Freire, P. (2005) *Pedagogy of indignation*, Boulder, CO: Paradigm Publishers.

Freire, P (2007a) *Education for critical consciousness* London: Continuum.

Freire, P. (2007b) *Daring to dream: Toward a pedagogy of the unfinished* (ed D. Macedo), Boulder, CO and London: Paradigm Publishers.

Freire, P. (2018) *Pedagogy of the oppressed, 50th anniversary edition* (trs M. Bergman Ramos), with Introduction by D. Macedo and Afterword by I. Shor, New York: Bloomsbury Academic.

Freire, P. and Faundez, A. (1992) *Learning to question: A pedagogy of liberation*, New York: Continuum.

Freire, P. and Macedo, D. (1993) 'A dialogue with Paulo Freire', in P. McLaren and P. Leonard (eds) *Paulo Freire: A critical encounter*, London: Routledge, pp 169–76.

Friends of the Earth and C40 Cities (2018) *Why women will save the planet* (2nd edn), London: Zed.

Fromm, E. (1962) *Beyond the chains of illusion*, London: Abacus.

Gamble, D.N. and Weil, M.O. (1997) 'Sustainable development: the challenge for community development', *Community Development Journal*, vol 32, no 3, July, pp 210-22.

Giddens, A. (1998) *The Third Way: The renewal of social democracy*, Cambridge: Polity Press.

Giroux, H.A. (1993) 'Paulo Freire and the politics of postcolonialism', in P. McLaren and P. Leonard (eds) *Paulo Freire: A critical encounter*, London: Routledge, pp 177-78.

Giroux, H.A. (2006) *Stormy weather: Katrina and the politics of disposability*, Boulder, CO: Paradigm Publishers.

Giroux, H.A. (2009) *Youth in a suspect society: Democracy or disposability?*, New York: Palgrave Macmillan.

Giroux, H.A., Lankshear, C., McLaren, P. and Peters, M. (1996) *Counternarratives: Cultural studies and critical pedagogies in postmodern spaces*, New York and London: Routledge.

Godrej, D. and Ransom, D. (2016) '10 economic myths' in K.-A. Mendoza, *Austerity: The demolition of the welfare state and the rise of the zombie economy*, Oxford: New Internationalist, pp 193–223.

Goodman, A., Johnson, P. and Webb, S. (1997) *Inequality in the UK*, Oxford: Oxford University Press.

Gordon, D. and Pantazis, C. (1997) 'Breadline Britain in the 1990s: the full report of a major national survey on poverty', *Poverty*, Journal of the Child Poverty Action Group, no 98, Autumn, pp 21–2.

Graham, H. and Jones, J. (1992) 'Community development and research', *Community Development Journal*, vol 27, no 3, July.

Graham, M. (1999) 'Some thoughts about the philosophical underpinnings of Aboriginal worldviews', *Worldviews: Environment Culture Nature*, 3(2), pp 106-113.

Graham, M. (2007) *Black issues in social work and social care*, Bristol: The Policy Press.

Gramsci, A. (1971) (ed & trs Q. Hoare and G.N. Smith) *Selections from prison notebooks*, London: Lawrence & Wishart.

Gramsci, A. (1988) *Gramsci's prison letters* (trs and intro H. Henderson), London: Zwan.

Griffiths, M. (2003) *Action for social justice in education: Fairly different*, Maidenhead: Open University Press.

Habermas, J. (1989) *The structural transformation of the public sphere: An inquiry into a category of bourgeois society*, Cambridge: Polity Press.

Hall, B. (2012) '"A giant human hashtag": learning and the Occupy Movement' in B. Hall, D.E. Clover, J. Crowther and E. Scandrett (eds) *Learning and education for a better world: The role of social movements,* Rotterdam: Sense, pp 127–39.

Hall, B. and Tandon, R. (2014) 'No more enclosures: knowledge democracy and social transformation', in *Transformation: Where Love Meets Social Justice*, 20 August, available at https://www.opendemocracy.net/transformation/budd-hall-rajesh-tandon/no-more-enclosures-knowledge-democracy-and-social-transformat

Hall, B. and Tandon, R. (2017) 'Decolonisation of knowledge, epistemicide, participatory research and higher education', *Research for All*, vol 1, no 1, pp 6–19, DOI 10.18546/RFA.01.02

Hall, S. (1996a) 'The meaning of new times', in D. Morley and K.-H. Chen (eds) *Stuart Hall: Critical dialogues in cultural studies*, London: Routledge, pp 222-36.

Hall, S. (1996b) 'What is this "black" in black popular culture?', in D. Morley and K.-H. Chen (eds) *Stuart Hall: Critical dialogues in cultural studies*, London: Routledge, pp 468-78.

Hall, S. (1996c) 'Gramsci's relevance for the study of race and ethnicity', in D. Morley and K.-H. Chen (eds) *Stuart Hall: Critical dialogues in cultural studies*, London: Routledge, pp 411-41.

Heron, J. (1981) 'Experiential research methodology', in P. Reason and J. Rowan (eds) *Human inquiry: A sourcebook of new paradigm research*, Chichester: Wiley, pp 153–66.

Higgins, P. (2010b) 'Stopping the juggernaut', *New Internationalist*, no 437, November, pp 23-4.

Hill Collins, P. (1990) *Black feminist thought: Knowledge, consciousness and the politics of empowerment*, London: Unwin Hyman.

Hirshon, S. with Butler, J. (1983) *And also teach them to read*, Westport, CT: Lawrence Hill and Co.

Hoare, Q. and Smith, G.G. (1971) 'Introduction' in A. Gramsci, *Selections from prison notebooks*, London: Lawrence & Wishart.

Hoffman, J. (1984) *The Gramscian challenge: Coercion and consent in Marxist political theory*, Oxford: Blackwell.

Holst, J. (2006) 'Paulo Freire in Chile, 1964–1969: *Pedagogy of the oppressed* in its socio-political economic context', *Harvard Educational Review*, vol 76, no 2, Summer, pp 243–70.

Holub, R. (1992) *Antonio Gramsci: Beyond Marxism and postmodernism*, London: Routledge.

hooks, b (1989) *Talking back: Thinking feminist, thinking black*, Boston, MA: South End Press.

hooks, b (1993) 'bell hooks speaking about Paulo Freire – the man, his work' in P. McLaren and P. Leonard (eds) *Paulo Freire: A critical encounter*, London: Routledge, pp 146–54

hooks, b (2000) *Feminism is for everybody: Passionate politics*, London: Pluto Press.

Hope, A. and Timmel, S., with Hodzi, C. (1984) *Training for transformation: A handbook for community workers* (Books 1-3), Zimbabwe, Gweru: Mambo Press.

Horton, M. and Freire, P. (1990) *We make the road by walking: Conversations on education and social change* (eds B. Bell, J. Gaventa and J. Peters), Philadelphia, PA: Temple University Press.

Hustedde, R. and King, B. (2002) 'Rituals: emotions, community faith in soul and the messiness of life', *Community Development Journal*, vol 37, pp 338–48.

ISSC (International Social Science Council), IDS (Institute of Development Studies) and UNESCO (United Nations Educational, Scientific and Cultural Organization) (2016) *World Social Science Report 2016, Challenging Inequalities: Pathways to a Just World*, Paris: UNESCO Publishing.

Jacobs, S. (1994) 'Community work in a changing world', in S. Jacobs and K. Popple (eds) *Community work in the 1990s*, Nottingham: Spokesman, pp 156-74.

Kahn, R. (2008) 'Towards ecopedagogy: weaving a broad-based pedagogy of liberation for animals, nature, and the oppressed people of the earth', Research Gate, https://www.researchgate.net/publication/228784808_Towards_ ecopedagogy_Weaving_a_broad-based_pedagogy_of_liberation_for_animals_ nature_and_the_oppressed_people_of_the_earth

Kane, L. (2008) 'The world bank, community development and education for social justice', *Community Development Journal*, vol 43, no 2, April, pp 194–209.

Kemmis, S. (2006) 'Participatory action research and the public sphere', *Educational Action Research*, vol 14, no 4, December, pp 459–76.

Kemmis, S. (2009) 'What is to be done? The place of action research?',Keynote address presented to the Collaborative Action Research Network (CARN) Annual Conference, Athens, Greece, 29 October–1 November.

Kenway, J. (2001) 'Remembering and regenerating Gramsci', in K. Weiler (ed) *Feminist engagements: Reading, resisting, and revisioning male theorists in education and cultural studies*, London: Routledge, pp 47–65.

Kirkwood, G. (1991) 'Freire methodology in practice', in *Roots and branches* (series of occasional papers), vol 1: *Community development and health education*, Milton Keynes: Open University Health Education Unit.

Kirkwood, G. and Kirkwood, C. (1989) *Living adult education: Freire in Scotland*, Milton Keynes: Open University Press.

Kirkwood, C., and Kirkwood, G. (2011) *Living adult education: Freire in Scotland* (2nd edn), Rotterdam: SensePublishers.

Kothari, U. (2001) 'Power, knowledge and social control in participatory development', in B. Cooke and U. Kothari (eds) *Participation: The new tyranny*, London: Zed books, pp 139–52.

Kuenstler, P. (ed) (1961) *Community organization in Great Britain*, London: Faber & Faber.

Ladson-Billings, G. and Tate, W.F. (2006) 'Toward a critical race theory of education', in H. Lauder, P. Brown, J. Dillabough and A.H. Halsey (eds) *Education, globalization and social change*, Oxford: Oxford University Press, pp 570–85.

Lamont, T (2017) 'Trapped: the Grenfell Tower Story'. Available at www.gq-magazine.co.uk

Lather, P. (1984) 'Critical theory, curricular transformation and feminist mainstreaming', *Journal of Education* vol 166, no 1, pp 49–62.

Lawner, L. (1979) (introduced, selected and translated) *Letters from prison by Antonio Gramsci*, London: Quartet Books.

Ledwith, M. (2005) *Community development: A critical approach* (1st edn), Bristol: The Policy Press.

Ledwith, M. (2010) 'Antonio Gramsci and feminism: the elusive nature of power', in P. Mayo (ed) *Gramsci and educational thought*, Chichester: Wiley-Blackwell, pp 100–13.

Ledwith, M. (2016a) *Community development in action,* Bristol: Policy Press.

Ledwith, M. (2016b) 'Emancipatory Action Research as a critical living praxis: from dominant narratives to counternarratives' in L. Rowell, C. Bruce, J.M. Shosh and M. Riel (eds) *The Palgrave international handbook of action research*, London: Palgrave Macmillan, pp 49–62.

Ledwith, M. (2018a) 'Reclaiming the radical agenda: Paulo Freire in neoliberal times' in *Concept: The journal of contemporary community education practice theory,* vol 9, no 3, Winter, pp 15–25.

Ledwith, M. (2018b) 'Paulo Freire and the politics of disposability: creating critical dissent dialogue' in A. Melling and R. Pilkington (eds) *Paulo Freire and transformative education: Changing lives and transforming communities*, London: Palgrave Macmillan, pp 29–42.

Ledwith, M. and Asgill, P. (1998) 'Black and White women working together: Transgressing the boundaries of sisterhood' in M. Lavalette, L. Penketh and C. Jones (eds) *Anti-racism and social welfare*, Aldershot: Ashgate, pp 211–34.

Ledwith, M. and Asgill, P. (2000) 'Critical alliance: Black and White women working together for social justice', *Community Development Journal*, vol 35, no 3, July, pp 290–9.

Ledwith, M. and Asgill, P. (2007) 'Feminist, anti-racist community development: critical alliance – local to global', in L. Dominelli (ed) *Revitalising communities in a globalising world*, Aldershot: Ashgate, pp 107-22.

Lewis, M. (2000) 'Interrupting patriarchy: politics, resistance, and transformation in the feminist classroom', in I. Shor and C. Pari (eds) *Education is politics: Critical teaching across differences, postsecondary*, Portsmouth, NH: Heinemann, pp 82–106.

Little, R.M. and Froggett, L. (2010) 'Making meaning in muddy waters: representing complexity through community based storytelling', *Community Development Journal*, vol 45, no 4, October, pp 458-73.

Lockhart, J. (1999) 'Re-examining Paulo Freire and his relevance for community intervention: the source of my "surprise"', in D. Scott and T. Ireland (eds) *'Vidas secas: Lutas fecudas': Community and development in the Brazilian Northeast*, London: Whiting & Birch.

Lorde, A. (1980) 'Age, race, class and sex: women redefining difference', in M. Evans (ed) (1994) *The woman question*, London: Sage Publications, pp 36–41.

Lorde, A. (1984) *Sister outsider*, New York: The Crossing Press.

Low, T. (2011) *Climate change and Queensland biodiversity. An independent report commissioned by Department of Environment and Resource Management (Qld)*, Queensland Government, Brisbane.

Lowrey, A. (2018) *Give people money*, London: WH Allen.

Mack, J. and Lansley, S. (1985) *Poor Britain*, London: George Allen & Unwin.

Mackie, R (1980) (ed) *Literacy and revolution: The pedagogy of Paulo Freire*, London: Pluto.

Marcuse, H. (1991) *One-dimensional man* (2nd edn), London: Routledge.

Maruyama, M. (1981) 'Endogenous research: rationale', in P. Reason and J. Rowan (eds) *Human inquiry: A sourcebook of new paradigm research*, Chichester: Wiley, pp 227–38.

Mason, J. (2002) *Researching your own practice: The discipline of noticing*, London: Routledge.

Mason, P. (2017) 'The violence in Charlottesville shows the far right has started a cultural war – and we must stop them now', *The Guardian*, 15 August.

Mason, P (2018) 'The meaning of Marxism today', *The New Statesman*, 4–10 May, pp 27–31.

Mayo, P. (1999) *Gramsci, Freire and adult education: Possibilities for transformative action*, London: Zed Books.

Mayo, P. (2004) *Liberating praxis: Paulo Freire's legacy for radical education and politics*, London: Praeger.

Mayo, P. (2010) 'Antonio Gramsci and his relevance to the education of adults', in *Gramsci and educational thought*, Chichester: Wiley-Blackwell, pp 21-37.

McCormack, C. with Pallister, M. (2009) *The wee yellow butterfly*, Glendaruel: Argyll Publishing.

McCormack, C. (nd) 'Raising kids in Easterhouse helped me to teach the world, says Cathy McCormack'. Available at: www.dailyrecord.co.uk [accessed 25 January 2019]

McIntosh, A. (2001) *Soil and soul: People versus corporate power*, London: Aurum.

McIntosh, P. (2004) 'White privilege: unpacking the invisible knapsack', in M. Anderson and P. Hill-Collins (eds) *Race, class and gender: An anthology*, Belmont, CA: Wadsworth Publishing.

McLaren, P. (1995) *Critical pedagogy and predatory culture: Oppositional politics in a postmodern era*, London: Routledge.

McLaren, P. (2000) *Che Guevara, Paulo Freire and the pedagogy of revolution*, Oxford: Rowman & Littlefield.

McLaren, P. (2002) 'Afterword: a legacy of hope and struggle', in A. Darder, *Reinventing Paulo Freire: A pedagogy of love*, Boulder, CO: Westview, pp 245-54.

McLaren, P. (2009) 'Critical pedagogy: A look at the major concepts' in A. Darder, McLaren, P. and Leonard, P. (eds) (1993) *Paulo Freire: A critical encounter*, London: Routledge.

McLaren, P. (2015) 'Reflections on Paulo Freire, critical pedagogy, and the current crisis of capitalism' in M. Peters and T. Besley (eds) *Paulo Freire: The global legacy*, New York: Peter Lang.

McLaren, P., Finschman, G., Serra, S. and Antelo, E. (1998) 'The specter of Gramsci: revolutionary praxis and the committed intellectual', *Journal of Thought*, Winter, pp 1–33.

Mendoza, K.-A. (2016) *Austerity: The demolition of the welfare state and the rise of the zombie economy*, Oxford: New Internationalist

Metcalf, S. (2018) 'Neoliberalism: the idea that swallowed the world' in *The Guardian*, 18 August 2017, modified on Friday 9 February 2018. Available at www.theguardian.com

Milne, S. (undated) 'Fifty years on, Labour discovers a guru', *The Guardian*.

Milne, S. (1994) *The enemy within: MI5, Maxwell and the Scargill affair*, London: Verso.

Monbiot, G. (2017) *Out of the wreckage: A new politics for an age of crisis*, London: Verso.

Monbiot, G. (2019) 'Could this local experiment be the start of a national transformation?', *The Guardian,* 24 January.

Moore, M.C. (1988) 'The development of a needs assessment for summer orientation students through the use of a modified Delphi Technique', *Retrospective Theses and Dissertations 16725*, Iowa, IA: University of Iowa.

Mosbacher, M. and Wiseman, O. (2016) *Brexit revolt: How the UK voted to leave the EU,* London: The New Culture Forum.

Nairn, T. (1982) 'Antonu su gobbu', in A. Showstack Sassoon (ed) *Approaches to Gramsci*, London: Writers and Readers, pp 159–79.

Novak, T. (1988) *Poverty and the state*, Milton Keynes: Open University Press.

O'Brien, T. (2018) 'Adult literacy organisers in Ireland resisting neoliberalism', *Education and Training, Special Issue: Adult Education transformation and social justice*, vol 60(6).

O'Donohue, J. (2004) *Beauty, the invisible embrace: Rediscovering the true sources of compassion, serenity and hope*, New York: HarperCollins.

Okri, B. (2015) *A way of being free* (UK edn), London: Head of Zeus.

Opie, A. (1992) 'Qualitative research, appropriation of the "other" and empowerment', *Feminist Review*, no 40, Spring, pp 52–69.

Oppenheim, C. and Harker, L. (1996) *Poverty: The facts*, London: Child Poverty Action Group.

Page, M. (1997) *Women in Beijing one year on: Networks, alliances, coalitions*, London: Community Development Foundation.

Pearce, J., Howard, J. and Bronstein, A. (2010) 'Editorial: Learning from Latin America', *Community Development Journal*, vol 45, no 3, July, pp 265–75.

Perraudin, F. (2019) 'Extinction Rebellion arrests pass 1,000 on eighth day of protests', *The Guardian*, 22 April.

Pheterson, G. (1990) 'Alliances between women: overcoming internalized oppression and internalized domination', in L. Albrecht and R. Brewer (eds) *Bridges of power: Women's multicultural alliances*, Philadelphia, PA: New Society Publishers, pp 34–48.

Piketty, T. (2014) 'Save capitalism from the capitalists by taxing wealth', *The Financial Times*, 28 March, available at ft.com

Pitchford, M. with Henderson, P. (2008) *Making spaces for community development*, Bristol: The Policy Press.

Polonski, V. (2016) 'Impact of social media on the outcome of the EU referendum', available at https://www.referendumanalysis.eu/eu-referendum-analysis-2016/section-7-social-media/impact-of-social-media-on-the-outcome-of-the-eu-referendum/

Popple, K. (1995) *Analysing community work: Its theory and practice*, Buckingham: Open University Press.

Randall, R. and Southgate, J. (1981) 'Doing dialogical research', in P. Reason and J. Rowan (eds) *Human inquiry: A sourcebook of new paradigm research*, Chichester: Wiley, pp 349-61.

Ransome, P. (1992) *Antonio Gramsci: A new introduction*, London: Harvester Wheatsheaf.

Ravangai, S. (1995) 'The Freirean model of applied theatre and performance', paper for Theatre for Development Conference, University of Zimbabwe, Research Gate.

Raworth, K. (2018) *Doughnut economics: Seven ways to think like a 21st-century economist*, London: Random House.

Reagon, B. (1983) 'Coalition politics: turning the century', in B. Smith (ed) *Home girls*, New York: Kitchen Table – Women of Color Press, pp 343-58.

Reason, P. (1994a) 'Inquiry and alienation', in P. Reason (ed) *Participation in human inquiry: Research with people*, London: Sage Publications, pp 9-15.

Reason, P. (1994b) 'Human inquiry as discipline and practice' in P. Reason (ed) *Participation in human inquiry*, London: Sage, pp 40-56.

Reason, P. and Bradbury, H. (eds) (2001) *Handbook of action research: Participative inquiry and practice*, London: Sage Publications.

Reason, P. and Rowan, J. (eds) (1981) *Human inquiry: A sourcebook of new paradigm research*, Chichester: Wiley.

Reside, A.E. et al (2013) *Climate change refugia for terrestrial biodiversity: defining areas that promote species persistence and ecosystem resilience in the face of global climate change*, National Climate Change Adaptation Research Facility, Gold Coast (with James Cook University and Commonwealth Science and Industry Research Organisation).

Ridge, T. (2004) 'Putting children first: addressing the needs and concerns of children who are poor', in P. Dornan (ed) *Ending child poverty by 2020: The first five years*, London: Child Poverty Action Group, pp 4-11.

Riggs, L. (2014) 'What it's like to be the first person in your family to go to college', *The Atlantic* 13 January. Available at: https://www.theatlantic.com/education/archive/2014/01/what-its-like-to-be-the-first-person-in-your-family-to-go-to-college/282999/

Rikowski, G. and McLaren, P. (1999) 'Postmodernism in educational theory', in D. Hill, P. McLaren, M. Cole and G. Rikowski (eds) *Postmodernism in educational theory: Education and the politics of human resistance*, London: The Tuffnell Press, pp 1–9.

Riordan, S. (2008) 'NGOs: the *sine qua non* of adapting to climate change in Africa', in J. Blewitt (ed) *Community, empowerment and sustainable development*, Totnes: Green Books, pp 33–58.

Roderick, I. with Jones, N. (2008) 'The converging world', in J. Blewitt (ed) *Community, empowerment and sustainable development*, Totnes: Green Books, pp 17–32.

Ross, C. (2018) 'How to create a leaderless revolution and win lasting political change' in *The Guardian*, 13 December. Available at www.theguardian.com

Rowan, J. (1981) 'Dialectical paradigm for research', in P. Reason and J. Rowan (eds) *Human inquiry: A sourcebook for new paradigm research*, Chichester: Wiley, pp 93–112.

Rowan, J. and Reason, P. (1981) 'On making sense', in P. Reason and J. Rowan (eds) *Human inquiry: A sourcebook of new paradigm research*, Chichester: Wiley, pp 113–40.

Roy, A. (2003) 'Confronting empire', available at ratical.org/ratville/CAH/AR012703.html [accessed 22 January 2019].

Rude, G. (1980) *Ideology and popular protest*, London: Lawrence & Wishart.

Rutter, M. and Madge, N. (1976) *Cycles of disadvantage*, London: Heinemann.

Santos, B. de Sousa (2007) 'Beyond abyssal thinking: from global lines to ecologies of knowledge', *Eurozine*, vol 33, pp 45–89.

Sayer, A. (2016) *Why we can't afford the rich*, Bristol: Policy Press.

Schutzman, M. and Cohen-Cruz, J. (eds) (1995) *Playing Boal: Theatre, therapy, activism*, London: Routledge.

Scottish Education Department (1975) *Adult education: The challenge of change* (Alexander Report), Edinburgh: HMSO.

Sewell, S. (2014a) *Women and the environment: An indicative study on Tamborine Mountain,* James Cook University, Queensland. Available through James Cook University Research Online (public access).

Sewell, S. (2014b) *Rainforest women: Hilda Geissmann Curtis, Judith Wright McKinney, Joy Guyatt on Tamborine Mountain*. Beaudesert Times Printing.

Shaw, M. (2004) *Community work: Policy, politics and practice*, Hull and Edinburgh: Universities of Hull and Edinburgh.

Shor, I. (1992) *Empowering education: Critical teaching for social change*, London and Chicago, IL: University of Chicago Press.

Shor, I. (1993) 'Education is politics: Paulo Freire's critical pedagogy', in P. McLaren and P. Leonard (eds) *Paulo Freire: A critical encounter*, London: Routledge, pp 24–35.

Shor, I. (2000) '(Why) education is politics', in I. Shor and C. Pari (eds) *Education is politics: Critical teaching across differences, postsecondary*, Portsmouth, NH: Heinemann, pp 1–14.

Shor, I. (2018) 'Afterword' in P. Freire, *Pedagogy of the oppressed: 50th anniversary edition,* New York: Bloomsbury, pp 185–8.

Shor, I. and Freire, P. (1987) *A pedagogy for liberation: Dialogues on transforming education*, London: Bergin & Garvey.

Showstack Sassoon, A. (1987) *Gramsci's politics* (2nd edn), London: Hutchinson.

Southgate, J. and Randall, R. (1981) 'The troubled fish: barriers to dialogue', in P. Reason and J. Rowan (eds) *Human inquiry: A sourcebook of new paradigm research*, Chichester: Wiley, pp 53–62.

Spretnak, C. (1993) 'Critical and constructive contributions of ecofeminism' in P. Tucker and E. Grim (eds) *Worldview and ecology*, Philadelphia, PA: Bucknell Press, pp 181–9.

Steedman, C. (2000) *Landscape for a good woman: A story of two lives* (2nd edn), London: Virago.

Tandon, R. (2008) 'Participation, citizenship and democracy: Reflections on 25 years of PRIA', *Community Development Journal*, vol 43, no 3, pp 284–96.

Tandon, R. (2013) *Global Democracy Requires Knowledge Democracy*, blog, http://unescochair-cbrsr.org/index.php/2013/09/15/globaldemocracy-requires-knowledge-democracy/ [accessed 1 October 2016].

Tandon, R. (2014a) *Knowledge democracy: Reclaiming voices for all*, http://unescochair-cbrsr.org/unesco/pdf/Lecture_at_Univ_Cape_Town-August%20-2014.pdf [accessed 30 September 2016].

Tandon, R. (2014b) 'Global challenges', in GUNi (eds), *Knowledge, engagement and higher education: Contributing to social change*, Basingstoke and New York NY: Palgrave Macmillan

Tandon, R., Hall, B., Lepore, W. and Singh, W. (2016) *Knowledge and Engagement: Building Capacity for the Next Generation of Community Based Researchers*, Victoria BC: University of Victoria, http://unescochair-cbrsr.org/pdf/resource/Knowledge%20&%20Engagement_26-09-16_pdf%20ver-mail.pdf [accessed 4 November 2016].

Taylor, P. (1993) *The texts of Paulo Freire*, Buckingham: Open University Press.

The Climate Institute (2010) *Climate of the nation: Australians' attitudes towards climate change and its solutions*, August 2010, Sydney, New South Wales.

Thompson, N. (2007) *Power and empowerment*, Lyme Regis: Russell House.

Thompson, N. (2016) *Anti-discriminatory practice* (6th edn), Basingstoke: Palgrave Macmillan.

Thompson, N. (2017) *Promoting equality: Challenging discrimination and oppression in the human services* (4th edn), London: Macmillan.

Torres, C.A. (1993) 'From the *Pedagogy of the oppressed* to a *luta continua*', in P. McLaren and P. Leonard (eds) *Paulo Freire: A critical encounter*, London: Routledge, pp 119–45.

Torres, M. and Reyes, L. (2011) *Research as praxis: Democratizing education epistemologies*, New York: Peter Lang.

Treleaven, L. (2001) 'The turn to action and the linguistic turn: towards an integrated methodology', in P. Reason and H. Bradbury (eds) *Handbook of action research: Participative inquiry and practice*, London: Sage Publications.

Tyler, I. (2013) *Revolting subjects: Social abjection and resistance in neoliberal Britain*, London: Zed

Tyler, I. (2015) 'The sociology of stigma: Why research stigma today?'. Available at stigmamachine.com

Visvanathan, S. (2009) 'The search for cognitive justice'. Available at http://bit.ly/3ZwMD2

Walby, S. (1992) *Theorizing patriarchy*, Oxford: Blackwell.

Walby, S. (1994) 'Post-postmodernism? Theorizing gender', in *The Polity reader in social theory*, Cambridge: Polity Press.

Weekes, K. (ed) (2009) *Privilege and prejudice: Twenty years with the invisible knapsack* (with Foreword by Peggy McIntosh), Cambridge: Cambridge Scholars Publishing.

Weiler, K. (1994) 'Freire and a feminist pedagogy of difference', in P. McLaren and C. Lankshear (eds) *Politics of liberation: Paths from Freire*, London: Routledge, pp 12–40.

Weiler, K. (1995) 'Freire and a feminist pedagogy of difference', in J. Holland, M. Blair and S. Sheldon (eds) *Debates and issues in feminist research and pedagogy*, Clevedon: Multilingual Matters/Open University, pp 23–44.

Weiler, K. (ed) (2001) *Feminist engagements: Reading, resisting, and revisioning male theorists in education and cultural studies*, London: Routledge.

Weiler, K. (2009) 'Feminist analysis of gender and schooling', in A. Darder, M.P. Baltodano and R.D. Torres (eds) *The critical pedagogy reader* (2nd edn), New York: Routledge, pp 217–39.

Wilkinson, R. and Pickett, K.E. (2009) *The spirit level: Why more equal societies almost always do better*, Harmondsworth: Allen Lane.

Wilkinson, R. and Pickett, K. (2018) *The inner level: How more equal societies reduce stress, restore sanity and improve everyone's well-being*, UK: Allen Lane.

Williams, F. (1989) *Social policy: A critical introduction*, Cambridge: Polity Press.

Williams, P. (1991) *The alchemy of race and rights*, Cambridge, MA: Harvard University Press.

Williams, Z. (2012) 'The Saturday interview: Stuart Hall', *The Guardian*, 11 February.

Winter, R., Sobiechowska, P. and Buck, A. (eds) (1999) *Professional experience and the investigative imagination: The art of reflective writing*, London: Routledge.

Wood, Z. (2019) '"I did the right thing": Richer Sounds boss has no regrets', *The Guardian,* 18 May.

Young, A. (1990) *Femininity in dissent,* London: Routledge.

Younghusband, E. (1959) *Report of the working party on social workers in the local authority health and welfare services,* London: HMSO.

Index

Note: Page locators in *italic* refer to figures.